Creativity and Strategic Innovati Management

Many organisations in both the private and public sector are confronted with stiff challenges as they face rapid changes in the business environment. Understanding the causes of these changes is essential if organisations are to fashion suitable management responses. In a highly competitive and globalised scenario, business creativity provides the spark that fosters the development and implementation of innovation and organisational change.

Increased understanding of the concepts of business creativity and strategic innovation management provides valuable insights into how organisations can change to meet new challenges. The book aims to:

- Explain the nature of the acceleration in discontinuous change that is affecting the Western business environment;
- Emphasise the importance of taking a strategic approach to management responses to encourage creative and innovative skills;
- Indicate how a detailed strategic plan can be developed to support organisations intent on profitable survival in the twenty-first century.

This textbook will be the perfect accompaniment to postgraduate courses on innovation management and creativity management. The wide-ranging approach means that the book will also be useful supplementary reading on a range of courses from management of technology to strategic management.

Malcolm Goodman is Senior Teaching Fellow at Durham University, UK.

Sandra Dingli is Director of The Edward de Bono Institute for the Design & Development of Thinking at the University of Malta, Malta.

Creativity and Strategic Innovation Management

Malcolm Goodman and Sandra Dingli

LONDON AND NEW YORK

First published 2013
by Routledge
2 Park Square, Milton Park, Abingdon, Oxon OX14 4RN

Simultaneously published in the USA and Canada
by Routledge
711 Third Avenue, New York, NY 10017

Routledge is an imprint of the Taylor & Francis Group, an informa business

British Library Cataloguing in Publication Data
A catalogue record for this book is available from the British Library

Library of Congress Cataloging in Publication Data
Goodman, Malcolm.
Creativity and strategic innovation management / Malcolm Goodman and Sandra Dingli.
    p. cm.
1. Creative ability in business. 2. Diffusion of innovations—Management.
3. Technological innovations—Management. 4. Organizational change—Management.
I. Dingli, Sandra M., 1952- II. Title.
    Hd53.G6643 2012
    658.4'063 – dc23   2012004478

ISBN: 978-0-415-66354-0 (hbk)
ISBN: 978-0-415-66355-7 (pbk)
ISBN: 978-0-203-10437-8 (ebk)

Typeset in Times New Roman
by Cenveo Publisher Services

MIX
Paper from
responsible sources
FSC   FSC® C004839
www.fsc.org

Printed and bound in Great Britain by
TJ International Ltd, Padstow, Cornwall

Contents

Tables

Figures

Prologue

Business people and those who study business live in times of rapid and discontinuous changes in the business environment triggered by a complex set of factors. Businesses that used to operate on safe ground now experience periodic and violent shifts and aftershocks in their environment. These shocks have been intermittent for some time but since the beginning of the twenty-first century have been happening more regularly and more forcefully. Management are faced by two serious questions. Are the contextual disturbances periodic and on the way out? Or are they a permanent phenomenon? Most now accept they are here to stay and so present a serious challenge to organisations. This text explores how top management and hence organisations can respond effectively by changing the way they do things – by seeking to get to grips with business creativity and strategic innovation.

The text is presented in four Parts:

- Part I The challenge of changing times
- Part II Preparing a response
- Part III Innovation from theory to practice
- Part IV Managing change

and provides theoretical and practical argument to facilitate understanding and to encourage practice. Real learning is a result of both education and practice. The former on its own might enable students to pass multi choice computer tests but practice builds know-how. Each chapter in the text features a common typology that progresses from:

- context to
- key principles to
- practice
- and finally to action.

To aid readers' understanding of the material each chapter contains a summary, discussion questions, a case exercise and reference sections.

A surprising number of people confuse creativity and innovation. The former is necessary for innovation but not sufficient. It provides the spark, the idea, that is progressed and actioned by innovation. Part I Chapters 1 to 3 and Part II Chapters 4 to 7 focus on business creativity. Part III Chapters 8 to 12 cover topics that relate to innovation. As many organisations seek to meet the challenges of modern business conditions there is growing interest in managing change. Part IV Chapters 13 to 16 outline and discuss the key topics of interest as identified by practitioners.

Business creativity techniques are fun and rewarding but are a skill. As such they require a commitment to practice. The text introduces some basic techniques (see Chapter 5). Be bold, overcome initial inhibitions and give it a go and you will be pleasantly surprised by the result. Whilst IT can assist the generation of creative ideas it should be regarded only as a tool. As such its usefulness depends on the timing, place and skill with which it is used. Innovation too is a skill set and IT is a particularly useful tool as it greatly assists the development and use of supportive networks.

The Epilogue presents a figure that summarises the key pointers that emerge from the argument of the text, all of which are conditional on a clear and likely new working definition of management.

Sandra Dingli
University of Malta

Malcolm Goodman
Durham University

Acknowledgements

Many have contributed in various ways to the process of writing this book. We would like to thank, in particular, Abi Goodman for the artwork that appears on the facing pages of each of the four parts of the text; Jill Goodman and Andrew Jeffrey for proof reading and copy editing. We are also grateful to our respective universities for exposing us to practitioners and students over the years.

Finally, this book is dedicated to our patient families and friends who have put up with the long hours we spend at our computers.

Sandra Dingli
University of Malta

Malcolm Goodman
Durham University

Part I

The challenge of changing times

Corporates sit in a meeting room Having discussions with biscuits and views. All turn away from 'impending doom', (Look at the screen for Breaking News).

1 The changing business environment

Can anything that is useful be accomplished without change?
(Emperor Marcus Aurelius)

If I have seen further it is by standing on the shoulders of giants.
(Isaac Newton)

Introduction

Organisations of all kinds, large and small, private and public are experiencing profound changes in their business environment during the opening decades of the twenty-first century. Many organisations are being affected by developments in their operational arenas and markets that are severely challenging managers. Natural resources and energy supplies are becoming more expensive. Advances in technology have revolutionised connectivity leading to the rapid expansion of virtual markets. In addition shifts in the economic fortunes of individual nation states and their consequent social and political ramifications, together with an emerging shift in global power dynamics as developing economies rival established ones, have all presented organisations with the necessity of seriously reviewing their established *modus operandi*.

Chapter 1 sets the scene and provides an overview of the complexity of the shifting sands of the business environment. This provides a platform for the text which addresses the equally complex matter of how organisations should identify, innovate and develop new ways of operating that are in tune with challenges they face.

Context

What is change?

Everything and everyone is exposed to change. It is a feature of the natural world and dictates the arena or environment in which the human race pursues its existence. At a basic level, change may be defined as 'the movement away from a present state towards a future state' (George and Jones, 1995).

It is useful to think of change metaphorically as a set of Russian dolls. The outer doll, which contains all the others, is the macro-environment that affects us all. The inner dolls can be taken to symbolise constituent or micro-environments that impact on our lives resulting from political, economic, socio-cultural and technological factors. In the opening decades of the twenty-first century increasing concerns over the fate of the physical environment

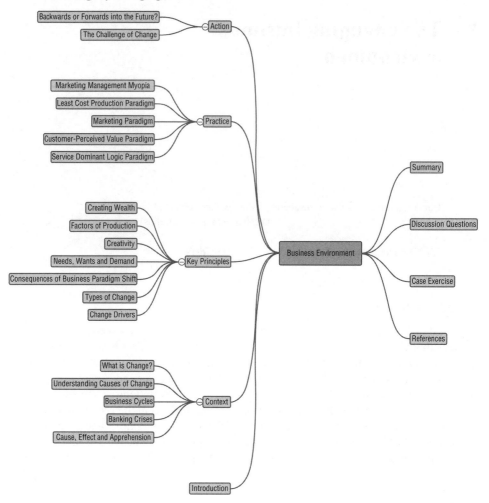

Figure 1.1 Explaining the changing business environment.

are being voiced by many as global warming, land use concerns, food provision and a rising world population are topics that feature daily in the world's media.

The *Concise Oxford English Dictionary* (OED) defines *change* both as a noun and as a verb. Used as a noun change is defined as 'becoming different', 'an alteration or modification (i.e. a change in someone's facial expression)' and 'a new experience'. As a verb the OED declares that change concerns action that 'makes (something) different'. Change then, is both about a state of being and about action to alter it.

The macro-environmental factors that shape change can move in either small, almost imperceptible ways (incremental change) or in an explosive tsunami-like way and radically change the *status quo* in minutes. Change, whether incremental or radical (and we usually face a mixture of both) is a paradox of recorded history. Sometimes the environment changes positively and sometimes negatively. Theories about change have been exercising the human intellect for thousands of years. In that time there have been many explanations and stories

Figure 1.2 Russian dolls.

about how change happens. Much of the recorded wisdom tells you *what* to do, but not necessarily *how* to do it. It provides both a challenge and a threat to human endeavour. Individuals and organisations that cope with the challenges brought about by change can be considered winners and those that fail to adjust their responses inevitably face a progressive and sometimes sudden deterioration in their perceived well-being.

The annual rotation of the earth results in changing seasons for some latitudes and changing weather patterns for others as violent rain and wind storms appear suddenly from clear blue skies. These seasonal changes trigger responses that are staggering in their enormity. For example, deciduous trees shed their leaves and close down for the winter, to bloom again in the spring. Some animals change their coats and others hibernate. Humans also change their ways and respond to climatic and weather changes, by varying their clothing at different times of the year or by seeking to regulate experienced extremes of cold, heat and discomfort brought about by wind and rain. Our well-being depends upon actively managing such changes. Change can manifest in a more dramatic way through metamorphosis, for example, which requires a complete change of state and represents a severe shock to the *status quo* (in this case requiring a sleeping phase to cope with change).

Understanding the causes of change

To respond effectively to rapid change, it is necessary to understand the underlying causes. There is a considerable volume of literature that shows that change has provided a major challenge to organisations since the Industrial Revolution (Grey, 2003). It is not something that is needed periodically; it is a business constant (Graetz *et al.*, 2006). Specific changes in an organisation's internal structure and external markets often derive from wider changes in society, economics or technology. Change takes place both 'out there' in the tangible and physical world and 'in here' in the internal world of our mind, with all our memories, thoughts and ideas. The world appears both 'objective' and 'subjective'. A change project starts from the subjective, inside our imagination, and gradually works out into the reality of managing other people and organising things in the world.

General trends in society, politics and demography touch everyone. In recent years these have resulted in upsurges in the pensioner, youth and consumer markets; a shift in emphasis from community to a more individualistic society; and ageing populations. The tides of economics change sometimes imperceptibly and sometimes abruptly. Markets and monetary flows can fluctuate, competitive ways can alter dramatically, and technology and innovation can fracture established patterns. Technological advance in the twenty-first century is accelerating and is expected to accelerate exponentially. In particular the revolution in information technology (IT) is having a profound impact on the business environment. In addition many companies are facing increased challenges from ecological and ethical forces.

Businesses and organisations operate in a global arena in response to meeting the needs of the developing world as well as those of the developed world. To achieve profitable business many organisations are following the trend of commoditisation together with the outsourcing of goods and services to achieve low market prices. This can result in their risking criticism in their domestic markets by tacitly accepting ethical practices abroad that would not be regarded as acceptable at home.

The development of information technology and the escalating shift towards it has had and continues to have a revolutionary effect on the dissemination of most forms of information and business functional activity. Digitisation is also shaping social attitudes and choices through the popularity of social networking platforms such as *Facebook* and *Twitter* which together with sites such as *YouTube* enable organisations to get ever closer to discovering customers' perceived value expectations. The purchasing patterns of Wal-Mart and IKEA have transformed the face of retailing with deep impacts across the global economy. *Google* has transformed global advertising.

In addition to these macro environmental changes many businesses have been severely affected by the 'on the ground' paradigm change from sellers' markets to buyers' markets.

Table 1.1 Key general forces that cause contextual change affecting businesses in the developed economies

Socio-cultural forces	Economic forces	Technological forces	Environmental forces
Ageing populations	More global capital flows – emergence of China and India as major economic powers	Improvements in communication	Global warming
Growth of youth markets	Fewer tariffs	Improvements in transportation	Carbon footprint
Trend toward individual-centred society	Rising consumer debts	Development of global IT networks	Rising cost of fossil fuels
Rise of consumerism	More countries linked to capitalism	Commoditisation	Increased government legislation e.g. EU clean air dictates
	Privatisation Slower domestic growth for developed economies		

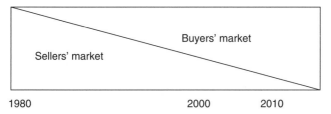

Figure 1.3 Business environment changes.
 Note: Horizontal axis indicates the speed of transition from sellers' to buyers' market conditions.

The former are characterised by demand for goods and services generally being in excess of the supply. This has been the case in many developed countries for several decades and can be described as 'business management's heaven'. The successful business response was to increase the volume of products and services placed on world markets to achieve a very profitable return. The latter, a buyers' market, is characterised by the supply of goods and services being in excess of the demand. This can be imagined as 'business management's hell' as competition is fierce and businesses need to be careful to meet the expectations of customers who have a wide choice of suppliers.

The combination and interaction of all these forces explains why so many businesses and organisations have experienced a sudden change in their real-time operating environments at an ever increasing pace since the turn of the millennium. These new external conditions have severely challenged both private sector and public sector organisations.

Business cycles

A business cycle is the periodic but irregular up-and-down movement in economic activity, measured in terms of real gross national product (GNP) and other macroeconomic variables. Parkin and Bade (2011) argue that a business cycle is not a regular, predictable or repeating phenomenon, like the swing of a clock's pendulum. Its timing is random and to a large extent unpredictable. A business cycle is identified as a sequence of four phases:

1. Contraction (a slowdown in the pace of economic activity);
2. Trough (the lower turning point of a business cycle, where a contraction turns into an expansion);
3. Expansion (a speed up in the pace of economic activity);
4. Peak (the upper turning point of a business cycle).

A recession occurs if a contraction is severe enough. A deep trough is called a slump or a depression.

Business cycles, according to the International Encyclopaedia of Economics, refer to 'time periods of rising prices, employment, and output that are followed by declines in these macroeconomic quantities'. There are two streams in business cycle research, one generating 'theory based cycles' and another generating 'data based cycles'. The first stream of research establishes theories which attempt to explain why and how business cycles arise in an economic system. The second stream of literature is more focused on methods of identifying, measuring and describing the business cycles. Scholars from this stream, notably those in the National Bureau of Economic Research (NBER) and the Economic Cycle Research

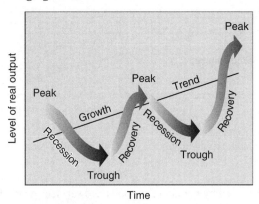

Figure 1.4 Business cycle troughs and peaks.

Institute (ECRI), argue that properly understanding business cycles relies first on collecting and studying observable data.

For Schumpeter (1939), the decisive driving force for an economy undergoing the alternating stages of prosperity, recession, depression and recovery is innovation. Three 'approximations' built up by Schumpeter are meant to explain how entrepreneurs' innovative behaviours bring about the emergence, the intensification and the simultaneity of the cycles.

Financial crisis of the opening decade of the twenty-first century

The financial crisis of 2007 to the present is one triggered by a liquidity shortfall in the United States' banking system. It has resulted in the collapse of large financial institutions, the bailout of banks by national governments, and downturns in stock markets around the world. It is considered by many economists to be the worst financial crisis since the Great Depression of the 1930s. It has contributed to the failure of key businesses, declines in consumer wealth estimated in the hundreds of trillions of US dollars, substantial financial commitments incurred by governments, and a significant decline in economic activity. Many causes have been suggested, with varying weight assigned by experts. Both market based and regulatory solutions have been implemented or are under consideration, while significant risks remain for the world economy over the next decade.

The collapse of the housing bubble, which peaked in the US in 2006, caused the values of securities tied to real-estate pricing to plummet thereafter, damaging financial institutions globally. Questions regarding bank solvency, declines in credit availability, and damaged investor confidence had an impact on global stock markets, where securities suffered large losses during late 2008 and early 2009. Economies worldwide slowed during this period as credit tightened and international trade declined. Critics argued that credit rating agencies and investors failed to accurately price the risk involved with mortgage-related financial products, and that governments did not adjust their regulatory practices to address twenty-first century financial markets. Governments and central banks responded with unprecedented fiscal stimulus, monetary policy expansion and institutional bailouts.

Advanced economies are braced for a tsunami of red ink. Economists have singled out Portugal, Ireland, Italy, Greece and Spain as spending too much for too long on the back of too cheap loans. But these countries are not alone, and now the good times are over most industrialised economies are struggling with inflated national debts. Most developed economies have spent the last decade living beyond their financial and demographic means, blowing the budget surpluses they enjoyed ten years ago. After the banking crisis struck in 2008, billions in bailouts inflated government debt. The banking crisis became a credit crunch and prompted economic recession. The fiscal crisis followed close behind.

While populations in many industrialised countries are aging and shrinking, their social security systems are still designed for relatively young, fertile populations with comparatively short life expectancies. These systems have become unsustainable, says the World Economic Forum (WEF). 'Current social systems are sacrificing future generations' money to sustain this generation', says Sheana Tambourgi, head of the WEF's Risk Network (WEF, n.d.). US spending, for example, has left future generations of Americans with a shortfall of 66 trillion dollars. 'Systems need to lengthen working lives, raise the age of retirement, and reduce healthcare spending by spending more effectively on prevention rather than treatment', Tambourgi argues. The report's authors cite the Scandinavian model of mixed public–private provision of some social services as one of the few positive exceptions.

In the immediate future the most likely effects of fiscal crises will be increased unemployment, especially amongst the young. Unemployment in the Eurozone is expected to rise dramatically in 2012/13 and joblessness could spread worldwide if trade does not pick up, threatening social and political stability in some regions such as the Middle East.

One remedy for indebted countries is a crash diet. Ireland and France have slashed spending and President Obama said when presenting his budget that the era of 'Monopoly money' was over and that governments should 'live within their means'. Having come to the aid of Greece in 2010 the EU also had to bail out Ireland in November and is keeping a watchful eye on the heavily indebted Italian, Portuguese and Spanish economies. Whilst the banking fraternity loudly claim that countries should admire their special cognitive skills, Daniel Kahnemann, winner of the Nobel Economics prize, dramatically exploded this as a cognitive illusion. The probability of successful trading he found largely to be governed purely by chance, as with rolling dice. Many have also lost confidence in the ability of economists' theories and practices to guide national economic policies and the profession itself has cried '*mea culpa*' (Wollensky, 2010).

Cause, effect and apprehension

Change is everywhere in business, and people do not appear to be very happy about it. But it is not just nostalgia, or laziness, that causes the negative reaction. Change is rarely managed well. What do managers get wrong about change? There is quite a long list:

- They underestimate how long it will take people to accept change.
- They fail to recognise how difficult it is to spread the message that change may be necessary or unavoidable.
- They do not understand what change feels like beyond the boardroom or the top management table.
- If they are successful in getting the organisation to accept the need for change, they forget to explain that the new direction or mission may change again and possibly quite soon.

The UK Cabinet Office recently made a set of predictions on the forthcoming business decade. It foresees the real emergence of an 'e-economy' with faster, nimbler firms driven by technology. It foresees large companies shrinking to more manageable scales. The report, called '2020 vision', highlights the emergence of a much greater dependency on IT and mobile commerce by 2020, as access points and connection speeds increase exponentially and entrepreneurs seek to tap further into the low overheads that virtual business offers.

This new industrial revolution is on its way and will continue to be fuelled by the growth in technology. Technological uptake has been growing since the development of the PC in the early 1980s and is nowadays overtaken by smartphones, tablets and m-commerce. This is the future. This is the way that consumers expect businesses to trade.

Although access to funding remains a major issue for SMEs, in order to grow within the current economy, it is essential that smaller businesses embrace the digital opportunities available. Many tools can be free of charge; take Twitter or Facebook for instance. Furthermore, at the time of writing it is anticipated that, for the London 2012 Olympics, millions of highly connected tourists will use search engines and social networks to find the best deals around for travel, food, leisure, gifts and accommodation.

Whether you are working with social media, such as Twitter, Facebook, YouTube or LinkedIn, the ways in which you reach and connect with your customers online is more than ever critical for your business. Put it this way, ignoring this fact is putting your business at risk. The good news is that digital marketing is not as complicated and inaccessible as some may say. Anyone can be successful even with a very limited budget and minimal resources.

Key principles

Creating wealth

In this era that is affected by far reaching change in the business environment wise companies and organisations will refocus their view of business from a tendency to emphasise costs and prices to one that places a greater significance on successfully meeting consumers' perceived values. In other words, discover, develop and provide what consumers want instead of assuming that the least cost production paradigm should dominate their activities.

The pursuit of profit, and by implication corporate wealth, is seen by many to be influenced by standard economic theory. It is the art of successfully combining the traditional economic factors of production, land, labour and capital. While this provides a sensible direction to modern corporate activity it needs to be expanded to include a philosophy and a functional expertise that can foster and deliver innovative solutions to the growing customer preference for products and services that align to their perceived values rather than for standardised offerings. This calls for the inclusion of creativity as a key factor of production.

Factors of production

The term factors of production relates to the key variables that according to conventional economics go into making goods and services. Table 1.2 presents a brief summary of the three conventionally accepted factors plus additional ones that are particularly relevant in the twenty-first century business environment.

Dean and Kretschmer (2007) argue that in most developed economies economic and social relations are undergoing radical change, expressed in concepts such as 'knowledge economy', 'weightless economy', 'post-industrial society' or 'information society'. Ideas, inventions and innovations are becoming of major importance as companies strive to find their way in highly competitive global markets. Intellectual capital has come of age and the literature suggests the arrival of a distinct new factor of production – human capital – that

Table 1.2 The factors of production

Factor	Description
Land	Refers to physical land and other natural resources, e.g. the land that a building is constructed on, oil that is extracted from under the sea, the land, forests, and fish reserves. Providers of land receive rent.
Labour	Refers to physical and mental effort – e.g. stacking shelves in a supermarket, or calculating the final financial accounts of a company. Providers of labour receive wages.
Capital	Exists at two levels. First of all we have financial capital. But more importantly, this is used to purchase physical capital that goes into making other things. Physical capital consists of machinery, equipment, tools, etc. Providers of capital receive interest.
Enterprise	Is the skill of combining the other factors of production. Entrepreneurs are the risk takers that set up and run business enterprises. Entrepreneurs receive profit.
Creativity	Creativity is a core competency for leaders and managers and one of the best ways to set companies apart from the competition. Corporate creativity is characterised by the ability to perceive the world in new ways, to find hidden patterns, to make connections between seemingly unrelated phenomena and to generate solutions. Generating fresh solutions to problems, and the ability to create new market offerings, processes for a changing market, are part of the intellectual capital that give a company its competitive edge (Bilton, 2007). Creativity is a crucial part of the innovation equation.

replaces or perhaps supplements the traditional view of land, labour and capital as the key factors for generating wealth. Ideas can be regarded as a form of capital that can be exploited in post-production economies and wise organisations should value it (Bowman and Swart, 2007).

Current approaches that position human capital as central to value generation in knowledge based industries obscure the importance of the relational nature of knowledge production. That is, separable and embodied forms of capital are interdependent in value creation and capture processes. Bowman and Swart identify a relational form of capital, *embedded* capital, which they argue is *the* critical resource in knowledge based industries such as professional services firms, because it takes into account the contributions of agency and interdependency in the value capture process. These dimensions have previously been overlooked by the conventional resource based view of the firm. Examples of embedded capital include brand value, processes and procedures.

Creativity

Organisations that seriously intend to develop a strategic approach to innovation need to facilitate and sustain cultures that encourage creativity in order to generate ideas (Bowman and Swart, 2007). A steady flow of ideas feeds the invention, innovation process. But what is creativity? Is it a form of magic that only certain individuals can perform? It is open to all who are prepared to experiment in thinking 'out of the box' to produce new, novel or original ideas and solutions (Goodman, 1995). According to the IBM 2010 Global CEO Study, which surveyed 1,500 Chief Executive Officers from 60 countries and 33 industries worldwide, CEOs believe that, 'more than rigour, management discipline, integrity or even vision – successfully navigating an increasing complex world will require creativity'. 'The effects of rising complexity calls for CEOs and their teams to lead with bold creativity, connect with customers in imaginative ways and design their operations for speed and flexibility to position their organisations for twenty-first century success' (IBM, 2010).

The literature on intellectual capital (Dean and Kretschmer, 2007) suggests that a distinctly new factor of production – intellectual or human capital – has arrived on the scene that replaces or supplants the traditional factors of land, labour and capital. In addition to the growing importance of creativity to the developed economies, developing countries are competing on creativity as well as cost and this will dynamically change business everywhere (*The Economist*, 2010). Recognising the trend, IBM now offers free consulting to 100 cities worldwide as they have enormous challenges and need to harness innovation, creativity and technical know-how to tackle long-standing, tough issues and plan for the future.

The Nomura Institute of Japan (www.nri.co.jp/english/) has an interesting and different view of the key factors of production and classifies four areas of economic activity:

1. Agricultural
2. Industrial
3. Informational . . . and now through the evolution of technology
4. Creative: constant innovation.

Needs, wants and demand

As the twenty-first century enters its second decade people all over the world are expecting more out of life. Despite the emergence of the global economy millions still live out their lives below the official United Nations breadline. Basic needs to sustain life such as food, water, shelter and security are yet to be met in many countries. The technological revolution that has launched the digital age is fuelling peoples' wants for products and services that will improve their standard of living, but the onward march of global communications often frustrates people who now know about the availability of such things but find it difficult or are unable to afford (demand) them.

Consequences of the business paradigm shift

The consequences of this paradigm change are profound and are summarised below:

*   There is more competition.
*   Therefore the customers of organisations have a choice of provider/supplier.
*   This tends to result in them demanding more for their money (as they see it).
*   This results in on-costs to hard pressed providers/suppliers.
*   Which results in a new business view of value – it is now heavily influenced by buyers and has resulted in the evolution of the concept of consumer-perceived value (Kotler *et al.*, 2009) as a key determinant of business success.
*   This increases the importance of the marketing approach to business and stresses the importance of innovation if organisations are to prosper in their operations.
*   Wise organisations seriously pay more than lip-service to research and development (R&D) and ring-fence or at least defend them from pressures to agree to reduce R&D budgets.

Types of change

Change can be either continuous and mainly incremental or discontinuous, when it bursts into the business arena and is characterised by sudden shifts in strategy, or structure, or culture and typically all three (Senior and Fleming, 2006; Balogun and Hope Hailey, 2008). An example is provided by the privatisation of publicly owned utilities.

Change, whether incremental or radical, is inevitable in an organisation. Change in social systems, in particular the formal organisation, may be defined as a planned or unplanned response to pressures and forces from the natural environment and mostly the activities of people. Managers are constantly challenged to respond to threats and opportunities in their organisation's environment. In order to meet these challenges, they must often change, adapt or even completely transform their organisations. To manage these organisational changes, theorists have found it instructive to categorise change. The three types of change that occur most frequently in organisations are incremental, transitional and transformational (Anderson and Anderson, 2001).

Incremental change

Incremental change or 'first-order' change is essentially about adaptation and assumes that organisations adjust to relatively minor variations in their *modus operandi* automatically without having to face any serious challenges. This mode of change is small and gradual and is easily operated by individuals, groups and managers. Some writers argue that all change, short of life or death, is incremental and so should draw a gradual response (Fox-Wolfgramm *et al.*, 1998).

If a company decided to improve its processes, methods or performance standards this would be considered more of a developmental change. Companies are continually processing developmental change to some degree in order to stay competitive. This type of change should cause little stress to current employees as long as the rationale for the new process is clearly conveyed and the employees are educated in the new techniques. When major change is required, such as the decision to close a division, employees may be more likely to accept the change if the company has attempted to implement developmental change as the first step in streamlining the business. The employees could see that the company has attempted different strategies before determining that closing the division is the only option.

Transitional change

Describes the progress changes an organisation makes as it journeys from the realisation that change is happening and that new and usually radical responses (Laughlin, 1991) must be implemented over a defined period of time. Transitional change involves a fundamental change in behaviour, attitude and belief so that people meet the challenges of the environment. Transitions are a core part of the dynamic of organisational change. Transitional change is more intrusive than developmental change as it replaces existing processes or procedures with something that is completely new to the company. The period when the old process is being dismantled and the new process is being implemented is called the transitional phase. A corporate reorganisation, merger, acquisition, creating new products or services, and implementing new technology are examples of transitional change. Transitional change may not require a significant shift in culture or behaviour but it is more challenging to implement than developmental change.

The outcome of transitional change is unknown so employees may feel that their job is unstable and their own personal insecurities may increase. Education in the new procedures should be commenced at each stage of the new process. This will allow employees to feel that they are actively involved and engaged in the change. As employees' level of engagement in the new procedure increases, their resistance to change may decrease. Management should be cognisant of the impact and stress these changes will have on their employees. The company should continue to inform the employees of their status and offer support in helping them deal with the personal adjustments they will be forced to make.

Transformational change

Transformational change implies radical change with the aim of improving service quality and/or reducing costs. It develops new and different ways of working. Transformational change requires strong leadership. For a transformational change project to succeed it has to be a leader's top priority. Transformational change occurs after the transition period. It may involve both developmental and transitional change. It is common for transitional and transformational change to occur in tandem. When companies are faced with the emergence of radically different technologies, significant changes in supply and demand, unexpected competition, lack of revenue or other major shifts in how they do business, developmental or transitional change may not offer the company the solution it needs to stay competitive. Instead of methodically implementing new processes, the company may be forced to drastically transform itself.

Change drivers

As we have seen, change has a multitude of causes that present us all with challenges as we seek to sustain and improve our standards of living. If we want to analyse change in organisations, a good idea might be to look at the change drivers – and how people feel about them. A good place to start is by encouraging people to brainstorm the change drivers which they think are important. Then encourage them to rank them, discuss them and express their fears about them.

   During the Newspaper Association of America and American Society of News Editors' 'Capital Conference' in 2008 senior executives from Dow Corning, Eastman Kodak and Procter & Gamble discussed their respective company's responses to contextual change. The six key points on which they were all agreed were:

1. The need for a crisis or some kind of 'burning platform' to motivate transformational change;
2. A clear vision and strategy that allows room for iteration;
3. A recognition that transformation is a multi-year journey;
4. A need to put the customer or consumer at the centre of the transformation equation;
5. The critical importance of demonstrating to sceptics that different actions can lead to different results;
6. The need to over-communicate to employees, customers, stakeholders and shareholders.

Practice

Marketing and management myopia

As peoples' standard of living increases and as world markets change from sellers' to buyers' markets so firms and organisations need to seek a new balance between the often competing approaches of market effectiveness (provide what consumers want) and market efficiency (with due regard to the wise use of funds and scarce resources). This places a great deal of importance on the need for organisations to be realistic and accept the desirability of adopting a marketing philosophy as they fashion suitable functional initiatives to meet the challenges of fiercely competitive markets. Ignoring the importance of this philosophy is highly dangerous. It is no good for providers to present to the market a product or service that has been efficiently supplied if it fails to meet the expectations of customers.

As world markets have been heavily challenged by the forces of change discussed in this chapter organisations that fail to place the concept of *market effectiveness* before that of *market efficiency* are in reality living in past sellers' markets. They are trapped in a world that is fast becoming a dream and are suffering from management myopia.

Least cost production paradigm

The least cost production paradigm is closely associated with the concept of market efficiency and makes a great deal of sense when trading organisations are exposed to sellers' markets. Producing as much as possible as cheaply as possible generally results in highly profitable rewards. If the private sector is enjoying a steady and reliable flow of revenue and profit this usually leads to a strong tax-take by national and local authorities which provides considerable resources for public sector spending.

Once private sector markets start to experience the paradigm change from sellers' to buyer's markets increasing pressure is placed on tax yields which in turn places a strain on public sector budgets. If the state or local authorities have inflated their spending during favourable seller's markets or as part of a strategy to win votes overall national indebtedness can increase alarmingly. Matters assume an even greater concern if the merchant banking fraternity have over reached themselves. Financial crisis results and periods of austerity set in as organisations struggle to reduce their indebtedness.

In such times as these there is a strong tendency for the concept of efficiency – highly focused attention to cutting costs – to dominate decisions.

Marketing paradigm

At some point in its development, every industry can be considered a growth industry, based on the apparent superiority of its product. But in case after case, industries have fallen under the shadow of mismanagement. The emphasis is usually on selling, not marketing. This is a mistake, since selling focuses on the needs of the seller, while marketing concentrates on the needs of the buyer. In this widely quoted and anthologised article, first published in 1960, Levitt (2004) argues that 'the history of every dead and dying "growth" industry shows a self-deceiving cycle of bountiful expansion and undetected decay'. But, as he illustrates, memories are short. The railroads serve as an example of an industry whose failure to grow is due to a limited market view. Those behind the railroads are in trouble not because the need for passenger transportation has declined or even because that need has been filled by cars, aeroplanes and other modes of transport. Rather, the industry is failing because those behind it assumed they were in the railroad business rather than the transportation business. They were railroad oriented instead of transportation oriented, product oriented instead of customer oriented. For companies to ensure continued evolution, they must define their industries broadly to take advantage of growth opportunities. They must ascertain and act on their customers' needs and desires, not bank on the presumed longevity of their products. In short, the best way for a firm to be lucky is to make its own luck. An organisation must learn to think of itself not as producing goods or services but as doing the things that will make people want to do business with it. In every case, the chief executive is responsible for creating an environment that reflects this mission.

When seller's markets get weaker so the concept of market effectiveness becomes of greater importance to the private sector. Companies need to place an ever increasing emphasis on providing the right market offerings for their markets (Grönroos, 1996). Often this results in increased expenditure, as consumers usually want more for their money, at a time when firms' finances are under a great deal of strain. To continue to provide the 'usual package' whilst ignoring increasingly difficult trading conditions is a dangerous practice.

Public sector organisations also find that they are required to meet high 'fit for purpose' values and find that as their income stream comes under increased pressure they are faced with stiffer and stiffer challenges.

Customer-perceived value paradigm

The customer-perceived value (CPV) paradigm (as argued by Ravald and Grönroos, 1996; Grönroos, 1996; Yang and Peterson, 2004; Kotler *et al.*, 2009) is a consequence of the paradigm shift from sellers' to buyers' markets. Customers want more value as they perceive it from private sector providers. They usually continue to expect at least the same level and quality of services to be provided by public sector authorities. Essentially CPV is defined as customer-perceived quality (CPQ), what customers expect to experience, relative to customer-perceived price (CPP), what they are prepared to pay for it. Whilst buyers' preferences in the private sector are significantly affected by the offerings of competitors, in the case of the public sector they are imposed by the degree or lack of degree of available public funds. In essence the customer takes what is provided, which is usually determined by cost issues.

Service dominant logic paradigm

Over the course of the last 20 years many marketing authors have argued the case for a new view of marketing that stressed the importance of moving away from the product-centred view. Grönroos, (1994); Gummesson, (1994); Varki and Rust, (1998); Pine and Gilmore, (1998); and Vargo and Lusch, (2004) have developed the leading views expressed in the literature to identify their new view of Service Dominant logic (S-D logic). This places the emphasis firmly on the concept of effectiveness and argues that product and services must be integrated to provide an effective experience for a buyer who has a wide choice of providers.

In many respects the CPV paradigm and the S-D logic paradigm are opposite sides of the same coin. The CPV approach emphasises the importance to providers and buyers of offering the right package (tangible and intangible attributes, i.e. product and service attributes) necessary to attract custom in buyers' markets. The S-D logic approach stresses the importance of service. Whilst this is important, if a customer receives an impressive service from a provider but for a poor quality product the CPV will be low.

Action

Backwards or forwards into the future?

When confronted with the challenge of discontinuous change, organisational management faces two basic decisions. The first is simply to ignore it, walk away and hope that returning swallows in spring will once again restore the good times. Many managers in organisations rose through the ranks in the softer business conditions of seller's markets and therefore can lack the foresight and skills to change the 'company way'. If the forces of discontinuous change intensify this response pattern inevitably leads to disappointing organisational performance and ultimately catastrophic failure.

The second decision is to accept the new reality and seek to change the way the organisation operates. This means coming to terms with complex management challenges. It means being willing to learn new tricks.

The challenge of change

In *The Dance of Change: The Challenges of Sustaining Momentum in Learning Organizations*, Senge and his colleagues (1999) identify ten challenges of change, grouped into three categories:

1.   Challenges of initiating change
2.   Challenges of sustaining momentum
3.   Challenges of system-wide redesign and rethinking.

The ten items amount to what the authors call 'the conditions of the environment that regulate growth':

Challenges of initiating change

1.   *'We don't have time for this stuff!'* People who are involved in a pilot group to initiate a change effort need enough control over their schedules to give their work the time that it needs.
2.   *'We have no help!'* Members of a pilot group need enough support, coaching and resources to be able to learn and to do their work effectively.
3.   *'This stuff isn't relevant.'* There need to be people who can make the case for change – who can connect the development of new skills to the real work of the business.
4.   *'They're not walking the talk!'* A critical test for any change effort: the correlation between espoused values and actual behaviour.

Challenges of sustaining momentum

1.   *'This stuff is . . .'* Personal fear and anxiety – concerns about vulnerability and inadequacy – lead members of a pilot group to question a change effort.
2.   *'This stuff isn't working!'* Change efforts run into measurement problems: early results don't meet expectations, or traditional metrics don't calibrate to a pilot group's efforts.
3.   *'They're acting like a cult!'* A pilot group falls prey to arrogance, dividing the company into 'believers' and 'nonbelievers'.

Challenges of system-wide redesign and rethinking

1.   *'They never let us do this stuff.'* The pilot group wants more autonomy; 'the powers that be' don't want to lose control.
2.   *'We keep reinventing the wheel.'* Instead of building on previous successes, each group finds that it has to start from scratch.

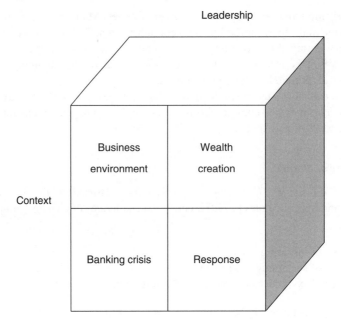

Figure 1.5 Context and leadership.

3.   *'Where are we going?'* The larger strategy and purpose of a change effort may be obscured by day-to-day activity. Big question: can the organisation achieve a new definition of success?

Summary

This chapter has opened the text with a discussion of how change affects the fortunes of business organisations and warns of the danger of management and marketing myopia. Senior management need to be alert to the dangers of business environmental trends and to respond swiftly. The current and foreseeable discontinuous change that is impacting on business organisations emphasises the importance of continually reappraising the business environment and presents them with a severe set of challenges if they are to successfully grow their businesses. As this text will argue in subsequent chapters business creativity and innovation are vital for the successful management of change (Andropoulos and Dawson, 2009). Organisations and strategic leaders that look for success, excellence and technological vanguard have to face the concept of 'Innovation Management' as a development perspective with a domain of conceptual autonomy.

Discussion questions

1.   Why does change present such a problem to organisations these days?
2.   What causes change?
3.   What is creativity and why is it important in times of discontinuous change?
4.   Briefly describe the main types of change.
5.   What is the customer-perceived value paradigm and why is it important in strong buyers' markets?

Case exercise

Gobur Caravans is a small company located in north Norfolk in the UK and has been manufacturing and marketing a range of folding caravans since the 1970s. Folding caravans are attractive to keen caravaners who do not have a great deal of storage space for a caravan. They are also safer to tow owing to their lower profile which also results in greater fuel economy.

The company has designed a range of caravans that cover the entry, middle and top market segments in their small factory in the village of Melton Constable. Despite the tendency of the caravan industry to be particularly sensitive to the health of the UK economy the business has grown over the years to assume a unique niche position in the UK caravan market.

The folding caravans are all hand-made and finished to a high standard before being put up for sale. Most of the new models are built to customer specifications. The firm also sells pre-owned models which are displayed on its factory site. In most cases Gobur sells these on a commission basis. Other manufacturer's caravans are also sold on a commission basis. As the business developed, a small extras retail shop has offered a range of optional caravan items such as wheel locks, steps, water carriers and so on.

Gobur employs less than ten full-time staff and a small number of part-time workers. The business is run in a supportive family style. The managing director has a sound knowledge of the mechanics of the caravan business and an open and welcoming customer manner.

As can be expected from a small company hand crafting its products, Gobur's models are priced at a premium and are more expensive to buy new than conventional closed top caravans. Although the company has advertised modestly in the leading UK caravan magazines and attended most of the leading UK caravan trade exhibitions and shows it has fashioned a niche market position within the UK caravan market.

Since the 1970s the UK caravan market has experienced a high degree of consolidation. Gobur has not sought to join any other group of manufacturers, preferring to cultivate its niche market position.

The business environmental paradigm change has resulted in fierce competition in the caravan market. Customers are demanding more and more for their money, causing the leading companies to seek an appropriate balance between expected quality and price and therefore costs of production and marketing. In 2011 Pennine, well known as a trailer tent specialist, entered the folding compact caravan market offering a superior specification than Gobur at a 20 per cent price lower price. There are also early warnings that a large French manufacturer (Trigano) is about to enter the folding camper market.

The management at Gobur are aware of the potential dangers to their niche market position but confident that despite their price disadvantage they will hold their own as through the years *down turns* and their associated problems have always been followed by *up turns* and their associated opportunities. Business is essentially about standing firm and waiting for the return of better market conditions.

Task

Write a brief memo to Gobur's managing director explaining the consequences of the business environmental paradigm change.

References

Anderson, D. and Ackerman-Anderson, L.S. (2001) *Beyond Change Management: Advanced Strategies for Today's Transformational Leaders*, San Francisco, Jossey-Bass/Pfeiffer.

Anderson, L.S. and Anderson, D. (2001) *The Change Leader's Roadmap*, San Francisco, Wiley.

Andropoulos, C. and Dawson, P. (2009) *Managing Change, Creativity and Innovation*, London, Sage.

Balogun, J. and Hope Hailey, V.H. (2008) *Exploring Strategic Change*, 3rd edn, Harlow, FT/Prentice Hall.

Bilton, C. (2007) *Management and Creativity*, Oxford, Blackwell.

Bilton, C. and Cummings, S. (2010) *Creative Strategy: Reconnecting Business and Innovation*, Oxford, Blackwell.

Bowman, C. and Swart, J. (2007) 'Whose human capital? The challenge of value capture when capital is embedded', *Journal of Management Studies*, Vol. 44, Issue 4, pp. 488–505.

Carniero A. (2008) 'When leadership means more innovation and development', *Business Strategy Series*, Vol. 9, Issue 4, pp. 176–84.

Chien-Hsin L., Sher, P.J. and Hsin-Yu, S. (2005) 'Past progress and future directions in conceptualizing customer perceived value', *International Journal of Service Industry Management*, Vol. 16, Issue 4, pp. 318–36.

Dean, A. and Kretschmer, M. (2007) 'Can ideas be capital? Factors of production in the post-industrial economy', *Academy of Management Review*, April, Vol. 32, Issue 2, pp. 573–94.

The Economist (2010) 'Developing countries are competing on creativity as well as cost. That will change business everywhere', 15 April.

Erickson, G.S. and Rothberg, H.N. (2000) 'Intellectual capital and competitiveness', *Competitive Review*, Vol. 10, Issue 2, pp. 192–98.

Erickson, T. and Nerdrum, L. (2001) 'Intellectual Capital: A human capital perspective', *Journal of Intellectual Capital*, Vol. 2, Issue 2, pp. 127–35.

The Financial Times (2004) 'Creative Business', 25 May.

Fox-Wolfgramm, S.J., Boal, K.B. and Hunt, J.G. (1998) 'Organizational adaptation to institutional change: A comparative study of first-order change in prospector and defender banks', *Administrative Science Quarterly*, Vol. 43, pp. 87–126.

IBM (2010) 'Capitalizing on complexity: Insights from the 2010 IBM global CEO study'. www.ibm.com/services/us/ceo/ceostudy2010/index.html, accessed 17/04/12.

George, J. and Jones, G. (1995) *Understanding and Managing Organizational Behavior*, Boston, Addison-Wesley.

Goodman, M.R.V. (1995) *Creative Management*, Harlow, Pearson.

Graetz, F., Rimmer, M., Lawrence, A. and Smith, A. (2006) *Managing Organisational Change*, 2nd Australian edn, Brisbane, Wiley.

Grey, C. (2003) 'The fetish of change', *Tamara: Journal of Critical Postmodern Organization Science*, Vol. 2, Issue 2, pp. 1–19.

Grönroos, C. (1994) 'From scientific management to service management', *International Journal of Service Industry Management*, Vol. 5, Issue 1, pp. 5–16.

Grönroos, C. (1996) 'Relationship marketing: Strategic and tactical implications', *Management Decision*, Vol. 34, Issue 3, pp. 5–10.

Grönroos, C. and Ravald, A. (2011) 'Service as business logic: Implications for value creation and marketing', *Journal of Service Management*, Vol. 22, Issue 1, pp. 5–22.

Gummesson, E. (1994) 'Service management: An evaluation and the future', *International Journal of Service Industry Management*, Vol. 5, Issue 1, pp. 77–97.

Kahnemann, D. (2011) 'The hazards of confidence', *Brad DeLong*. http://delong.typepad.com/sdj/2011/10/daniel-kahnemann-the-hazards-of-confidence.html, accessed 17/04/12.

Kotler, P., Keller, K.L., Brady, M., Goodman, M.R.V. and Hansen, T. (2009) *Marketing Management*, 1st European edn, Harlow, Pearson.

Laughlin, R.C. (1991) 'Environmental disturbances and organisational transitions and transformations: Some alternative models', *Organizational Studies*, Vol. 12, pp. 209–32.

Levitt, T. (2004) 'Marketing myopia', *Harvard Business Review*, July/August, Vol. 82, Issue 7/8, pp. 138–49.

Parkin, M. and Bade, R. (2011) *Foundations of Economics*, 5th edn, Harlow, FT/Pearson,

Pine, II, B.J. and Gilmore, J.H. (1998) 'Welcome to the experience economy', *Harvard Business Review*, July/August, Vol. 76, Issue 4, pp. 97–105.

Ravald, A. and Grönroos, C. (1996) 'The value concept and relationship marketing', *European Journal of Marketing*, Vol. 30, Issue 2, pp. 19–30.

Rivett, K.G. and Kline, D. (2000) 'Discovering new value in intellectual property', *Harvard Business Review* (January–February). http://hbr.org/2000/01/discovering-new-value-in-intellectual-property/ar/1, accessed 11/4/12.

Schumpeter, J.A. (1939) *Business Cycles: A Theoretical, Historical and Statistical Analysis of the Capitalist Process*, New York, McGraw-Hill.

Senge, P., Kleiner, A., Roberts, C., Ross, R., Roth, G. and Smith, B. (1999) *The Dance of Change: The Challenges of Sustaining Momentum in Learning Organizations (A Fifth Discipline Resource)*, London, Nicholas Brealey Publishing.

Senior, B. and Fleming, J. (2006) *Organizational Change*, 3rd edn, Harlow, FT/Prentice Hall, Chapters 1–2.

Vargo, S.L. and Lusch, R.F. (2004) 'Evolving to a new dominant logic for marketing', *Journal of Marketing*, January, Vol. 68, Issue 1, pp. 1–17.

Varki, S. and Rust, R. (1998) 'Technology and optimal segment size', *Marketing Letters*, Vol. 9, Issue 2, pp. 147–67.

WEF (n.d.) The World Economic Forum is an independent organisation committed to improving the state of the world by engaging business, political, academic and other leaders of society to shape global, regional and industry agendas. http://www.weforum.org/, accessed 17/04/12. See also http://www.weforum.org/s?s=Scandinavian+model, accessed 17/04/12.

Wollensky, J. (2010) 'Wanted: The right sort of genius', *Modern Power Systems*, December. http://www.modernpowersystems.com/story.asp?sectionCode=85&storyCode=2058777, accessed 11/4/12.

Yang, Z. and Peterson, R.T. (2004) 'Customer perceived value, satisfaction, and loyalty: The role of switching costs', *Psychology & Marketing*, October, Vol. 21, Issue 10, pp. 799–822.

2   Key business decisions

The man who is denied the opportunity of taking decisions of importance begins to regard as important the decisions he is allowed to take.

(C. Northcote Parkinson, 1958)

Nothing is more difficult, and therefore more precious, than to be able to decide.

(Napoleon Bonaparte)

Introduction

A basic definition of business decisions would imply that they simply involve choosing among alternative responses. However, a fundamental shift in the underlying state of the business environment challenges organisations to respond in one of two ways. The first is to do little in terms of their fundamental approach to their business environment in the hope of riding out the storm. If the complex disturbances in the business environment are incremental a contextual recovery may well provide the prospect of a business recovery. However, if the disturbances amount – as explained in the previous chapter – to a major environmental paradigm shift, organisations need to re-evaluate their *modus operandi*. In most cases this will involve considering a mix of incremental and radical response changes.

Whilst study of the S-curve (see 2.3.6) provides a conceptual understanding of what business decisions are needed the following concepts address the necessary responses. The concept of business effectiveness addresses the need to do the right thing in the new business environment. The concept of efficiency addresses issues concerned with the wise use of funds and resources. Radical responses address the changes that will be needed and sustained to meet the environmental challenges. This will demand a committed approach to thinking outside the previous sellers' market paradigm box (business creativity) to secure effective and efficient business practice in order to foster the growth of innovation and entrepreneurship.

Context

Time frame issues

Organisations have never faced a more turbulent, complex or changing environment than they do today, whether in social, political, economic, technological or ecological terms. Customers are more demanding; product lifecycles are shorter; technologies are constantly

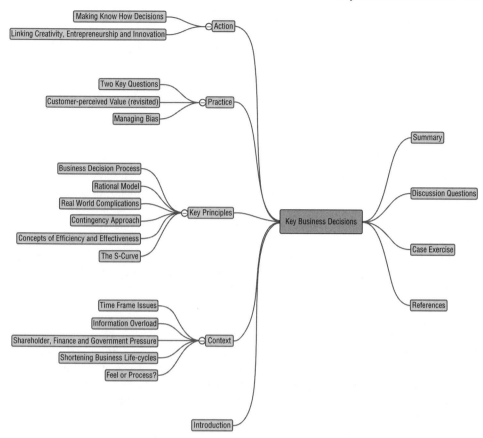

Figure 2.1 Exploring key business decisions.

changing. Managers must continuously scan the competitive environment. All of us have to make decisions every day. Some are relatively straightforward and simple; others are quite complex. A business decision can be defined as a purposeful selection from among a set of alternatives in the light of a given task objective. Decision making is not a separate function of management but is intertwined with other functions, such as planning, co-ordinating and controlling. These functions all require decisions to be made. For example, at the outset, management must make a critical decision as to which of several possible strategies should be followed. Such a decision is often termed a *strategic* decision because of its long-term impact on the organisation. Also, managers must make several lesser decisions, tactical and operational, all of which are important to an organisation's performance and health.

Business decision making in a predominantly buyers' market environment is difficult. Three macro level elements (Friga and Chapas, 2008), clearly differentiate decision making today:

1. Information overload
2. Shareholder, finance and government pressure
3. Shortening business lifecycle times.

All decisions are about problems and these are evident at three levels:

1. *Macrocontext* draws attention to global environmental trends, the state of buyers' markets;
2. *Mesocontext* attends to organisational cultures and structure;
3. *Microcontext* addresses the immediate decision environment – the organisation's employees, staff board and so on.

Information overload

The abundance of information and the complexity of modern search tools yield a flood of data that can easily overwhelm individual decision makers. Essential information provided by a useful business intelligence system which covers both contextual issues – the state of the market – and competitive business intelligence is needed in buyers' markets if management are to take perceptive tactical and strategic decisions (Vasilopoulos, 2010). Managers can quite easily become confused with too much information unless they are trained in knowledge management skills. Data is data and true decision making expertise is about the effective use of information in addressing management problems.

Shareholder, finance and government pressure

The rise and expectations of worldwide capital markets has led to a relentless drive to achieve short-term financial results, often at the expense of longer term considerations. In the private sector the pursuit of growth at any cost has resulted in the demise of many companies. Small and medium sized businesses (SMEs) are experiencing tighter and tighter payback deadlines from financial institutions. Public sector organisations are increasingly expected to maintain services in the light of funding cuts.

Shortening business lifecycles

The time to market and overall business cycles have shortened to a level unimaginable in the closing decades of the twentieth century. Individuals alone and in meetings, have to make decisions at an ever increasing pace. These decisions can so easily be made on the basis of precedent, leaving organisations floundering as the accustomed and expected results fail to materialise.

Feel or process?

In relatively unchallenging times, such as the long period of sellers' markets that was in evidence for much of the last half of the twentieth century, many key decisions were made in a relatively casual manner as such interventions stood a high chance of success. Many low risk decisions were often taken by *feel* with a tendency to be largely influenced by financial factors (the concept of effectiveness as discussed below). Decisions with a higher level of risk and commitment have usually been made by the application of *process* techniques. Difficult decisions usually involve much more than 'off the cuff' responses and typically involve such issues as:

- Uncertainty – many essential facts may be unknown;
- Complexity – demanding attention be given to several inter-related factors;

- High risk consequences – impact of the decision may be of crucial significance;
- Alternatives – each possesses its own set of uncertainties and consequences;
- Interpersonal issues – that are difficult to predict.

With these difficulties in mind it is wise to make complex decisions by using clear process techniques that usually lead to consistent, high-quality results. We discuss a selection of some of the most popular in the following section. In many cases in today's turbulent business environments it is pertinent to combine both 'feel' and 'process' techniques.

Key principles

Business decision process

Business decision making in today's sellers' markets is difficult. Except in the case of simple problems, it involves more than a simple act of selecting a response from a number of alternatives. It requires the application of a process that may take time initially, but which will speed up with experience. Many organisations suffer from a lack of systematic decision making. The decision making process can be explained clearly to staff, sponsors and stakeholders. People tend to be happier to implement decisions when they have participated in them.

Figure 2.2 presents an example of a typical seven-step approach to business decision making.

Step one concerns a clear *identification of the problem* and addresses the issue of the current situation and the desired one (Nagurney *et al*., 2002). For example, in the case of a family decision, say to purchase a new TV, the main task is to acquire one that works. In contrast managers in organisations face a more complex task. Key factors in the purchase of a new machine tool (Sayer, 2002) would include the following issues:

- expected financial return,
- technical excellence,
- compatibility with existing production facilities and staff.

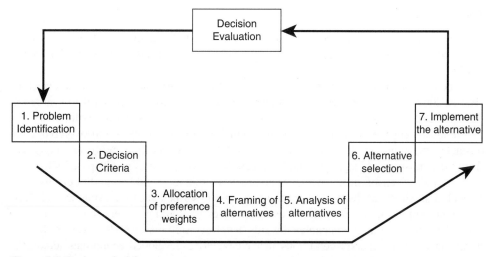

Figure 2.2 Business decision process.

Step two follows once the problem has been framed clearly and concerns the *decision criteria* that would influence the selection of a suitable purchase. Families, for example, might seek to obtain a new TV set that was technically up-to-date, had a clear, flat digital screen and appealing design. Managers intent on purchasing a machine tool would also be interested in the technical support, training and engineering support provided by the machine tool company (Figueira and Ray, 2002).

Step three addresses the issue that not all the identified decision criteria are of equal importance and so indicates preferences by allocating weights to decision criteria. In the case of the family TV set, for example, a strong preference might be placed on picture quality ahead of design. Managers may exhibit a strong preference for a branded provider of machine tools whose products they have been happy with in the past.

Step four involves *listing alternatives* that might be capable of solving the problem. The individual replacing the family TV draws up a list of selected brands that meet the family's purchase criteria. Management, whilst expressing a strong preference for one machine tool manufacturer, decide to evaluate this provider's product against the possible competitive products (Fazlollahi and Vahidov, 2001).

Step five can be termed *analysis of alternatives* and is where our potential imaginary family seeking a new TV and the organisational management team intent on the purchase of a new machine tool evaluate the list of possible alternatives. In both cases, though most likely in the case of the machine tool purchase, our potential buyers score the selected providers' products key criteria attributes, say on a scale of 1 to 10.

Step six follows and is where the key decision makers for both the domestic TV and the machine tool *select a provider.*

Step seven is the stage when purchases are made.

Finally, buyers, whether consumer or business-to-business, seek a satisfactory in-use purchase experience. Our imaginary family will assess the customer-perceived value they experience with their chosen TV and this will significantly influence their future buying decisions. An organisation purchasing a machine tool will carry out an *overall evaluation* of all aspects of the contribution of the purchase to their business.

Rational model

Individual or organisational decision making is assumed to be rational when those involved make consistent and value maximising selections within specified criteria. (DeYoung, 2002)

Rationality is the use of scientific reasoning and logical arguments to arrive at decisions (Burns, 2009). As widely applied, the scientific method is analytical (rather than synthetic), positivist and reductionist. The rational or scientific model allows for both evolutionary and revolutionary change, as well as exploitive and explorative contexts, and overcomes the obstacles impacting on objectivity (see Section 2.2.5). It is objective and theoretically free from the imposition of large egos and bureaucratic thinking (Friga and Chapas, 2008).

A business decision maker who was completely rational would be totally objective and logical in all stages of the decision making process described above. Davenport and Harri (2010) present a best practice guide to using analytics as a tool for leaders at every organisational level to drive their companies towards better decision making. However, in the predominantly sellers' market conditions that characterise developed economies today, the degree of outcome surety that the rational model demands rarely exists, as the precise result of every business decision alternative is unknown. Therefore, managers can only seek to assign probabilities to the likely success of their decisions. The conventional wisdom as expounded by adherents to the scientific method is well suited to the natural and exact sciences but unsuited to management charged with business decision making in highly competitive buyers' markets. A more appropriate input to decision making processes is *grounded theory* or what Kaplan (1998) termed *innovation action research*.

In the real world this results in the need to assess the degree of risk attached to decisions. Faced with this difficulty decision makers need to blend their rational approach to well framed problem statements with an ability to think 'outside the box' and harness the benefits that creativity can bring. Many still scoff when consultants recommend this and often reject such an illogical approach out of hand. However, if the existing responses fail to deliver in the current buyers' market environments then it can indeed make sense to explore new ways of thinking. Creativity can help managers generate ideas and interventions that are manifestly different from those of the past (mainly sellers' markets) but relevant to the challenges provided by buyers' markets. It can help greatly by enabling managers taking decisions to identify all viable alternatives. The management literature is replete with the successes of reductionist research. However, it is incomplete because it does not place sufficient attention on the process of generating high and consistent levels of customer-perceived value offering alternatives in today's highly competitive buyers' markets (Goodman, 1995).

Real world complications

Every day most of us make decisions that are in the strict sense of the term far from being rational. Economists have their model of the Rational Man (*homo economicus*) and lawyers have a similar concept known in the UK as 'the man on the Clapham omnibus'. In real life we all make decisions which are irrational in this sense. We make decisions on the basis of incomplete information and largely on the basis of intuition rather than scientific processes. At its best such behaviour is rational within the parameters of a simplified model that captures the essential features of the problem needing a business decision (Kuhberger *et al.*, 2001; Mintzberg and Westley, 2001; Dane, 2007; *McKinsey Quarterly*, 2010; Kandelwal and Tanje, 2010).

Contingency approach

The contingency approach posits the view that there is not necessarily a 'one-best-way' of managing and making business decisions. It maintains that the structures and practices of an organisation, and therefore its performance, are dependent (i.e. contingent) on the context that it faces. The main contingencies – situational variables – identified by its proponents are environmental uncertainty and dependence, technology and organisation size (Burns, 2009).

The contingency approach appeals to the 'if–then' formula and constitutes a break with the 'one-best-way' rational approach often favoured by organisations. Ambos and Schelgelmilch (2007) collected data from 134 German multinational companies' research and development units and found that the contingency approaches returned better results than the more traditional rational approaches. Research by Bradshaw (2009) found that a number of contingency factors were likely to be relevant for effective nonprofit organisations and their boards. Although all boards must fulfil certain critical roles and responsibilities, strategic choices could be made about adopting different governance configurations or patterns.

These choices could be meaningfully informed by understanding organisational contingencies such as, age, size, structure and strategy – and, even more important, by external contingencies and environmental dimensions, such as degree of stability and complexity. Bradshaw's research extends or layers contingency thinking beyond its traditional focus on an alignment between the external environment and the organisation's structure, to focus as well on the alignment of the organisation's governance configuration with its structure and environment.

Ambos and Schelgelmilch focus on control mechanisms used by multinational corporations (MNCs) to manage their extra-national R&D units. Drawing on the literature of both organisational power and contingency theory, their study develops and empirically tests a set of hypotheses aimed at explaining how headquarters control their overseas R&D units. Data collected from 134 R&D units of German MNCs serve to test the hypotheses. Results highlight the importance of the units' R&D mandate and its interdependence in explaining control mechanisms. Moreover, they indicate a relatively weak predictive power of political approaches compared to contingency approaches.

Sillince (2005) argues that attempts to adapt structure to contingencies will be unsuccessful unless there is also rhetorical congruence, which has two parts. First, rhetorical congruence exists if rhetoric is appropriate to contingencies. For example, decentralisation aimed at increasing local initiative will lead to more requests by headquarters for advice from subsidiaries. Second, it exists if the various rhetorical processes are in balance with one another.

When important projects fail, the investigation is often focused on the engineering and technical reasons for the failure. That was the case with NASA's Mars Climate Orbiter (MCO) that was lost in space after completing its nine month journey to Mars. Yet, in many cases the root cause of the failure is not technical, but managerial. Often the problem is rooted in management's failure to select the right approach to the specific project. The evolving field of project management contingency theory provides an opportunity to re-examine the concept of fit between project characteristics and project management, and offer deeper insights on why projects fail. Sauser *et al.* (2009) show that project management contingency theory can indeed provide new insights for a deeper understanding of project failure. Furthermore, it suggests implications for a richer upfront analysis of a project's unique characteristics of uncertainty and risk, as well as additional directions of research. Such research may help establish new and different conceptions of project success and failure beyond the traditional success factors, and subsequently develop more refined contingency frameworks. The results of such research may enable future project managers to rely less on heuristics and possibly lead to a new application of 'project management design'.

Despite the tremendous popularity and great potential, the field of Enterprise Resource Planning (ERP) adoption and implementation is littered with remarkable failures (Morton and Hu, 2008). Though many contributing factors have been cited in the literature, we argue that the integrated nature of ERP systems, which generally requires an organisation to adopt standardised business processes reflected in the design of the software, is a key factor contributing to these failures. We submit that the integration and standardisation imposed by most ERP systems may not be suitable for all types of organisation and thus the 'fit' between the characteristics of the adopting organisation and the standardised business process designs embedded in the adopted ERP system affects the likelihood of implementation success or failure. In this chapter, we use the structural contingency theory to identify a set of dimensions of organisational structure and ERP system characteristics that can be used to gauge the degree of fit, thus providing some insights into successful ERP implementations.

Propositions are developed based on analyses regarding the success of ERP implementations in different types of organisations. These propositions also provide directions for future research that might lead to prescriptive guidelines for managers of organisations contemplating implementing ERP systems.

Concepts of efficiency and effectiveness

The concepts of *efficiency* and *effectiveness* provide important guidance for business decision makers. *Efficiency* is essentially about bearing in mind the resource implications of possible alternative solutions. Good business decisions take into account more than short-term considerations wherever possible and relevant. For example, with buying decisions, *buying cheap* can result in *buying dear* if the pressures of the moment saddle the organisation with a problem solution that fails in the medium term and so calls for more funds to fix. Another practice to be considered very carefully by wise business managers in the public sector is the over use of Private Finance Initiatives. This may seem to be expedient in the short term, as it appears to be less of a strain on the Public Sector Borrowing Account, but can heavily mortgage into the future. Perhaps, a classic case of 'backwards into the future'?

The concept of *effectiveness* stresses the importance of achieving an optimum solution to a business problem. No half measures but a considered attempt to do what is necessary to fix a problem.

A balanced approach to these concepts should result in a sound business decision. The argument is essentially simple but it is both surprising and alarming that research around the world shows that many CEOs and managers have a poor track record with their business decisions (Finkelstein *et al.*, 2009).

The S-curve

Business decisions concerning the pursuit of innovation are either incremental or radical in nature and are subject inevitably to practical constraints. The progress of successful innovations can usefully be examined with reference to an S-shaped curve as depicted in Figure 2.3.

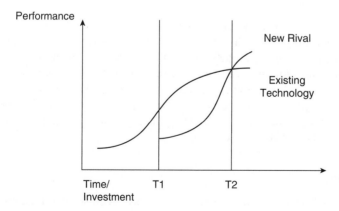

Figure 2.3 The S-curve: a comparison between an established and a new technology.
Source: M.R.V. Goodman, Durham University.

The curve is plotted in a two-dimensional plane and shows how the performance of a technology in terms of the concepts of market effectiveness and efficiency change over time. The horizontal axis summarises how an innovation develops in terms of time and investment. The vertical axis reflects some key dimensions of product performance or cost competitiveness. As evident from Figure 2.3 the pace of innovation changes with time. Most decisions tend to become incremental and progressively more and more costly.

When the rival technology emerges many view it as being inferior to the existing technology (position T1). Growing pains may be obvious for all to see and so many competitors may not identify it as a real threat. Most customers are also unsure about the value offered by the innovation and so pay it scant regard. As time passes and after further investment, the teething troubles associated with the innovation are addressed and manufacturing costs begin to fall. At point T2 the innovation matches the perceived value of the established technology and starts to return a superior level of performance. The scenario outlined above has three important lessons for decision makers:

1. Businesses seeking to protect their positions with the established technology increasingly face difficult decisions – the limpet strategy.
2. Pioneers in one generation of technology are not necessarily leaders in the next – the cautious strategy.
3. Businesses seeking to exploit innovations enjoy several advantages – innovative entrepreneurial strategy.

Limpet strategy

Companies that cling on to established technologies tend to be challenged by three options:

(a) Totally adopt the new technology and abandon the established technology;
(b) Retain their existing exploitation of the established technology and attempt to raise standards of performance by means of incremental investment;
(c) Retain their existing interest in the established technology but begin to invest in innovative technology to obtain the best of both worlds.

Option (a) is the most difficult to sustain and involves moving on to a new S-curve. It is also potentially the most dangerous decision to make. Option (b) means sticking with the established technology that usually attracts incremental business decisions to maintain the effective life of the innovation. As time passes these decisions make only marginal differences and organisations have to contemplate making radical decisions in order to move on to a new S-curve. Option (c) seems to make the most sense in times of discontinuous change as it enables an organisation to phase in the new technology whilst continuing to benefit as long as possible from the established technology.

Cautious strategy

There are several examples of organisations whose established technology has lost out to new and innovative technologies. When desktop computers took off the then dominant computer manufacturer – IBM – was displaced as market leader by Digital Equipment. Swiss watch manufacturers lost out to East Asian competition with the introduction of the innovative battery driven quartz watches. The well respected *Encyclopaedia Britannica* that ran to 30 plus printed volumes, gave way to innovative software packages such as Microsoft's Encarta which in turn was superseded by Internet-based encyclopaedias.

Innovative strategy

Several companies that have become household names started as small operations. Apple emerged from a garage. Hewlett-Packard, DEC, Intel, Microsoft, Dell and eBay all began in this way.

New processes, tools and practices are being introduced into software companies at an increasing rate. With each new advance in technology, software managers need to consider not only whether it is time to change the technologies currently used, but also whether an evolutionary change is sufficient or a revolutionary change is required (Nikula *et al.*, 2010).

Practice

Two key questions

1.   Can the challenges of business environmental change be managed successfully?
2.   Should the organisation reappraise and alter the way it does things?

The first question is the hang-on-and-do-nothing strategy often argued on the basis that every downturn in an organisation's business is always followed by an upturn. It is just a matter of making minor (or depending on the nature of the problem major) financial adjustments. Some consultants refer to this option as the 'coherence theory of truth'. However, in times of discontinuous change it is usually disastrous.

The second question makes more sense in today's business environment but is far more difficult for top management to achieve and calls for a real match between professional competence and rank. Sadly many organisations are led by management that honed their skills in a previous era (sellers' markets) or religiously follow the dictates of the established organisational culture. Whilst a rising executive may look through the glass clearly, political pressure – real and imagined – seems so easily to frustrate talent and results in the executive following the company ways, even it if means looking through a glass darkly.

Customer-perceived value revisited

A crucial consequence of the business environmental paradigm change (See Chapter 1) has been a transformation in the concept of *value*. In sellers' market conditions value was essentially regarded by many businesses as being about cost reduction and production expansion, effectively placing a heavy stress on the concept of *efficiency*. In buyers' market conditions value is firstly a matter of providing what customers perceive to have value. This places the concept of *effectiveness* before that of *efficiency*. The implication of this is profound, as it presents a severe challenge to the least cost production approach to management. Yesterday's business solutions cannot now automatically become the default decisions. If CEOs and senior management are to become proactive and seek new ways of conducting their businesses many consultants will confirm that a major problem resides in their attitudes, mindsets and paradigms. Biased argument is awash in organisations as they try to maintain the *status quo* by management myopia or through the deception that often results from biased thinking.

Managing bias

Before managers make key business decisions they should strive to avoid bias by responding to the following questions (Kahneman, Lovallo and Sibony, 2011):

Questions that decision makers should ask:

1.   Is there any reason to suspect motivated errors?
2.   Is the decision maker too emotionally involved with the issue?
3.   Are there any dissenting opinions (group)?

Questions that decision makers should ask the team making recommendations:

4.   Is the decision overemphasised by salient analogies (what has happened in the past)?
5.   Have all credible alternatives been considered?
6.   If the decision had to be made again what information would be needed and can some of it be acquired now?
7.   Where did the justifying numbers come from?
8.   Is a halo effect apparent? Charisma . . .
9.   Is the decision maker overly attached to past decisions?

Questions focused on evaluating the proposal:

10. Is the case overly optimistic?
11. Is the worst case scenario bad enough?
12. Is the decision maker overtly cautious?

Whilst key business decisions are ultimately the responsibility of top management, involving staff groups in the decision making process has the following distinct advantages:

*   It facilitates the analysis of information;
*   It generates more alternative solutions;
*   It leads to an increased acceptance of the final top management business decisions.

The downside factors are:

*   Group participation is inherently time consuming;
*   Groups can be heavily influenced by dominant minorities;
*   'Groupthink' (Janis, 1982) can cloud issues if the group feels threatened by possible solutions to the business problems being discussed.

Action

Making decisions – blending knowledge with experience

- Identify the real problem – what is the gap between what is happening and what should be happening?
- Analyse possible causes of problems and decide on the most likely cause – collect evidence for and against each possible cause. 'Score' each cause.
- Brainstorm possible solutions to the problem (apply creative thinking).
- Evaluate alternatives and decide on the most sensible (rational or creative response). Score each identified solution against key criteria such as cost, people, time and so on, and select the solution with the highest score.
- Anticipate what could go wrong. Draw up a 'Plan B'.
- Implement the decision. Who does what with what resources and when?

Linking creativity, entrepreneurship and innovation

If organisations are to take business decisions in the light of the second option in Section 2.4.1 and seek to become market or office leaders this requires a different kind of thinking as they approach business decisions. CEOs and managers will need to ensure that their business decisions reflect a suitable contextual combination of the concepts of efficiency and effectiveness. This will require a new thinking approach (see Chapter 4): to encourage, fund, develop and implement innovative business decisions. Managers will need to become entrepreneurs if they are to strike the right balance on the efficiency–effectiveness concept continuum.

Many in business life have a vague or ill-defined understanding of the terms creativity, entrepreneurship and innovation. Creativity forms the lead topic in Chapter 4 but can be taken for now to mean 'thinking outside the box' or being original. Entrepreneurship is about applying creativity and foresight to identify commercial opportunities or more efficient and effective ways of running an administrative office. Innovation is to do with fashioning new ideas to improve methods, to design and develop new products and services that contain appropriate levels of customer-perceived value.

Especially in times of discontinuous change, CEOs and senior managers need to ensure that their organisations are performing successfully. Doing what they have always done – if it is done efficiently – is not sufficient unless it is contextually effective. Enterprises that do not innovate inevitably age and decline.

To face today's business world with confidence managers must understand the linkage between creativity, entrepreneurship and innovation.

Summary

An organised and systematic decision making process usually leads to better decisions. Without a well defined process that includes both the analytical and feel approaches managers are in danger of making decisions that are based on insufficient information, analysis and interpretation. Many variables affect the final impact of business decisions. However, if managers establish strong foundations for decision making, generate good alternatives, evaluate these alternatives rigorously, and then check their decision making process, they will improve the quality of their decisions. The current business environment demands sound business decision making. It is not a time to shrink from this executive responsibility.

Discussion questions

1. What effect do shortening business cycles have on business decision makers?
2. Explain why so many successful businesses continue to be characterised by managers who make courageous business decisions.
3. Why might a total reliance on the rational, analytical approach to making business decisions be inadvisable in times of discontinuous change?
4. Explain why the concepts of effectiveness and efficiency are so important for business decision makers.
5. How might managers avoid bias in their business decisions?

Case exercise

The UK catalogue retailer Argos in the 1980s was led by Mike Smith, who presided over a senior management team who had been with Argos all their working lives. Argos had performed impressively up to this point and Mike was revered in the City. Suddenly Mike Smith began to slow down. He was a heavy smoker and nobody at the time realised that he was seriously ill. He tried to continue but he was diagnosed with an aggressive cancer and he stopped making business decisions.

This situation continued for a couple of years: day-to-day operating decisions but no formative decisions were made and the company started to underperform. As the CEO, Mike Smith remained in control. His management team had worked for him since the day he had started and had become 'yes-men'. There was no proactive, innovative debate at board level and no desire for change. Much to the frustration of a nonexecutive director who had been appointed in 1990 the board failed to respond to his entreaties for the necessity of introducing change. Eventually Mike Smith and the Financial Director had to take time off work but continued to pull the strings. Despite early support from the City Argos returned poor performances, leading the City to lose confidence in the firm.

Questions

1. What in your view are the main dangers of a CEO surrounding himself with yes-men when it comes to making business decisions?
2. How would you have advised Argos about the importance of taking business decisions to encourage, fund and develop innovative practices within the company?
3. Why do you think that research has indicated that CEOs and senior managers often make bad business decisions?

References

Amabile, T.M. (1997) 'Motivating creativity in organisations', *California Management Review*, Fall, pp. 42–52.
Ambos, B. and Schelgelmilch, B.B. (2007) 'Innovation and control in the multinational firm: A comparison of political and contingency approaches', *Strategic Management Journal*, May, Vol. 28, Issue 5, pp. 473–86.

Bradshaw, P. (2009) 'A contingency approach to nonprofit governance', *Nonprofit Management and Leadership*, Fall, Vol. 20, Issue 1, pp. 61–81.

Burns, B. (2009) *Managing Change*, 4th edn, Harlow, Prentice Hall.

Dane, E. (2007) 'Exploring intuition and its role in management decision taking', *Academy of Management Review*, Vol. 32, Issue 1, pp. 33–54.

Davenport, Thomas H. and Harri, J. G. (2010) 'Leading the way towards better business insights', *Strategic HR Review*, Vol. 9, Issue 4, pp. 28–33.

DeYoung, R. (2002) 'Practical–theoretical approach in the application of theory models of organizational behavior', *Journal of American Academy of Business*, March, pp. 361–3.

Fazlollahi, B. and Vahidov, R. (2001) 'A method for generation of alternatives by decision support systems', *Journal of Management Information Systems*, Fall, pp. 229–50.

Figueira S. and Ray, B. (2002) 'Determining the weights of criteria in the electre type of methods with a revised Simos' procedure', *European Journal of Operational Research*, June, pp. 317–26.

Finkelstein, S, Whithead, A. and Campbell, J. (2009) 'Think again: Why good leaders make bad decisions', *Business Strategy Review*, Vol. 20, Issue 2, pp. 62–6.

Friga, P.N. and Chapas, R.B. (2008) 'Make better business decisions', *Research Technology Management*, July/August, Vol. 51, Issue 4, pp. 8–16.

Goodman, M.R.V. (1995) *Creative Management*, Harlow, Prentice Hall.

Janis, I.L. (1982) *Groupthink*, Boston, Houghton Mifflin.

Kahneman, D., Lovallo, D. and Sibony, O. (2011) 'Before you make that big decision', *Harvard Business Review*, April, Kindle edition.

Kandelwal, P. and Tanje, A. (2010) 'Intuitive decision making in management', *Indian Journal of Industrial Relations*, July, Vol. 46, Issue 1, pp. 150–6.

Kaplan, R. (1998) 'Innovation action research: Creating new management theory and practice', *Journal of Management Accounting Research*, Vol. 10, pp. 89–118.

Kuhberger, A., Komunska, D. and Perner, J. (2001) 'The dysjunction effect: Does it exist for two-step gambles?', *Organizational Behaviour and Human Decision Processes*, July, pp. 250–64.

McKinsey Quarterly (2010) 'How we do it: Three executives reflect on strategic decision making', Cover article, Issue 2, pp. 46–57.

Mintzberg, H. and Westley, F. (2001) 'Decision making: It's not what you think', *MIT Sloan Management Review*, Spring, pp. 89–93.

Morton, N.A. and Hu, Q. (2008) 'Implications of the fit between organizational structure and ERP: A structural contingency theory perspective', *International Journal of Information Management*, October, Vol. 28, Issue 5, pp. 391–402.

Nagurney, A., Dong, J. and Mokhtarian, P.I. (2002) 'Multicriteria network equilibrium modelling with variable weights for decision-making in the information age with applications to telecommuting and teleshopping', *Journal of Economic Dynamics and Control*, August, pp. 1629–50.

Nikula, U., Jurvanen, C., Gotel, O. and Gause, D. (2010) 'Empirical validation of the classic change curve on a software technology change project', *Information and Software Technology*, Vol. 52, Issue 6, pp. 680–96.

Sauser, B.J., Reilly, R.R. and Shenhar, A.S.J. (2009) 'Why projects fail. How contingency theory can provide new insights – A comparative analysis of NASA's Mars Climate Orbiter loss', *International Journal of Project Management*, October, Vol. 27, Issue 7, pp. 665–79.

Sayer, J. (2002) 'Problem-solving success tips', *Business and Economic Review*, April/June, pp. 23–24.

Shlomo, M. and Srinivas, P. (2008) 'Bridging the chasm between management education research, and practice: Moving towards the "grounded theory" approach', *The Journal for Decision Makers*, January–March, Vol. 33, Issue 1, pp. 1–18.

Sillince, J.A.A. (2005) 'A contingency theory of rhetorical congruence', *Academy of Management Review*, July, Vol. 30, Issue 3, pp. 608–21.

Spanjol, J. and Tam, L. (2010) 'To change or not to change?: How regulatory focus affects change in dyadic decision-making', *Creativity and Innovation Management*, December, Vol. 19, Issue 4, pp. 346–63.

Stebbins, L.H. (2010) 'Development of reality system theory', *Journal of Business and Economic Research*, April, Vol. 8, Issue 4, pp. 1–22

Vasilopoulos, A. (2010) 'Development of a competitive business intelligence system', *Proceeding of the Northeast Business & Economics Association*, pp. 614–18.

Wang, C.W. and Horng, R.Y. (2003) 'The effects of creative problem solving training on creativity, cognitive type, and R & D performance', *R & D Management*, January, pp. 35–46.

3   Management revisited

A good manager is best when people barely know that he exists. Not so good when people obey and acclaim him. Worse when they despise him.

(Lao Tzu)

If you want to manage somebody, manage yourself. Do that well and you'll be ready to stop managing. And start leading.

(Anonymous)

The best executive is one who has sense enough to pick good men to do what he wants done, and self-restraint enough to keep from meddling with them while they do it.

(F.D. Roosevelt)

Introduction

Setting out to 'do things differently' in order to take business decisions that are both effective and efficient in the use of resources, calls for a re-evaluation of current response (management) practice in organisations. This chapter presents some common theoretical models of management and stresses the importance of defining management so that it can be understood by every individual in an organisation and applied to all their tasks. Many recognise that management practice needs to change but few organisations have a working definition of what management should do. This is significant as thought needs to be focused on 'doing'. Therefore the term 'managing' needs to be codified and communicated to individuals. Few organisations have a working definition of management let alone managing. This is a serious weakness that severely hampers well intentioned executive effort to boost business creativity and strategic innovation. This chapter presents ideas to assist organisations to avoid 'management myopia'.

Horse sense!

Literally the word 'management' comes from the French 'manège' (Italian 'maneggio') which derives from dressage exercises to train a horse in obedience and deportment in order to perform better than the competition. In this scenario the rider is firmly in the saddle and can urge or nag his or her mount by exercising persuasion, cracking the whip or using spurs. Managers in organisations can be likened to riders as they also find themselves in a competitive environment. Like the rider they employ a set of process skills to cajole and encourage people to assist them to complete tasks effectively and efficiently.

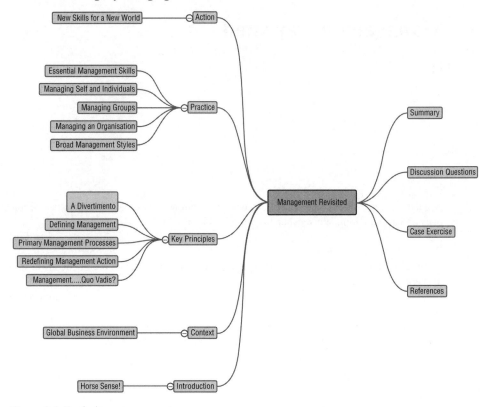

Figure 3.1 Exploring management.

Context

Global business environment

Dressage trainers have to train and prepare their horses and riders to perform in whatever kind of competitive environment they meet. Similarly, managers need to acquire a skill set to enable them to operate in real-world conditions. The business environment is their stage and in common with the horse rider they have to successfully conquer both the contextual arena and the competition. Keen novice riders can approach specialists and seek to be taught how to become successful in dressage competitions. The necessary skill sets both for the horse and the rider are known and codified.

Key principles

A divertimento

Leaving the dressage metaphor aside, learning the basic skills of management can present quite a challenge. Most know what is usually meant by the term management but relatively few can answer these questions:

- What skills are necessary to master individual effort?
- What skills are necessary to co-ordinate and control the efforts of others?
- What skills are required to manage organisations?

When individuals wish to learn to drive they naturally want to know what this involves. In most countries it is necessary to pass a driving test with both a cognitive and a practical component. All driving schools can describe in detail what has to be learnt and assessed. If this was not the case learning the necessary skills would be very difficult. What is more, imagine what it would be like for an individual wishing to learn how to qualify to drive if every person spoken to said that something different needed to be learnt and examined.

As seen in the previous chapter (Section 2.4.1), if individuals and organisations want to change the way they operate they will need to have a common understanding of management. Strange as it may seem few organisations have a standard definition that is known by all 'on board'. If this were the case in the UK navy then operations in trouble contexts would be a disaster. Is management just a broad set of magical skills that enable people to get things done individually or collectively, efficiently and effectively? Part science and part art? How can an honest enquirer learn the key skills?

A group of students were asked in a seminar at Durham University recently to define management and then to list in five minutes the words they thought best identified the key skills a manager should command. Tables 3.1 and 3.2 present a summary of the results.

The students were then asked to see if their parents who were or had experienced management could define it. When they reported a week later the consensus was close to their earlier expressed understanding. Neither the students or their parents identified management as being about behaviour. The results of this small experiment were alarming as most are exposed to management activity (good, indifferent and bad) on a daily basis. Management like marketing seems to be in the ether. Marketing can be defined, it is both a philosophy and a set of action skills. Management, curiously, does not have a widely accepted definition. This is a real problem when business responses need to change to cope with the challenges of a highly volatile business environment.

The seminar attracted the interest of both students and most parents who were embarrassed at not being able to define management in a practical way. Both parties delved into management texts but many were frustrated at the depth of skill exposition and the relevance of broad definitions for expressing action in current contextual conditions. Many asked whether business schools would have the answer. Several parents who had attended

Table 3.1 Student seminar survey I

Definition of management
Getting thing done by others . . . was a general understanding

Table 3.2 Student seminar survey II

Skills	*Focus*	*Performance*
IT	Context	Individual
Communication	Task	Group
People skills	Resources	Organisation
Leadership		
Professional		

these organisations rated them very poorly on the practical skills. One parent remarked 'the school I attended spoke a lot about management but I was distressed to see that they hardly ever practised it'. Scholarship does have a place in the evolutionary definition of management and some schools are engaging with practitioners to sharpen their practical understanding (Hughes *et al.*, 2011). Schein advocates getting alongside managers through a process he terms 'humble enquiry' to better understand their world and so be in a better position to blend academic and practitioner thinking on management (in Lambrechts *et al.*, 2011).

Private moments of doubt and fear come even to managers who have spent years on the job. Any number of events can trigger them: an initiative going poorly, a lukewarm performance review, a daunting new assignment.

As the balance of economic power swings inexorably towards the East and bearing in mind recurrent economic crises, Western managers could learn much from Eastern management approaches (Ming-Jer and Miller, 2010). The world is looking for fresh ideas and new perspectives. Business reality has transformed from 'West leads East' to 'West meets East'. A thriving Chinese business culture represents not only a source of economic partnership but a potential fount of managerial wisdom that can help renew Western economies. Unfortunately, the cultural distance between East and West makes Chinese examples too different, and at times inappropriate, for Western firms to emulate. 'Chinese' thinking, with its emphasis on balance and self–other integration, offers the promise to bridge global divides and facilitate the formation of global-minded executives.

Defining management

For a noun that is in common parlance, 'management' is surprisingly difficult to explain. Many business people call themselves managers. So what is a manager? Some would say that a manager is a manager. Or perhaps a manager is someone who is in a management position. Then some regard management as a rank or badge and dream about rising in an organisation through the management hierarchy to achieve high corporate office. Perhaps some light can be shed on the matter by considering what managers do. The verb 'managing' suggests coping or perhaps contriving to accomplish something by the thoughtful choice of certain responses. If this is the case, then any individual can be a manager, as we all have a personal responsibility to cope with the problems of everyday life. The key words here are *thoughtful*, *choice*, *problems* and *responsibility*.

The ideal individual manager then assumes *responsibility* for coping with his or her own *problems* by a process (*management*) that includes *thinking*, understanding and the deliberate selection (*choice*) of appropriate responses. Managers think and managers act but our thinking and our choice of response may not always be strictly rational. We often exercise our *judgement* largely on intuitive grounds or through habitual responses. At the same time we are not always well *organised* and so may adopt a reactive rather than proactive individual management style.

However, we are social beings and much of our life involves *interacting* with other people. Few individuals are an island. Managing our individual affairs frequently involves a responsibility to manage others – for example, parents assume the responsibility for managing the early lives of their offspring. When we are at work we are all individual managers, in the sense described above, but usually find ourselves in some positions where we are expected to manage others.

The term *management* can be viewed from a number of perspectives:

- The organisation and coordination of the activities of an enterprise in accordance with certain policies and in the achievement of defined objectives, that is, the process of being managed or managing.

Management is often included as a factor of production along with machines, materials and money. According to the management guru Peter Drucker (1909–2005), the basic task of management is twofold: marketing and innovation. Modern management owes its origin to the sixteenth-century enquiry into low efficiency and failures of certain enterprises, conducted by the English statesman Sir Thomas More (1478–1535). As a discipline, management consists of a set of functional skills.

- The executives who have the power and responsibility to make decisions to administer business and public organisations.

The size of management can range from one person in a small organisation to hundreds or thousands of managers in multinational corporations. In large organisations the board of directors formulate policy which is then implemented by the CEO. Some business analysts and financiers accord the highest importance to the quality and experience of the managers in evaluating an organisation's performance.

- Leading a team to achieve planned objectives.
- A corporate rank in an organisation.

The term *management* thus refers to both a title (position in an organisation) and a set of functional skills. Ideally both these descriptors should be effectively combined in the performances of managers. However, this is not always the case, as some adopt a mind set of entitlement in the rank and demonstrate poor functional skills. There are many of these in important positions in organisations having been promoted during easier business conditions (sellers' markets) or as a reward for long or loyal service. Others possess considerable functional skills that have been honed over the years but have failed to update their skill sets in a relevant manner to meet the challenges presented by today's business environment. This would logically imply that several organisations may have executives in powerful and important positions who are insufficiently skilled to cope effectively with modern business life. Worse still they may actually restrict the contributions of young staff for fear of being professionally embarrassed. This 'what I have I hold' approach to management is in a way a natural human response but it is not a professional one. It can lead to such managers and their organisations becoming myopic and blaming external events such as Eurozone crises, casino banking, the royal wedding in the UK in 2011 or the weather, for their problems.

Clearly, external or contextual events do impact on business life and require the right, considered, application of necessary functional skills. Here it is useful to revisit the vehicle driving metaphor of section 3.3.1. A successful driver has to pass both a cognitive and a practical test to be successful. Managers should constantly update their cognitive skills and learn to cope with contextual problems by constantly practising and refining their skills. Crashing a vehicle and claiming that the accident was caused by rain is bad driving and unprofessional.

Primary management processes

Much of the academic literature is based on the supposition that managers think and act rationally and declares that the main functional skills of management follow the five principles described by Fayol (1916):

- Planning (mission/strategy planning, objective setting);
- Organising (time, work and decision-making);
- Leading (setting direction, aligning the team, motivating and inspiring);
- Controlling (correcting errors, disciplining, appraising);
- Achieving (putting it all together and getting things done effectively and efficiently).

For managers to be both effective and efficient in practising Fayol's basic set of functional skills they need to acquire and become proficient in:

- Conceptual skills – the ability to analyse and evaluate complex situations;
- Interpersonal skills – the ability to relate to and work with people individually and in groups;
- Technical skills – the ability to apply required technical skills;
- Political skills – the ability to liaise successfully with other managers in the organisation and to build professional networks – a task that has benefited greatly from social networking sites such as Facebook, LinkedIn and Twitter.

The above cluster of functional and general skills form a template for assessing managerial competencies (Agut and Grau, 2002).

Table 3.3 Principles divided into the major management activities

Management function	Management activities
Planning	Forecasting
	Developing objectives
	Programming
	Scheduling
	Budgeting
	Developing procedures
	Developing policies
Organising	Developing organisational structure
	Delegating
	Developing relationships
Leading	Decision making
	Communicating
	Motivating
	Selecting
	Developing people
Controlling	Developing performance
	Measuring performance
	Correcting performance

Management involves people and thrives on interaction. It is relational and most people like being treated as people. This seems at first an obvious point to make but with the increasing dominance of ICT in modern business, people are losing face-to-face interaction through excessive management by email. There is growing interest amongst the most progressive organisations in the principles of humanistic management (Spitzeck, 2011). It is sometimes said, by people who have not really been into the matter, that the humanistic approach is too soft and too people-oriented, but in fact humanistic consultants always emphasise the importance of doing justice to the task as well as to the people involved.

Redefining management action – control or lead?

Putting the emphasis on control – micromanagement

Many managers needlessly over-manage, over-scrutinize and over-frustrate employees. Such meddlesome bosses are now called micromanagers. A micromanager can be much more than just a nuisance in today's complex organisations. The bothersome boss who second guesses every decision a subordinate makes, frets about the font size of the latest progress report, or inspects all of his or her employees' emails not only frustrates and demoralises his or her harassed workers, but seriously damages the productivity of the organisation and, over the long run, may jeopardise the organisation's survival. Unfortunately, micromanagement is a fact of management life. Micromanagement was practised and recognised well before we labelled it as an organisational pathology. In 1946, Peter Drucker called for a 'democracy of management' whereby organisations decentralise and delegate more decision making authority to employees. In 1960, Douglas McGregor described a Theory X manager as one possessing many of the characteristics of the modern micromanager, 'one who is poor at delegating but one who believes he delegates well' (White, 2010).

Putting the emphasis on leadership – fundamental management competencies

A reasonable approach to learning how to practise management skills is indicated in Figure 3.2. Essentially it concerns *working with people* and in this context leadership is of paramount importance. This is true whether management takes place at the individual, group or organisational level. Anyone who cannot motivate him- or herself will find it difficult to convincingly lead others. Self-discipline and determination are essential aspects of personal motivation. Evident and continuous leadership skills result in effective and efficient group teamwork and motivation levels.

The next priority after mastering practical working with people skills is to apply a clearly understood *managing method*. This involves delegation which is an important skill that is often abused. Sound delegation entails:

- Clearly communicating a task to an individual or group;
- Clearly explaining any necessary skills;
- Keeping an eye on the individual or group as the task is tackled.

Walking away after a muddled communication of the task and then blaming an individual or group if things go wrong is too common. This approach is not delegation but abdication and is a totally destructive management practice. The other basic management

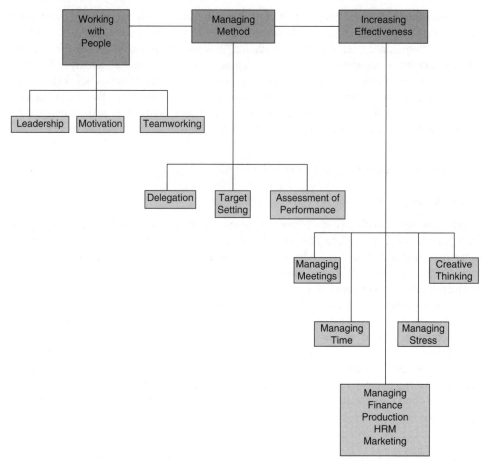

Figure 3.2 Putting the emphasis on leadership.
          Source: M.R.V. Goodman, Durham University.

method skills include setting targets and assessing performance truthfully and as positively as possible.

Dynamic managers constantly seek ways to *increase efficiency*. This requires giving attention to effective and efficient ways of running meetings, and to time and stress management. The contemporary business environment usually requires people in management positions to display and encourage creative thinking (see Chapter 4). This is necessary because many of the traditional models and practices can lose their edge and effectiveness. In addition, wise organisations re-evaluate their vision and study the impact of the consequences of the business paradigm change from sellers' to buyers' market conditions (see Chapter 1).

Management: quo vadis?

Many see management mainly as a position that is a statement of authority. The decades of sellers' markets encouraged 'top-down' activity. Organisations were run by managers on behalf of owners, public boards or shareholders. Apart from owners of SMEs, authority for the larger private sector and public enterprises resided in distant bodies many of which did not take part in the day-to-day running of the organisation. Technical advances in communication and computerisation have had a substantial effect on management practice. Whilst few would deny the benefits this has brought, many would recognise the creeping depersonalisation that has resulted from the escalation in many organisations of management by email.

In sellers' markets control was everything and management didn't like surprises. Organisations (and hence people) could be run automatically and management became obsessive with detailed planning and reporting systems. However, as every weather forecaster knows, such practice can be illusory as to measure is not necessarily to control. Sound managers will keep their eyes on the road all the time – they do when they drive their company cars – if they fail to do this in times of shifting environmental paradigms they run a real danger of becoming myopic.

As the decade progresses traditional hierarchical management structures are giving way to network models. Honed supply chains are being replaced by value chains. The entitlement culture is dying. There are no more jobs for life. The role of management needs to be seen in a new way so that people are seen as the most important resource that organisations command and not merely names on a payroll and an expendable resource. Responsible organisations will find ways to affirm this perception, and discover how to value and recharge their staff.

Management needs to accept that responses and experiences that served well in yesterday's world may not be best for today. New thinking is required and an acceptance that it is essential for managers to be prepared and to do something about introducing different attitudes and operating cultures. Of course it is best to keep what is seen to be good practice in current conditions but those in authority also need to encourage themselves and their staff to learn new skills. To this end wise organisations are increasingly investing in knowledge management, recognising that an organisation's value derives from knowledge, *know-how* and intellectual capital and competencies. The short-termism that has been so much a feature of the last 30 years is being increasingly challenged as the present and the future are seen not to be separate but as being intertwined. Business creativity is needed as never before to help organisations become positively differentiated but is often hampered in its execution by the mindset that management is essentially about operational and control matters.

Practice

Essential management skills

Section 3.3.1 above posed three questions to assist aspiring and existing managers to equip themselves with essential skills to enable them to practice successfully in the current environment:

- What skills are necessary to master individual effort?
- What skills are necessary to co-ordinate and control the efforts of others?
- What skills are required to manage organisations?

The next three sections draw from interviews with practitioners and from academic material and argument presented in this chapter to provide a guide to individual, group and organisational managers.

Managing self and individuals

Table 3.4 Basic individual management skills

Management skill set	Specific skills	Tasks
Contextual awareness	Identify business environment	1. Sellers' market 2. Buyers' market
Creative thinking	Creative problem solving	See Chapter 4

Organising self/ individual	Task scheduling	1. Make a list of tasks
		2. Identify the tasks that are essential for effective performance – active tasks
		3. Identify those tasks that are essentially reactive
		4. Establish priorities in the light of:
		
		  • Importance
		  • Urgency
		
		5. Schedule sufficient time for active tasks and allow time for reactive tasks

Managing groups

Table 3.5 Summary guidelines for group managers

Management skill set	Specific skills	Tasks
Contextual awareness	Identify business environment Information search	1. Sellers' market 2. Buyers' market Interpretation
Creative thinking	Creative problem solving	See Chapter 4
Organising other people	Delegation	1. Which task? 2. Who does it? 3. Brief people and train them 4. Establish priorities 5. Inform others 6. Be available for advice 7. Check progress 8. Support staff at all times
From management to managing (or leading)	Leadership	Managers should be leaders – leadership is about discovering answers to questions others have yet to contemplate not about repeating someone else's answers

Managing an organisation

Top managers should follow the guidelines outlined in Tables 3.5 and 3.6. CEOs are advised to make selecting the members of a senior management team among their first priorities, to make sure that such teams focus on a set of priorities where their group decision making is essential and to address the group dynamics of their team (Kruyt *et al.*, 2011). CEOs also

Table 3.6 Summary guidelines for top management

Management skill set	Specific skills	Tasks
Contextual awareness	Identify business environment	1. Sellers' market 2. Buyers' market
Creative thinking	Creative problem solving	See Chapter 4. Good top management do not attempt to manage creativity, they manage for creativity, by providing a work environment and culture that allows creativity to flourish. Top managing for creativity means taking most of what we know about management, standing it on its head and putting the concept of effectiveness before that of efficiency.
Avoiding management myopia	Revelations	1. Exercise vision 2. Declare mission 3. Prepare corporate plan and set goals 4. Define responsibilities 5. Set standards 6. Agree tasks
Establish a creative culture	Prepare organisation for change	Empower individuals and groups
Ethical operation	Corporate Social Responsibility (CSR)	Operate ethically and with regard to CSR

need to take care to see that talented executives do not hold back for fear of exposing the limitations of those in leadership positions (DeLong and DeLong, 2011).

As business becomes increasingly competitive organisations can, sometimes without realising it is happening, slip into management actions that are ethically questionable. Research on business ethics communication and behaviour indicates a relatively clear, positive link between open workplace dialogue about ethical issues and ethical conduct. Empirical research by Leila Trapp (2011) revealed that discussing ethical issues was influenced by two main factors: employee conceptualisations of business ethics and the level of inter-collegial trust, credibility and confidence. An evident and lasting high level of trust in an organisation is an important influence on motivation. In addition, socially responsible management pays due to regard to minimising any harmful effects of its operations on the internal and external environment as well as pursuing a less than cynical CSR policy.

Broad management styles

The way in which managers behave determines the way in which individuals and groups will behave towards them. So much of a manager's job is concerned with acquiring and fine tuning a set of interactive skills. Basically there are two broad styles open to a manager: the *autocratic* style and the *democratic* style.

Autocratic style

The *autocratic* style is characterised by behaviour choices that are designed to compel people to do what they are told. Sometimes this style is necessary – for example in an emergency when people are shocked or there is no time for argument and debate. Exercised constantly this hard, authoritarian behaviour usually upsets people. Practised by the uncaring manager this management style can be a cynical power game that damages individuals and groups, and inflicts untold harm on organisational management performance.

Democratic style

The *democratic* style fosters staff participation and can empower an organisation by encouraging staff to apply their knowledge and expertise. Practised by a caring manager this style can do much to release the creative skills of employees and associates. Exercised cynically, when managers front the 'false charm' in order to manipulate people, this style tends to promote low trust and loyalty.

Is there one correct style? It is difficult to answer this question purely in terms of these opposing style categorisations. Different contextual stimuli will favour different responses. In practice these two styles describe opposite polls and there are many 'styles' between them. As they choose their responses to different stimuli over time managers will be 'unofficially classified' by their peers and staff. Their management style will be interpreted as OK or not OK – trustworthy or essentially political. Managers serve several individuals including subordinate staff, peers, senior management, high ranking company officers and, frequently, external publics or customers. Each of these individuals and groups will form their own judgement based on *what they see* as consistent responses.

Action

New skills for a new world

Private moments of doubt and fear come even to managers who have spent years on the job. Any number of events can trigger them: an initiative going poorly, a lukewarm performance review, a daunting new assignment. Hill and Lineback (2011) have long studied the question of how managers grow and advance. Their experience brings them to a simple but troubling observation: most bosses reach a certain level of proficiency and stay there – short of what they could and should be. Why? Because they stop working on themselves. Hill and Lineback offer three imperatives for managers who seek to avoid this stagnation:

1. Manage yourself – who you are as a person, the beliefs and values that drive your actions and especially how you connect with others all matter to the people you must influence.
2. Manage your network. Effective managers know that they cannot avoid conflict and competition among organisational groups; they build and nurture ongoing relationships.
3. Manage your team. Team members need to know what's required of them collectively and individually and what the team's values, norms and standards are.

Increasingly managers at all levels will be required to do much more than just implement the plans declared by top management. They will be expected to define problems facing their organisations in a rapidly changing and increasingly complex world of business and to communicate these to top management. Information search and interpretation will continue to be key skills.

Summary

Management is both a rank in an organisation and a set of skills that can be practised at the individual, group and top management (organisational) levels. Good managers learn first to manage themselves successfully before attempting to lead others. They encourage, facilitate and sustain effective and efficient team-working toward a common vision.

Discussion questions

1. Explain what is meant by the term *management*.
2. What is the difference between the concept of efficiency and the concept of effectiveness?
3. Describe the five primary management processes.
4. What are the basic guidelines for managing self or an individual?
5. What are the basic guidelines for managing groups?
6. Briefly describe the main tasks of top management.

Case exercise

Sarah Jones works for a local authority in the UK and is based in a large open plan office situated on a modern trading estate. Sarah is English and holds a degree in history from a North of England university. Ever since early experiences working in school and university vacations Sarah had been fascinated by management practice.

She firmly believed that the art of successful management was to get the job done both effectively and efficiently whilst valuing the contributions of staff. She had attended a civil service graduate apprenticeship prior to her move to the local authority. Her tutors had taught her well and all the temporary in-house internships in London had been both informative and enjoyable.

Her first impression of the office was one of unorganised chaos. Individuals did not seem to know what they were supposed to do and every one she spoke to seemed to be submerged by work and on the receiving end of poor and distant management activity. Staff were demotivated and some were in the habit of venting their frustrations by deliberately giving local council tax payers a difficult time.

Robert Mitford, a retired university lecturer, established a partnership with his wife and ran a small business that concentrated on part-time teaching and the authorship of business texts. Tom Duddlestone, a fellow graduate in his second year in the office, assumed responsibility for Mitford's account. Sarah could not help but notice how badly he treated Mitford. Her concern first surfaced when Tom requested him to pay tax at on the basis of his property having four bedrooms when it only had two and a small box room. Mitford queried this and enclosed photographs of the bedrooms and the original surveyor's report he had commissioned when the house was purchased five years ago. He sent the letter by recorded delivery and marked it 'urgent'. His letter was ignored. Three weeks later he wrote again requesting a reply to his queries in ten days and informed the local authority that if he heard nothing after that he would take the matter to his solicitor.

Sarah was dismayed by Tom's attitude which she felt was partially explained by the organisation's policy of refusing to let tax payers know who was dealing with their account. She discussed Mitford's case with Tom during a lunch break and expressed her concern at the way he was treating the retired lecturer. Tom listened to her attentively and then dismissed her argument, retorting that the senior management placed a heavy stress on efficiency which they measured in terms of the number of tax demands posted each week. Official policy was to demand as much as possible and if the tax payer complained to deliberately delay responding quickly, collect the money by the due date and deal with any appeals at their leisure.

Mitford's threat to involve his solicitor acted as a catalyst so that his case was treated promptly and effectively. Tom reported it to his manager, who immediately blamed him for the problem and threatened to have him disciplined. Sarah was pleased to see that Mitford's case was dealt with in two days. Her satisfaction was dampened by Tom's immediate dismissal and the revelation of the existence of a highly political blame culture.

Task

Public sector organisations are often in monopoly positions and in the case of tax authorities can enforce their demands with the full force of the law. The blame culture and concentration on the concept of efficiency in raising money was distressing to the pensioner featured in the case. Imagine that you have been asked by the local authority to advise how they might improve their management processes. What guidelines would you suggest?

References

Agut, S. and Grau, R. (2002) 'Managerial competency needs and training requests: The case of the Spanish tourist industry', *Human Resource Development Quarterly*, Spring, pp. 31–51.

DeLong, T. and DeLong, S. (2011) 'Managing yourself. The paradox of excellence', *Harvard Business Review*, April, Kindle edition.

Fayol, H. (1916) *Industrial and General Administration*, Paris, Dunod.

Hill, L.A. and Lineback, K. (2011) 'Are you a good boss: Or a great one?' *Harvard Business Review*, January/February, Vol. 89, Issue 1/2, pp. 124–31.

Hughes, T., Bence, D., Grisoni, L., O'Regan, N. and Wornham, D. (2011) 'Scholarship that matters: academic–practitioner engagement in business and management', *Academy of Management Learning & Education*, March, Vol. 10, Issue 1, pp. 40–57.

Kruyt, M., Malan, J. and Tuffield, R. (2011) 'Three steps to building a better top team', *McKinsey Quarterly*, Issue 1, pp. 113–17.

Lambrechts, F.J., Bouwen, R., Grieten, S., Huybrechts, J.P. and Schein, E.H. (2011) 'Learning to help through humble inquiry and implications for management research, practice, and education: An interview with Edgar H. Schein', *Academy of Management Learning & Education*, March, Vol. 10, Issue 1, pp. 131–47.

Leila Trapp, N. (2011) 'Staff attitudes to talking openly about ethical dilemmas: The role of business ethics conceptions and trust', *Journal of Business Ethics*, November, Vol. 103, Issue 4, pp. 543–52.

Ming-Jer, C. and Miller, D. (2010) 'West meets East: Toward an ambicultural approach to management', *Academy of Management Perspectives*, November, Vol. 24, Issue 4, pp. 17–24.

Mintzberg, H. (1973) *The Nature of Managerial Work*, New York, Harper Row.

Spitzeck, H. (2011) 'An integrated model of humanistic management', *Journal of Business Ethics*, March, Vol. 99, Issue 1, pp. 51–62.

White Jr., R.D. (2010) 'The micromanagement disease: Symptoms, diagnosis, and cure', *Public Personnel Management*, Spring, Vol. 39, Issue 1, pp. 71–6.

Part II

Preparing a response

4   Thinking revisited

It is an old maxim of mine that when you have excluded the impossible, whatever remains, however improbable, must be the truth.

(Sir Arthur Conan Doyle)

Discovery consists of seeing what everybody has seen and thinking what nobody has thought.

(Albert von Szent-Györgyi)

Introduction

The challenges organisations face as a result of the business environmental paradigm change discussed in Part I call for fresh thinking. The portfolio of management responses, that was both effective and efficient in the era of sellers' markets (collectively referred to as the least-cost production/supply paradigm) needs to be revised in order to respond successfully to the different problems posed by buyers' markets. In most cases this requires a radical change in thinking. This is the essence of business creativity and the process starts with a review of thinking at the individual level. The chapter describes the physiology of the brain and discusses how the process of thinking occurs. Once the fundamentals of thinking have been explored the next task is to apply the key principles to the individual's problem-solving practice. This requires both mental flexibility and a tolerance of ambiguity and is fundamentally a personal journey of discovery. Practical exercises are included to assist individuals to realise the need to evaluate their thinking approach to business problems.

Nasruddin

Mullah Nasruddin was once attempting to repair something, without apparent success, when an onlooker asked scornfully, 'Do you know what you're doing?'

Nasruddin replied, 'No, that's why I'm doing it'.

The field of creativity research is rich with examples from the lives of remarkable individuals, but lacks an accepted framework for approaching the many issues that arise when trying to make more general sense of the data. To produce such a framework is an important aim of this chapter.

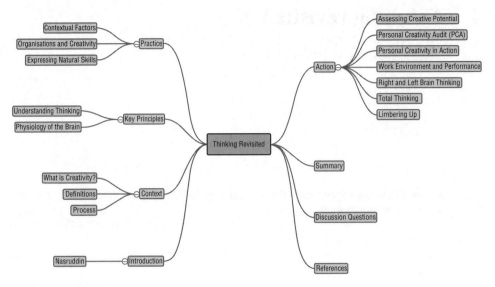

Figure 4.1 Thinking revisited.

Context

What is creativity?

Creativity is a natural gift and part of the wholeness (*gestalt*) of every individual. It can and should be encouraged. This offers the individual the opportunity to derive more satisfaction out of life. Understanding creativity is difficult if we strive to define it in rules and try to put it in a box. By its very nature it is unpredictable, unique, infectious and real. Most, excepting those with closed minds, can quickly appreciate it when they see it. True creativity has a beauty of its own that often defies logical explanation. So are civilisations all over the world in danger of losing their way by attempting to justify creativity? Can it be bottled, concentrated in a pill and swallowed? Is it possible to control it by logic alone? Or is it a mysterious force that seems to bless us in puzzling, usually joyful, ways?

Creativity is a unique force that distinguishes the higher orders of fauna, such as *Homo sapiens* from the rest of Creation. Other creatures are capable of expressing creativity and creative thought. Squirrels, for example, can do amazing things in pursuit of food. Humans, however, are generally accepted to be the most advanced form of created life. So the way in which humans think would seem to hold promise if we are fully to appreciate human creativity and fully achieve our individual potential to express it. The next section explains how the human brain works. Prepare to be surprised.

Definitions

Creativity has been defined as the generation of new ideas by approaching problems or existing practices in innovative or imaginative ways. It is stated that creativity involves re-examining assumptions and re-interpreting facts, ideas and past experience. It is also reported that a growing interest in creativity as a source of competitive advantage has developed in recent years (Banks *et al.*, 2002; Dundon, 2002). It is an imaginative process with outcomes that are original and of value. One way to find out more about creativity is to ask people about their conception of a creative person. Whether they are lay people or experts in a field, people have implicit theories about what it means to be creative. They usually identify personality and cognitive elements such as:

- Connects ideas;
- Sees similarities and differences;
- Is flexible;
- Has aesthetic taste;
- Is unorthodox;
- Is curious, inquisitive;
- Questions accepted ways of doing things.

Another way to tease out the governing conditions of creativity is to look at paradigm case examples of what the most creative people do, just as in studying effective schools we might start by studying existing effective schools, or study detergents by looking at the best-selling detergents. Much research has gone into trying to understand creativity better by looking at the way creative minds work (Gardner, 1997). By studying exemplars of creativity such as world-famous writers, artists or inventors we might find a set of necessary and sufficient conditions which defined their creativity. We then might want to try to recreate those conditions in our homes, schools, businesses and communities. We all have the mental resources to be creative (see Chapter 5).

Process

Research into the habits of creative people reveals certain common characteristics. They:

- Generate ideas;
- Are flexible in their thinking, experiment and seek variation;
- Strive for originality;
- Provide examples of their work.

Generate ideas

Creative people tend to have lots of ideas. They do not limit their thinking to a few ideas; they want more ideas and better ideas. The more they have the greater the likelihood that some of them will work. Some ideas will go wrong. As Edison, the inventor of the telephone said, he needed 100 ideas for he knew that 99 of them might be wrong. Inside the oyster of an idea may be a pearl. Creative people do not discard ideas simply because they seem at first to be a bit odd or unworkable. Output of ideas spurs further ideas, each of which may have an unexpected potential. Creative people are rarely half-hearted. They make an effort to keep thinking, to become absorbed, immersed in and fascinated by the subject in hand for the ideas to flood in. When Tolstoy was writing a novel he said he 'knew' all his fictional characters inside out because he had thought so much and generated so many ideas about them.

Are flexible in their thinking, experiment and seek variation

Creative people are able to overcome the mental blocks to their thinking through being flexible and divergent. Some of these blocks include the tendency to think that:

- There is only one right way to do things;
- We know all there is to know;
- It is wrong to experiment with new ideas.

Being creative means not having to be stuck with one idea, one approach, one way of doing things. It is having the ability to move from a known way to a new way, being willing to change your ideas or views if you need to. Creative people have a thirst for knowledge. They use imagination to play with ideas. They are willing to experiment. The French mathematician Poincaré said 'Experiment is the sole source of truth'. It is also the source of all creativity. Creative people are curious, open-minded and have the confidence to try new ideas.

Strive for originality

Creative people strive for originality by thinking of novel ideas, finding new solutions to problems or creating their own unique ways or plans for doing things. They extend their thinking through a process of elaboration. They are willing to improve on an original idea, so that what they add improves on or takes further the original idea. Elaboration is shown in the number and quality of different ideas used to add on to the original idea, expanding on existing knowledge, extending an idea to make it more complex or build a unique feature into a given situation. They try alternatives and don't give up easily. They have 'stickability' – they know that creativity often requires a tremendous struggle for a vision to be realised. The painter Turner said 'My paintings bring me nothing but pain. The reality is so immeasurably below the conception'.

Provide examples of their work

Creative people work hard and continually to improve ideas and solutions, by making gradual alterations and refinements to their works. Contrary to the mythology surrounding creativity, very, very few works of creative excellence are produced with a single stroke of brilliance or in a frenzy of rapid activity (Breen, 2004). Here is Beethoven describing his way of working: 'I carry my thoughts with me for a long time, often for a very long time before writing them down. . . I change many things, discard others and try again until I am satisfied; then, in my head, I begin to elaborate the work. . .the underlying idea never deserts me. It rises, it grows. I hear and see the image in front of me from every angle' (Gruber and Wallace, 1999).

Newton claimed that what enabled him to make discoveries in mathematics and science was his ability to concentrate intently on a problem for hours, days and weeks on end. Research shows that experts in any creative field take about ten years of practice before they produce a masterwork (Sternberg and Lubart, 1999). Creative excellence in any field seems to require long-term interest and investment of effort.

The problem with studying paradigm cases of creative people who have excelled in their field is that they are vulnerable to paradigm shift (Kuhn, 1975). Thus the analysis may fit well with the works of preceding artists who were imbued with a reverence for the tradition they were working in, but it may not fit the works of revolutionary creative thinkers. The old ways of study may not fit new technologies. We may not be able to reinvent the future by copying the traditions of the past. Creative people can learn from a past tradition but may need to move beyond that tradition to achieve the most creative expression of their ideas. They may need to move into new paradigms, new ways of thinking.

Most acknowledge that creativity exists. Many can name a creative person, alive or dead, though it is amazing how many people seem to think that creativity and the afterlife go together! This chapter asserts that all individuals are naturally creative and that this is by design and not an accident of birth. Of course, some are more creative than others. However, we all have tremendous potential. The curious thing is that many of us keep our creativity under wraps. Perhaps this is because many of us find it easier this way. Many individuals and groups seem to radiate a latent hostility toward creative people. This makes about as much sense as the author of this text trying to convince you that you do not exist! Curiously, when Western wealth-creation activities were primarily facing a supply gap, the pearl of great price was not creativity or innovation but compliance. The pursuit of order has a strong attraction for many – usually those doing the ordering – and is necessary for some of the adventures of life. If it becomes the norm – the way things are done at all times – it restricts the *creative force*. Practised to excess it can sometimes lead to a dangerous myopic condition. As the forces of change are 'neutralised' or managed for administrative convenience and short-term advantage so the real, long-term cost becomes staggering. Suddenly in a series of unstoppable shifts the contextual factors impacting on wealth creation undeniably enter a period of explosive change. The result is a dangerous crisis that frequently does not play the game by the rules. As instability is met by complacency and living standards are threatened. What is needed is a new management approach that is contextually aware.

In such a predicament we can place our trust in man's ingenuity, but only if it is given sufficient space. All over the West there are many potentially like Richard Branson, Colonel Sanders, Chester Carlson and Alan Sugar. Ordinary individuals just need to believe that it can happen. A vital first step is for an individual to rediscover his or her own creativity. It is hoped that many honest enquirers will be helped by this chapter.

Key principles

Understanding thinking

To realise the full potential of our brains it is helpful to briefly explore how the physiology works before assessing our creative thinking potential.

Physiology of the brain

By any account the human brain is an incredible machine. It controls all the activities and reactions of the body and is the centre of emotion, memory and personality. Whereas the heart is the functional centre, it is the pump that circulates our blood, it is the brain, the organic computer, that is the true expression of life. Whereas the heart enables us to be, the brain enables us to live. It is made up of millions of very small cells called *neurons*. The average individual has over ten thousand million of them (*Encyclopaedia Britannica*, 2006). There are two categories of cells: those that carry information to and from the body via the spinal cord and those that cross-connect the constituent parts of the brain. Basically there are three key parts to the brain: the *cerebrum*, the *cerebellum* and the *brain stem* or *medulla oblongata*, as shown in Figure 4.2.

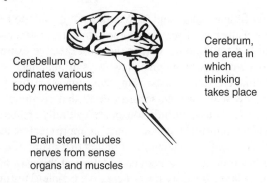

Cerebellum co-ordinates various body movements

Cerebrum, the area in which thinking takes place

Brain stem includes nerves from sense organs and muscles

Figure 4.2 Lateral view of cerebrum, cerebellum.
Source: M.R.V. Goodman, Durham University.

The brain is the co-ordinator of the nervous system and controls most of a person's conscious and unconscious actions. The *cerebrum* is the largest and most highly developed part of the brain and on inspection looks a little like a walnut. It consists of two approximately equal halves or lobes called the *cerebral hemispheres*. In humans this part of the brain is so large that it has had to be wrinkled, like a walnut, to fit into our shells or skulls. The surface of the *cerebrum* is referred to as the *cerebral cortex* or grey matter. Below the *cerebral cortex* is the white matter that is a mass of nerve fibres connecting the *cortex* with the body and other parts of the brain. Information flows into the brain from the body by a process known as *sensation*. Messages come from the skin, the muscles, the eyes, the ears, nose and other sense organs by the sensory nerves. The brain processes the information and then sends out responses along the *motor nerves* to the muscles of the body that control all the body movements. Different areas of the cortex control different parts of the body. Curiously the left side of the brain controls the right side of the body and vice versa, with the centre brain somehow co-ordinating this activity.

The cortex is the place that determines our awareness of the environment around us. The eyes look at the world and the ears listen but it is the cortex that sees, hears and understands. It decides what responses to trigger having evaluated the external stimuli. This is where trust or suspicion are determined and it is the centre of our creativity. The *cerebellum* is below the *cerebrum* (see Figure 4.2) and assists the cerebral cortex by providing fine control of intricate movements, such as walking, writing and driving. The *medulla oblongata*, or brain stem, connects the cerebrum and cerebellum to the spinal cord and so to the rest of the body. This part of the brain provides a largely automatic control of the body's internal organs.

The working brain – a synaptic wonder

Each brain cell or neuron is structurally independent. In other words, they do not come into contact with each other. They communicate with other cells by a subtle interchange of complex electrochemical signals. This process is known as *contiguity* and was first described by the Spanish scientist Ramon y Cajal in 1889. Each neuron has three distinct components: the cell body or *soma*; the main nerve fibre or *axon* which is the main exit of information transmitted by the cell; and a number of receiving branches or *dendrites*. Dendrites and axons range in size from a millimetre to one and a half metres in length. All along their length are little acorn-like shapes called *dendritic spines* or *synaptic buttons* that contain chemical material that provide the means for connections to be made between brain cells. This occurs when an electrical impulse travels through the liquid-filled space between two adjacent cells and connects their synaptic buttons.

The amount of activity going on in the brain is incredible. It can usefully be likened to the amount of traffic through a busy electronic telephone exchange. Incoming messages are automatically connected to a multitude of cells as the brain processes the input stimuli to produce a suitable response or outcome. This is the product of a complex evaluation procedure that co-ordinates the contributions of thousands of individual brain cells and produces a distinct electromagnetic routing or pathway that is known as a *memory trace*. If the same or similar stimulus or enquiry is repeated, then the brain automatically energises the memory traces it formed, thus speeding up the response time. This is the essence of *learning*. As each brain cell is capable of directing information to as many as 10,000 other brain cells in the same instant, the problem-solving potential at the individual's disposal is virtually infinite.

Practice

Contextual factors

Anyone is capable of responding creatively. The issue is to what end and how often. Of course some will be naturally more creative than others. Figure 4.3 illustrates some of the ways that ordinary everyday people exhibit creativity. The degree to which personal creativity occurs depends on a complex set of environmental or contextual factors. Social pressures, such as the pressure to conform to group norms, can either encourage or discourage creativity depending on the value placed on such activity by the dominant social rules.

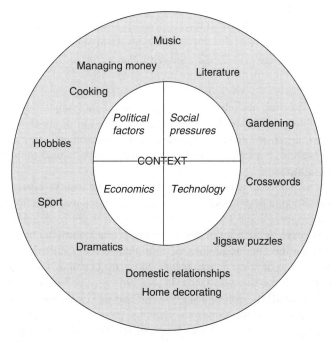

Figure 4.3 Activities that entail personal creativity.
  Source: M.R.V. Goodman, Durham University.

Technology can trigger creativity when a new and accepted (wanted) application suddenly appears. A useful example of this is provided by the development of the electric toothbrush that took off after the technology behind rechargeable batteries was perfected. Economic factors too can play their part, as many on low budgets know when they 'make a penny do the work of a pound'. Finally, political factors can influence creative responses. Examples of this include a variety of novel ways of 'getting round' – legally and otherwise – existing and proposed legislation. Take some time out and think of a handful of examples!

Whilst creativity will occur, to some degree, even when it is discouraged and opposed by organisations in society, its incidence increases if it is actively encouraged. This coaxing has to occur at two distinct levels: that of the individual and that of the social groups/organisations to which the individual belongs. An adult, like a child, needs to feel safe if he or she is to play creatively. Heightened tension and emotional pressure are bad for creativity. The individual has to experience a satisfactory level of safety and to trust the personnel around him or her. No trust, little creativity.

Organisations and creativity

Organisations cannot respond creatively. What they can do, though, is to actively encourage their individuals. Thus the incidence of creative activity is contextually governed by the degree of group and/or organisational support. At the individual level the vibes that are in the air have to be convincing. Corporate motherhood statements and other forms of 'chin music' are to no avail unless the 'place feels right'. When this is the case then the people will invoke the processes and creative responses will occur.

Expressing natural skills

Whilst it is true that all individuals possess creativity – it's a gift of nature – most of us fail to make the most of it. As creativity is a dynamic phenomenon, a force, we cannot learn to effectively improve our use of it by only studying the literature. If we realistically wish to develop our creative skills then we must be prepared *to have a go*. The first major challenge facing many individuals is to overcome their shyness and apprehension and let the genie out of the bottle. Starting with the knowledge that all individuals are creative is both reassuring and challenging. It provides comfort in that most of us are aware of our creative achievements, no matter what private beliefs we may harbour about their frequency, strength or durability. It presents a challenge in that most will readily accept that any skill can be developed by sustained exercise.

Car drivers have to overcome inhibitions and agree to take their first driving lesson. Then, despite the possibility of a few shocks and surprises, they need the resolution to see a driving tuition programme through and then to present themselves for examination. If successful most drivers then cease to put a lot of sustained effort into improving their general driving skills. Experience on the open road does develop their driving skills in some respects but also leaves them prey to developing bad habits. Most, for example, fail to continuously update their knowledge of the Highway Code. In short, many of us become lazy. We are easily satisfied with a relatively low level of achievement. Some of us later rue this, when a sudden challenge to our skill response leaves us wanting. As the environment on the roads is constantly changing we would be wise to keep our relative skill level high. Frequently the problems we face are the result of someone else's failings. Thus to survive on today's roads we need to be continuously both up-dating our own driving skills and learning how to cope with the mistakes of others. Passing the driving test and just driving is not sufficient. Likewise, making do with our natural creativity skill level is not enough.

Action

Assessing creative potential

If we are intent on discovering what we can do to improve our creativity, then it is helpful to start by getting a measure of *where* we are now. This can be achieved, to some extent, by recourse to an appropriate audit or inventory. An improvement programme can then build on this apparent skill level. It is important to realise that such 'tests' are not infallible measures of our creative performance. They merely confirm that we are creative and provide some indicative evidence of the use to which we consciously put creative skills. A subsequent running of the selected audit should then provide evidence of development.

There are a number of tests widely available that can help us to get a picture of our present level of creative activity. However, few were designed exclusively to reflect creative responses. Most are intended to reveal other personal characteristics such as psychological type (Myers-Briggs and McCaulley, 1988), personality (16PF, see http://similarminds.com/cattell-16-factor.html) and learning style (Kolb, 1984; Honey and Mumford, 1985) or team working attributes (Belbin, 1981). One, (Kirton, 1987) was developed to measure creative style.

Personal Creativity Audit (PCA)

The *Personal Creativity Audit* (PCA) was developed to provide evidence that individuals are creative and to give an indication of an individual's tendency to use creative skills in daily situations. Appendices 4.1 and 4.2 contain our PCA together with response and scoring instructions. For any such inventory to be useful it has to be capable of measuring *what* it is intended to measure and to be reliable in the responses that it elicits from respondents. However, some people will inevitably try to read the algorithm to deliberately register high scores rather than complete the inventory with a view to seeing what it says about them. Despite these reservations such inventories can provide a snapshot that can be illuminating.

Personal creativity in action

How do you think you can help yourself to release more of your natural creativity? Take a short break and try to jot down at least five ideas.

Here are a few exercises and ideas to help you develop your own creative thinking.

- How many potential uses can you think of for an ordinary paper clip?
- Irrespective of how good an artist you judge yourself to be, grab a piece of paper (A4 size is ideal) and try and draw a quick head and shoulders sketch of yourself. Now choose a hat from the options below.

  - Mexican hat
  - Top hat
  - Cloth cap
  - Deerstalker
  - Chef's hat

- Now draw your chosen hat on your head and shoulders.
- Why did you choose the hat you did? Express your reasons in a short sentence.

Would you have preferred to have chosen one of the other hats? If so, which one and why did you pass it by? If it was because you had doubts as to whether you could draw it have a go right now.

- How many uses can you think of for an ordinary builder's brick?

Now ponder on the following:

- 'According to all the laws of aerodynamics, a bumble bee cannot possibly fly. The bumble bee does not know this, so it goes ahead and flies anyway.' (Anonymous)
- 'When in doubt, make a fool of yourself. There is a microscopically thin line between being brilliantly creative and acting like the most gigantic idiot on earth. So what the hell, leap.' (Heimal, 1983)
- Play a track of your favourite music. How would you:

  o   Briefly describe it with words?
  o   With pictures?
  o   Can you hum it unaccompanied?

- Look out of the window and focus for half a minute on an object.

Now close your eyes. Think of something that has been troubling you today. Think about the object . . . make any connections? Get any good ideas? If not, try again, and you too can experience the *Eureka* effect!

Work environment and performance

No matter how we look at individual responses there is little doubt that the organisational work environment has a direct effect on performance. The role models, paradigms, reward systems, management culture, peer pressures, official and unofficial and psychological contracts all act to encourage some responses and to discourage others. This places – as will be explored, in Chapters 5, 6 and 7 – a considerable responsibility on individuals who seek to work in teams. Figure 4.4 summarises four response sets that we have discovered in our own research work in England. If an individual is working in an environment where the management are highly concerned about their own interests and give poor regard to the individual's interest, then this is likely to result in programmed, robotic responses from the member of staff. This situation is typified by people going through the motions to earn their corn and is unlikely to encourage a creative attitude to the job. Where management are concerned with the personal wishes of their staff this will trigger a reciprocal response from the individuals and will provide the opportunity for highly creative responses.

However, if these responses are not continuously encouraged and no action is seen to result then this can lead, sadly, to situations where the individual becomes disenchanted. If this occurs then the goose that laid the golden egg is effectively killed and the individual will slip into the damped innovation quartile and possibly to the robot quartile.

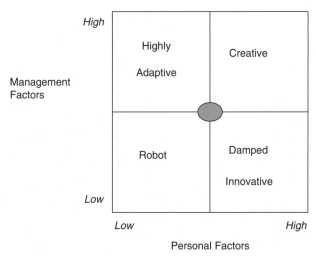

Figure 4.4 Individual response patterns resulting from interpreted management responses.
Source: M.R.V. Goodman, Durham University.

Whilst there is merit in an individual taking stock and seeking to discover a position on an audit such as KAI, MBTI or LSI, it must be remembered that these inventories only provide, at best, some indicative information. This must then be closely vetted for its contextual relevance – most people appear to be different at home than they are at work. Most psychometric tests carry error propensities resulting from a variety of factors such as environmental/ contextual issues, test procedures and classification typologies, and so on. Furthermore, some individuals may be discouraged by the results of such inventories and so withdraw into their shells, especially if they perceive that management are not very interested in them. Others may, unless carefully advised, believe that core behaviours and responses cannot be changed. Whilst this is true for the broad personality characteristics that tend to be set in the first 20 years of life, it is not true for several learnt behavioural responses that can be changed. Individuals can choose to change many of their behavioural responses such as learning and skill styles.

Right and left brain thinking

In right-handed people it is thought that the left brain lobe is the centre of logical thinking with the right lobe being the centre of creative thought. The pattern is reversed for left handed people. Maximum thinking potential lies in understanding the role that each lobe plays and then learning techniques to combine both in what this text terms *total thinking*. Many have sought to differentiate these two kinds of thinking. Table 4.1 presents a summary of the most commonly found distinctions.

We need both critical and creative thinking, both analysis and synthesis, both the parts and the whole to be effective in our thinking. We need reason and intuition, order and adventure in our thinking. We need creative thinking to generate the new, but critical thinking to judge it. The technological world enables us to access knowledge in abundance, but creativity is in short supply.

Having briefly described the workings of the brain it is time to return to the cerebral cortex to see how it handles the key intellectual components of thinking. The American

Table 4.1 Exploring logical and creative thinking

Logical left-brain thinking	Creative right-brain thinking
Analytic	Generative
Convergent	Divergent
Vertical	Lateral
Probability	Possibility
Judgement	Suspended judgement
Hypothesis testing	Hypotheses forming
Objective	Subjective
Single solution	Possibility of several solutions
Closed	Open-ended
Linear	Associative
Quantitative	Qualitative
Logical	Intuitive
Yes but	Yes and

Table 4.2 Cortical hemispheres

Left-brain functions	Right-brain functions
Written language	Insight
Number skills	3-D forms
Reasoning	Art awareness
Spoken language	Imagination
Scientific skills	Music awareness
Right-hand control	Left-hand control

psychologist Professor R.W. Sperry proposed that the two hemispheres of the cortex control separate, distinct intellectual enquiries (see Table 4.2).

The right hemisphere appeared to be active in the processing of the following:

- Rhythm
- Spatial awareness
- Gestalt (wholeness)
- Imagination
- Colour
- Dimension.

The left hemisphere, by contrast seemed to process an equally important but different pattern of memory traces covering a variety of learnt skills including:

- Language
- Logic
- Quantitative ability
- Sequential ability
- Linear ability
- Analytical ability.

Learning skills

When the range of skills – the ability to cut, develop and maintain complex memory trace sets – of both cortical hemispheres is combined, the individual has a dazzling potential to develop his or her thinking. The equipment is there for us to generate an amazing array of responses. The degree to which we are able to do this is a function of our thinking skills and our determination to improve them.

Many of us regard thinking as a natural skill and tend to get lazy in our approaches to information processing and problem solving. Effective thinkers take care of their grey matter as an athlete takes care of his or her physical skills. To do our best we need to look after our brains. If we look at the incredible human machine in computer terms, as a unit of hardware, then we can work towards getting the maximum from it by paying attention to how we put it to use. Thinking can be likened to the sustained development of software. The quality of output produced by computers is directly related to the quality of the input (in terms of clarity – the *what*); the method of processing it (software – the *how*); and the performance specification of the machine (individual ability). Whilst it is true that each individual has a different potential in terms of *what* can be achieved, as some are just cleverer than others, many of us can improve our thinking performance by making the best use of our potential. This can be achieved by thinking about thinking to select the most appropriate approach to solving a particular problem. Many of us try to get our brains to give us an instant answer or quick fix. We turn on our hardware and use the software already installed. If this can find the required collection of memory traces then this represents our thinking. Whilst this is probably in order for familiar problems this rather mechanistic or programmed approach will not serve us too well with rather more complex and/or infrequent problems. This requires *total* as opposed to *partial thinking*.

Total thinking

Total thinking, it is posited, occurs when we seek to focus the full power of our brain that we can activate on a problem. This means using the potential of both hemispheres of the cortex described above. Strange as it may seem, many people around the world choose to develop the skills in the left hemisphere to a higher level than those of the right hemisphere. This produces an over-dependence on logic as a key response to stimuli and the associated tendency to try to think in terms of programmed patterns. Over-dependence on such *partial thinking* can result from personal choice or from a perception that the intuitive, emotive and 'arty' skills such as colour, design, imagination, movement and sound are in general not the way to behave in public. This is curious as many of us actually take part in activities that utilise these skills in public as well as paying to view other people performing! Obviously there has been some sustained conditioning here that over time has resulted in the development of certain traditions or paradigms that preclude the regular adoption in our public lives of many right-brain skills.

Half-brained thinkers!

Both hemispheres of the cortex provide potentially powerful problem-solving power. In reality, all individuals will display a degree of *total thinking* in their private and professional lives as they are people. The issue is the degree. In most cases it is small, as individuals tend to select a thinking style that is usually highly biased to the left hemisphere, so in terms of degree are predominantly *partial thinkers*. Gifted artistic individuals can exhibit the reverse pattern. Both will fail to achieve the benefits that flow from a better-balanced use of total thinking. In many respects such people could, with tongue in cheek, be accused of half-brained thinking! Perfection, defined as a completely balanced total thinking approach to life, is very difficult to achieve. However, as the positive benefits from minor gains in our use of both left- and right-brained thinking are so immense all are capable of developing their problem-solving performance. The question is whether we choose to do so.

Limbering up

The next section sets out some ideas and routines designed to appeal to all those who genuinely wish – recognising that they are going to need to put some work into it – to develop their thinking performance. See if you can solve the problem posed below in five minutes – time yourself. If you think that you are happy with your answer after the five minutes are up, then turn to Appendix 4.3 to see if you have got the correct solution. If you are still puzzled, then have another go.

1. Four spies in trench coats sat in four facing seats.
2. They travelled the Beijing Express.
3. With two by the window and two by the aisle.
4. The arrangement was strange as you've guessed.
5. The British spy sat on Mr B's left.
6. Mr A had a tan coloured coat.
7. The spy dressed in olive was on the German's right.
8. Mr C was the only cigar-smoking man.
9. Mr D was across from the American spy.
10. The Russian, in khaki, had a scarf around his throat.
11. The British spy stared out of the window on his left.
12. So who was the spy in the rust coloured coat?

Summary

This chapter has revisited thinking. In the current business environment individuals, groups and organisations need to sharpen their thinking skills. Whilst core knowledge (general or specific) is necessary, in times of discontinuous change, it requires special thinking skills if it is to result in discoveries that are truly innovative. Total thinking is a process that enables the full power of people's brains to be applied to problems that result from the challenges presented by a dynamic and competitive business environment. Success cannot now be assumed to result by steadfastly using yesterday's processes and theories. The business world requires managers to develop a new way of doing things. This chapter has sought to show how thinking can be boosted if individuals, groups and top management personnel can learn to make use of both left- and right-brain thinking. This will enable them to discover a new expertise for today's challenging business context. Chapter 5 seeks to equip you with a set of practical thinking tools.

Discussion questions

1. How would you explain what creativity is to a fellow student or work colleague?
2. Name three living creative business people.

3.   What is meant by the term *total thinking*?
4.   What is the difference between logical thinking and creative thinking?

Case exercise

The toymaker: from lone apprentice to master craftsperson

From what to … help!

We invite you to picture a doting father who wants to give his daughter an extra special birthday present. However, he is of modest means and cannot afford to go to the local toy shop and purchase something nice. Faced with this problem he thinks of giving up his intention to buy a special present. This leaves him inwardly unhappy and ill at ease. He *knows that* this is not a solution that he can accept and so decides to dwell on the problem overnight. As the morning light streams into his room he awakes with a jolt and *knows that* he wants to build a doll's house for his daughter. Excited, he begins to think about such a project and experiences difficulty in picturing the finished article. Driven by a force that he cannot understand he gets up, sighs and feels a strong urge to open the bedroom curtains. As the full glory of the morning sun is revealed he blinks his eyes and looks over the garden below. The first thing that he notices is that his lawn is twice as high as his neighbour's; he shrugs his shoulders and commits himself to wrestling once more with the elderly and rather moody hover mower. To avoid the sun's rays, he looks sideways across his garden and suddenly realises that his eyes have come to rest on the new house that has just been built down the road. In a flash he is convinced that he wants to build a model of this house. Happy in his discovery of what he will build, he goes downstairs for breakfast. As he leaves the bright light in his bedroom and enters the relative darkness of the hall he becomes depressed. He is worried about how he is going to build the doll's house in time.

Aware of a very strong inner motivation, he looks for inspiration in his cornflake bowl. A few soggy flakes stare back at him from the bottom of the bowl and, intrigued, he stares back and is suddenly aware that his daughter would really like a doll's house with a thatched roof.

Getting started

After breakfast our man rushes out, gets into his car and reverses into the world. 'Backwards into the future' again he sighs as he speeds off down the road to buy a set of carpentry tools. A short while later he is back and proudly unpacks his new toolbox and tools. Picking up each tool, he imagines just what he could do if he could handle them as professionally as an expert. This is both exciting and almost immediately depressing. He feels nervous and exposed and now somewhat out of pocket but firmly decides to banish all self-doubt and go for it. Mastering a new skill set may be difficult but then so was learning to play the piano and how to drive. A cold shiver runs down his spine as he recalls that it took him ten years to learn how to play the piano! Oh, well, wrong example for he passed his driving test after ten lessons. Mm, he thinks, just 15 days to go.

That evening the garage light shines late into the night as he tries out his new tools. Some are easy to handle but others claim bits of his fingers as he struggles to come to terms with them. Spurred on by his determination to build the doll's house he enthusiastically assaults a piece of plywood only to find that it bends one way then the other and then jumps off his work bench and clouts him over the head. Cross at this unreasonable behaviour and in a crazy attempt to release his fretsaw blade from the offending plywood board he bashes it with his hammer. The board takes of again and smashes into his lamp, knocking it off the bench to the sound of shattering glass. Suddenly he is in the dark again. As his eyes refocus to the subdued light from the street lamp he realises that he will have to stop rushing at things and work within his capabilities. Imagination, top marks; tools, pretty good; technical proficiency with the tools, pretty basic. The thought of giving up once more flashes across his mind. No way, he thinks, for this is a task that he is going to complete and on time!

Assessing the situation

'In a word, depressing', he thinks, as he feels the pain from his bleeding and bruised fingers. There is something strangely informative about the semi-darkness in his garage. It seems to describe how he feels – a pale shade of grey instead of light, bright and active. So he decides to lighten up the garage with a tin or two of white emulsion and to fix up a couple of fluorescent lights. However, this would cost money and he knows he would have to plead his case with his wife for some extra cash for, as luck would have it, the current month is one when all the bills seemed to come in. He remains quietly determined to argue the case for some of the scarce household disposable income; he knows that this is going to challenge his existing order of things.

In the half light of his garage he begins to think about the whole business of combining ideas, tools and rather basic technique and is pleased to discover that he can build a doll's house as long as he works within the constraints of his limitations. Abandoning the idea of making a scaled down replica of the house down the road, he resolves to design a simpler structure that is within his capability. Hearing the chink of glass bottles on the milkman's van he resolves to leave things for the time being, take some time out and have a cup of coffee.

Staring into his cup as he stirs his coffee he searches for inspiration. Soggy cornflakes had given him an idea yesterday morning; perhaps his coffee would now. After a minute with nothing of any note happening he begins to be discouraged. Perhaps he should give it up. After all, one night working in the garage has resulted in very little to show for his pains except of course his injured fingers. Finding himself thinking about the story of Archimedes in his bath, he suddenly shouts *eureka* followed by *aha*. The circular movement of his coffee has led him to see that he will go round and round and make little progress unless he learns from the lessons of the night. He ponders on this for a while. Well, the tools are up to the job. His revised task seems sensible but his technical ability is still suspect. However, if he had learnt from his mistakes, and used the DIY carpentry book he had bought he would have made better progress. Keen to follow this line of thought he opens his diary and starts to list the lessons that he learnt that night.

A creative workshop

Two days later our father returns to the task of making a doll's house, having successfully obtained sufficient resources to brighten up his garage and install some effective lighting. As he settles down to work he disciplines himself into starting with a brief quiet time and resolves not to charge into his work. He remembers his childhood days when grand projects always seemed fun when they were tackled in a relaxed playful spirit rather than as a chore. Play was fun. Chores were boring. To add to the new environment in the garage he has brought in a portable disc player with a handful of his favourite music CDs. Now to work . . . no, just a minute. What did I learn from my experiences in the garage earlier in the week? Mm!

Three hours later much has been accomplished. The tools seem more friendly. The structure, though simple, is starting to emerge and he feels at peace with himself. So he decides to take time out and go to bed. He falls asleep almost as soon as his head hits the pillow but he can see the finished article in full colour and is sure that his daughter will be very pleased.

Master class

Ten years later our father has become a master toymaker and has achieved considerable fame throughout the country for his one-off and low volume designs. It seems amazing but it is true. He has acquired a reputation for both his quality of build and his designs, has left his old job in a solicitor's office and is now running his own business. Abigail, a keen young reporter, stops by, determined to find out how such creative people function. Content in his sense of fulfilment he is quite happy to talk to her.

He explains how he started and describes a couple of nights in his garage a decade before. As the conversation develops, the reporter can see clearly that his first doll's house was a significant event in his life. The master's main guides were:

1. A determination to prevent himself from restricting the flow of his and his staff's creative energies by the provision of a stimulating environment in which to work that served rather than strangled creative work.
2. A fascination with learning new skills and the patience to master them.
3. The ability to stop and quickly select the best tools for the job rather than be trapped in the repetitive boredom of always using the same techniques.
4. A determination to regularly think about the quality of *how* he and his staff worked as well as what they worked on. He was concerned to ensure that working practices were adapted to suit the needs of his markets rather than become enshrined in company mindsets.
5. Valuing the work of all his staff, encouraging them to work to the best of their capabilities when under pressure and to learn to develop their creative skills when time permitted.
6. Encouraging his staff to adopt a free rein in their design work. To practice total thinking unashamedly.
7. To build a climate of security and trust so that all felt free at all times to question the *status quo* in a positive way.
8. To seek inspiration from the natural world.

Task

Study the main master guides above. Then select a problem of your own that needs managing. Which of the eight master guides would you use and why?

References

Banks, M., Calvey, D., Owen, J., Russell, D. (2002) 'Art is: Defining and managing creativity in the new media SMEs', *Creativity & Innovation Management*, December, Vol. 11, Issue 4, pp. 255–64.
Belbin, M. (1981) *Management Teams: Why they Succeed or Fail*, Oxford, Heinemann.
Breen, W. (2004) 'The 6 myths of creativity', *Fast Company*, December, Issue 89, pp. 75–8.

Dundon, E. (2002) *Seeds of Innovation,* American Marketing Association, Chapter 1, 'Believe in creativity'.

Gardner, H. (1997) *Extraordinary Minds: Portraits of Four Exceptional Minds and the Extraordinary Minds in All of Us*, New York, HarperCollins.

Gruber, H.E. and Wallace, D.B. (1999) 'The case study method and evolving systems approach for understanding unique creative people at work', in Heppell, S. (ed.) *Handbook of Creativity*, Cambridge, Cambridge University Press.

Heimal, C. (1983) 'Lower Manhattan survival tactics', *Village Voice*.

Honey, P. and Mumford, A. (1985) *The Manual of Learning Styles*, Maidenhead, Peter Honey.

Kirton, M.J. (1987) *Adaption–Innovation Theory (KAI) – Manual*, 2nd edn, Hatfield, Occupational Research Centre.

Kolb, D. (1984) 'Problem management: Learning from experience', in Srvastra, Suresh and Associates (eds.), *The Executive Mind*, London, Jossey Bass.

Kuhn, T. (1975) *The Structure of Scientific Revolutions*, Chicago, University of Chicago Press.

Myers-Briggs, I. and McCaulley, M.H. (1988) *Myers-Briggs Type Indicator*, Consulting Psychology Press.

Sternberg, R.J. (2006) 'The nature of creativity', *Creativity Research Journal*, January, Vol. 18, Issue 1, pp. 87–98.

Sternberg, R.J. and Lubart, T.I. (1999) 'The concept of creativity: prospects and paradigms', in Sternberg, R.J. (ed.) *Handbook of Creativity*, Cambridge, Cambridge University Press.

Appendices

1: Personal Creativity Audit

Instructions

1.   Copy the questionnaire before attempting the audit.
2.   Answer the questions honestly and as quickly as you can by placing a tick or * in the box that fits most closely your most likely characteristics.
3.   Do not confer with others as you are completing the audit exercise.

Table 4.3 Personal Creativity Audit

Q		Never	Sometimes	Fairly often	Regularly
1	Do you remember your dreams as images?				
2	How often do you devote time to hobbies?				
3	How often do you read?				
4	Do you like to stick to the rules?				
5	Do you listen to others' ideas?				
6	Do you inspire others?				
7	How often do you show a sense of humour?				
8	Do you take part in sporting activity?				
9	Are you a perfectionist?				
10	Are you an optimist?				
11	Do you have any ideas of your own?				
12	Are you courteous?				
13	How often do you hum and sing?				

Table 4.3 Cont'd

Q		Never	Sometimes	Fairly often	Regularly
14	Are you predictable?				
15	Do you like exercising administrative (rank) authority?				
16	Are you a good listener?				
17	Are you a resourceful person?				
18	Do you tend to work on one idea at a time?				
19	Do you welcome change?				
20	Do you have many original ideas?				
21	Do you actively promote them?				
22	Are you a loner?				
23	Do you like organisations with lots of rules and indentified procedures?				
24	Are you self-motivated?				
25	Are you a good problem solver?				
26	Are you good at improvisation?				
27	Do you prefer to adapt the ideas of others?				
28	Do you challenge rules if you think that they are silly?				
29	If people oppose your ideas do you give up promoting them?				
30	Do you use metaphors when communicating key points?				

2: Assessing performance

Instructions

1. Circle the Descriptor you selected (i.e. Never, Sometimes, Fairly Often or Regularly) in the table below.
2. Next add up your overall score and place it on the creativity spectrum in Figure 4.5.

Table 4.4 Personal Creativity Audit coding

Question	Never	Sometimes	Fairly Often	Regularly
1	1	2	3	4
2	1	2	3	4
3	1	2	3	4
4	2	4	3	1
5	1	2	3	3
6	1	2	3	4
7	1	2	3	4
8	1	2	3	4
9	1	2	3	4
10	1	2	3	4
11	1	2	3	4

(Continued)

Table 4.4 Cont'd

Question	Never	Sometimes	Fairly Often	Regularly
12	1	2	3	4
13	1	2	3	4
14	4	3	2	1
15	4	3	2	1
16	1	2	3	4
17	1	2	3	4
18	4	3	2	1
19	1	2	3	4
20	1	2	3	4
21	1	2	3	4
22	4	3	2	1
23	4	3	2	1
24	1	2	3	4
25	1	2	3	4
26	1	2	3	4
27	4	3	2	1
28	1	2	3	4
29	4	3	2	1
30	1	2	3	4

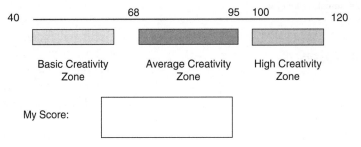

Figure 4.5 Personal creativity assessment spectrum.

3: Limbering up problem solution

The British spy has the rust coloured coat.

5 Learning new skills

Genius is one percent inspiration and ninety-nine percent perspiration.

(Thomas Edison)

O this learning, what a thing it is!

(William Shakespeare, *Taming of the Shrew*)

You can't solve the problem with the same thinking that's creating the problem.

(Albert Einstein)

Introduction

This is essentially a practical chapter. Having made the case for a new approach to thinking individuals are presented with a development programme to assist them to acquire the necessary knowledge and to develop expertise by applying it to problem solving. The chapter helps readers by presenting a Gateway Personal Creative Thinking Toolbox and encourages them to develop this in accordance with their respective needs.

Context

Challenge of change

A more competitive business environment presents top management with two clear options (Chapter 2, Section 2.4.1).

1. Ride out the storms and hope for a better tomorrow
2. Realise the need to do things differently.

The second option places a heavy stress on the need in the private sector to deliver *customer-perceived value* and in the public sector *best value* solutions. In both cases there is a need to acquire and practice new thinking skills.

Stimulating creative thinking

To think creatively individuals have to really believe that they enjoy the freedom to think in ways different from the accepted norms (the ways in which things are normally done). For this to happen regularly individuals should be given a succession of positive challenges and

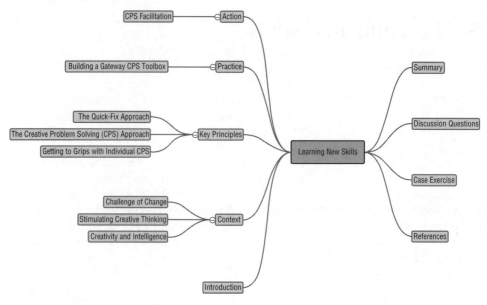

Figure 5.1 Exploring new skills.

be constantly encouraged to perform to the best of their abilities. 'Carrot and stick', excessively autocratic management styles tend to cause creative output to die away to residual levels. This reductionist approach in the management of creativity is the opposite of what is needed when organisations are battling for business in crowded markets. To achieve a consistent market edge creative thinking must be released and continuously supported.

Creativity and intelligence

Many people strongly associate creative thinking with intelligence. Like many things in life, this is both true and untrue. Research into this question has not as far as is known come up with any conclusive proof that intelligent people *per se* are generally more creative than individuals who would not see themselves as being intelligent. Then what is meant by intelligence? There is a body of evidence that suggests that creative people tend to have high intelligence quotas (IQs), but not all people with high IQs are creative. Many of the psychometric profiles that have been constructed have been built from data that has been recorded from tests that were originally intended to measure IQ levels. Several, notably Getzels and Jackson (1962), Torrance (1988) and Baron (1988), have tried to devise and validate tests (Sullivan and Ford, 2010) that can accurately detect and measure the presence or otherwise of creativity.

Creativity tests are typically divided into four main components:

1.   Divergent thinking
2.   Convergent thinking
3.   Artistic assessments
4.   Self assessments.

Divergent thinking (Guilford, 1967; Torrance, 1988) is the ability to consciously generate new ideas that branch out to many possible solutions for a given problem. These solutions or responses are then scored on four components:

(a) Originality – statistical infrequency of response
(b) Fluency – number of responses
(c) Flexibility – the degree of difference of the responses, in other words do they come from a single domain or multiple domains?
(d) Elaboration – the amount of detail of the response.

Convergent thinking is the ability to correctly hone in on the single correct solution to a problem. In creativity convergent thinking often requires taking a novel approach to the problem, seeing the problem from a different perspective or making a unique association between parts of the problem. These solutions are scored either correct or incorrect (Mednick, 2009).

Artistic assessments are the evaluations of an artistic product (e.g., painting, story, poem, musical composition, collage, drawing etc.). Evaluations are typically done by two or more judges who must be in near agreement on the creativity of the product.

Self assessments are people's responses to the amount of creativity they feel they exhibit.

Key principles

The creative problem solving approach

Note-taking skills

A problem that many of us face, whether at home or at work, is how to study efficiently. The student who has to summarise key information from articles and texts in a form that is user-friendly for memorising and understanding. The individual at work who has to write a brief summary report for management on a complex subject. In both cases *creative problem solving* (CPS) has a lot to offer. Note taking can be a long and painstaking exercise which can easily become frustrating when an individual later returns to his or her notes only to find that the passage of time has made them difficult to use. In common with Buzan and Buzan (1993) years of observing students reveals that there would appear to be three main styles of note taking:

1. *Narrative* – writing all selected information in narrative form.
2. *Listing* – recording interesting ideas as they occur.
3. *Outline* – seeking to arrange the material in a hierarchical sequence.

The *narrative* style demands a lot of writing and may be useful to those who are anxious to convince themselves that they really understand some taxing argument or theory. Generally speaking this style demands much recording effort and can be difficult to summarise for the purpose of revision or to write an essay or report. The *listing* style certainly saves on paper and on time, but may just produce copious columns of material that become difficult to handle later. The *outline* style is better, as the use of main and subheadings provides both order and visual variety for the brain.

However, such predominantly left-brain presentation, even if all three styles are combined, often results in the brain having to work hard to understand the key points. Many individuals find it hard going to make sense of such notes and may well have to devote a lot of time in getting to grips with the material. This is because the brain basically gets bored, as the styles of note making only effectively stimulate the left brain and almost ignore the right brain. For efficient brain activity – learning and thinking – to occur, the missing stimuli are essential, especially for recall and argument. Sadly, many individuals make notes in a format that is almost guaranteed to bore the brain into wandering off in an effort to find something interesting to do.

Memory friendly information

To study effectively it is necessary to input in the correct format for the brain to process. This means using both left- and right-brain stimuli. For example, we can produce better notes if we seek to:

- Use as few words as possible;
- Use analogies, metaphors;
- Use diagram, sketches;
- Use colour for picking out key words and in marking key sections of diagrams;
- Summarise notes, once prepared, in a predominantly right-brain style such as a mind map or rich picture.

Learning skills

For learning, as opposed to note taking, try using the sound capabilities of the right brain by the following measures:

- Convert important pieces of factual information into ghost lyrics to well known tunes and then do some humming. For example, if you were trying to remember Ohm's law consider setting it to the tune of the 'Rain in Spain' from Lerner and Lowe's musical *My Fair Lady*. (The unit of resistance is the OHM!) Record it, play it back for the rhythm.
- Select words that have a rhythmic flow rather than formal language. This is a technique that is often used by schoolchildren when they are swotting for exams. Here are a couple of examples:
  Remembering trigonometry formulae

  - tan = opp/adj or 'toads over act'
  - sin = opp/hyp or 'snakes only hiss'
  - cos = adj/hyp or 'cats always howl'

  Remembering the names and order of the planets

  - '*My v*et *E*ric *m*unched *j*am *s*andwiches *u*sually *n*ear *P*aris.' (*Mercury, Venus, Earth, Mars, Jupiter, Saturn, Uranus, Neptune and Pluto.*)

- Play music, to your taste, in the background as you study. This text was written to a mixture of classical, light and pop background music.

You can also seek to produce material that appeals to the visual skills of the brain. For example:

- Summary charts
- Mind maps
- Picture books
- Picture charts
- Broadsheets
- Designs.

Put them up on the walls of your study. The brain works best when it is well stimulated. This incredible machine is a true multimedia device. Try to provide sufficient stimuli to keep your brain interested and entertained. Then even the most potentially boring of tasks assumes a different hue. Escape from the grey world of predominantly left-brain note taking styles.

Getting to grips with individual creative problem solving

Organisations must be creative continuously to survive and thrive in today's highly competitive, rapidly changing environment. A century of creativity research has produced several descriptive models of creativity, and hundreds of prescriptions for interventions that demonstrably improve creativity. This section is based on an adaptation of the Nominal Group Technique first expounded by Delbecq *et al*. (1975), Rikards (1990) and VanGundy (1988).

Demonstration exercise: organising a perfect wedding

To illustrate how CPS can assist in *personal problem solving* (PPS), imagine that you wish to formulate some ideas for discussion with your family to plan for the big day. A useful CPS template to adopt to begin with is a simple, but powerful, three-stage approach (after Kolb, 1984 and Kreitner, 1980):

1. *Problem evaluation* – what is the problem?
2. *Idea generation* – process for generating and selecting apt ideas.
3. *Implementation* – converting thinking into action.

Now the Nominal Group Technique involves six basic steps:

(a) Private brainstorming
(b) Round robin collection of ideas
(c) Consideration of each idea
(d) Preliminary selection of ideas
(e) Consideration of chosen ideas
(f) Final choice.

In this case the problem is known, but it is good practice to state it, in as few words as possible, in a formal *problem statement*: planning the perfect wedding.

Now generate some ideas using an adaptation of the Nominal Group Technique.

PRIVATE BRAINSTORMING (AFTER STEVENS, 1988)

This is a widespread and popular process for generating ideas and the rules are widely known:

- List spontaneous thoughts – do not exercise any judgement.
- Write down everything, however trivial it may seem at first.
- Aim to record as many ideas as possible.
- Use ideas you have written down to stimulate other ideas.

A period of about five minutes is usually enough for this step:

Venue	Choir	Best man
Reception	Music	Ring
Guest list	Bridesmaid	Pageboys
Seating plan	Organ	Cost

ROUND ROBIN

Transfer your ideas to Post-It notes. Write out a separate Post-It slip for each idea (Figure 5.2).

MIND MAPPING (BUZAN AND BUZAN, 1993)

Now shade in the *problem statement* Post-It and place your Post-It note slips on a convenient surface, such as a wall or broad table top (see Figure 5.3).

CONSIDER EACH IDEA AND CLUSTER

Once your Post-It notes are in place examine them closely and look for ideas. This involves rearranging the Post-It notes into clusters. According to Tassoul and Buijs (2007) it is about

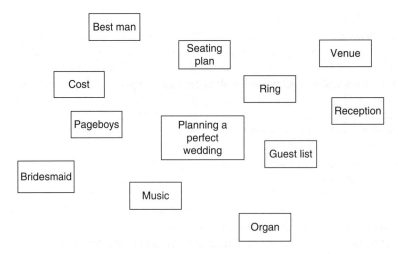

Figure 5.2 The perfect wedding mind map 1.

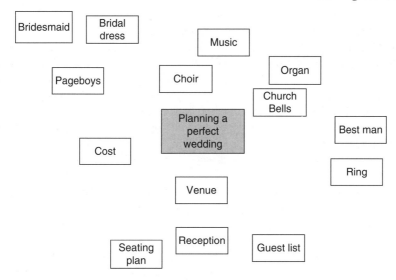

Figure 5.3 Planning the perfect wedding mind map 2.

expanding knowledge, about connecting ideas, and connecting ideas to problem statements, functionalities, and values and consequences. It is about building a shared understanding, in other words about 'making sense', an essential creative activity in the development of concepts and, although different from a more freewheeling divergent phase, can be as creative and maybe even more so. Four kinds of clusterings are distinguished: object clustering, morphological clustering, functional clustering and gestalt clustering. Object clustering is mainly aimed at categorising ideas into an over-viewable set of groups of ideas that appear to make sense (see Figure 5.3). The Post-It notes are particularly useful as they provide the facility to move ideas around and to experiment.

ANALOGY (RIKARDS, 1974)

Now if you should need to generate some more ideas select a tangible item at random, such as a picture, the view from the window, an outside tree. You may like to keep a pack of picture post cards of famous paintings, views or steam engines! Or, perhaps, you may find that listening to your favourite music helps. Explore your multimedia brain! Often you can jump straight from this stimulus and think of new ideas. For example, looking out of the window, you may notice that it is raining and then get the idea of making sure that a supply of umbrellas are available for the wedding day! (See expanded mind map in Figure 5.4.)

REVERSAL (RIKARDS, 1990)

Selecting ideas and inverting them often suggests additional useful ideas. Imagine the worst possible wedding. For example, the best man fails to turn up, the bride's car breaks down, one of the bridesmaids is sick over her dress. Now simply invert and place on a Post-It note, and add to the mind map. It is a simple technique but it works!

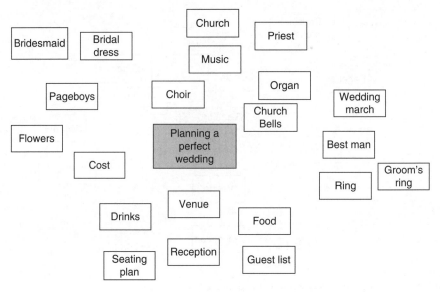

Figure 5.4 Planning the most perfect wedding mind map 3.

SHAPING

Now study the Post-It notes on your wall or table top and do some further clustering if neces-sary. Spend some time looking at the complete pattern that has evolved. Look at the problem statement again. Is there anything else that you would like to add?

PRELIMINARY SELECTION AND CONSIDERATION OF IDEAS

At this stage choose the most important matters and mark them with a green dot. For exam-ple, booking the church, settling on a venue for the reception. Now spend a few minutes writing out some brief guideline notes on your preliminary selection. For example, list some possible places in which to hold the reception, who you need to invite.

TIME-OUT (GOMAN, 1989; STEVENS, 1988)

Comparatively few problems really have to be 'solved' on the spot. Try to take time out to think about your notes. Many things that worry us are processed by the subconscious mind overnight when hopefully the conscious, worrying, mind is resting. Often gentle messages to our conscious minds, first thing in the morning, contain real pearls of wisdom.

Practice

Building a gateway CPS toolkit

Table 5.1 presents a creative problem-solving (CPS) starter toolbox. Pick a problem of your own and first try all the tools in sequential order. Start in Stage 1 by spending some time getting a clear statement of your problem, that is, an effective diagnosis (Okes, 2010).

Then resist any temptation to come to an immediate answer (the *quick fix* approach) and in Stage 2 generate as many ideas as you can. Many have found it helpful to collect ideas on

Table 5.1 Introductory CPS toolkit

Function stages	Action tool
1. Problem evaluation	State problem in as few words as possible
2. Idea generation	Private brainstorming
	Round robin
	Mind mapping
	Clustering
	Analogy
	Reversal
	Shaping
	Time-out
	Notebook
3. Implementation	Stage 1 – selection
	• Colour coding
	• Intuition
	• Advantages/disadvantages
	Stage 2 – final choice

Post-It notes. These facilitate the construction of mind maps, which provide a picture that appeals to the right-brain functions. Use the tools as described in the Perfect Wedding example to come up with as many ideas as you can.

Stage 3, implementation, starts with the application of a simple selection technique such as the use of coloured sticker dots to pick out very good ideas (green sticker dot) and good ideas (blue sticker dot) for the problem under investigation. Finally an idea is selected as the best – usually the one with the most green dots.

Introductory CPS toolkit

See Appendix 5.1 for further information and for an outline of the CPS toolbox used professionally in AJM Management Development over the last decade.

Action

CPS facilitation

CPS is necessary in all three dimensions of management, that is, individual, group and organisational. In each level facilitation is necessary.

Individual or personal CPS activity

The sequence in which individuals approach CPS is important. Considerable care should be taken in Stage 1 to ensure that the problem being tackled is clearly stated. The CPS tools that are used in Stage 2 can be used in the sequence they appear in Table 5.1 or some variation in the running order may be appropriate. It may, for example, be suitable to start with Reversal rather than Personal Brainstorming. The key action point here is to mix the tools to generate ideas. Using Post-It notes is helpful as it enables the individual to construct a mind map of the ideas and then to Cluster and Shape it more easily to see the big picture and apply a selection technique in Stage 3. The exercise should be carried out at speed with the individual moving smoothly between the Stage 2 tools.

Group CPS activity

This process is similar to that for an individual CPS session with the following differences. Preferably a trained CPS facilitator should act as moderator. The maximum number of participants should be kept to five or six and each should be encouraged to contribute and not to indulge in idle chatter. As with individual CPS, sessions should be fast paced with the facilitator moving smoothly through the tools of Table 5.1.

Organisational CPS activity

At top or senior management level a trained facilitator is essential and participants must enter into the spirit of CPS and especially resist any temptation to harness their functional skills to present a prescriptive solution rather than play along and generate ideas.

Summary

If managers at the individual, group or organisational level are to do things differently to successfully meet the challenges of the current business environment there must be a willingness to both accept and learn new ways of thinking. As Einstein has written, 'You can't solve the problem with the same thinking that's creating the problem'. Mastering CPS requires time and determination. Reflect on Handy's observation: 'Ask people . . . to recall two or three of the most important learning experiences in their lives and they will . . . tell you . . . of times when continuity ran out on them, when they had no past experience to fall back on, no rules or handbook'. The good news is that it pays handsome dividends.

Discussion questions

1. A curious enquirer has asked 'Is intelligence both a necessary and sufficient condition for acting creatively?' How would you frame your answer?
2. What are the four main components of creativity tests?
3. Name the three main styles of note taking.
4. List the three stages of the CPS process.
5. What are the six basic steps of the Nominal Group Technique?
6. Explain how CPS activity can be applied to individual, group and top management.

Case exercise

Graham Davy is the managing director of a medium-sized engineering company that manufactures metal and plastic components for the motor industry. The business suddenly experienced a downturn in its order book as economic conditions worsened in the UK and as the company's European markets were badly affected by the Eurozone crisis of 2011. Graham knew that he would soon have to start laying off valued staff if things did not improve in the next two to three months.

The outlook was gloomy as he sat at his desk thinking how he and his marketing director, Robin Wardle, could find work for the factory. As an avid fan of Arthur Conan Doyle stories Graham suddenly recalled an old maxim of Sherlock Holmes's: 'When you have excluded the impossible, whatever remains, however improbable, must be the truth'. New orders from the company's original equipment and after-sales customers were not going to materialise so all that remained was to look for other markets for the company's expertise. The problem was how to begin the search for new business.

Robin had recently returned from a marketing presentation in London where he had sat transfixed as one of the speakers introduced and explained how creative problem solving (CPS) could be applied in real businesses as opposed to case studies in university seminars. Intrigued by the possibilities of this new approach he remained nervous about recommending it to Graham as he was strictly a numbers man and could be quite dismissive of anything that appeared to him to be qualitative and 'airy fairy'. However, his resolve was stiffened by the sudden crisis with the forward order book. He decided to be brave and suggest to Graham that the company should try CPS.

As he had anticipated, Graham was at first reluctant but did agree that it was worth giving it a go. Robin wasted no time in securing the services of Anna Bridges who agreed to visit the factory and facilitate a CPS session. He was confident that the experiment would be beneficial but Graham was uncertain and had a hard task in keeping an open mind.

Anna duly arrived and to Graham and Robin's surprise immediately requested that no more than five people who the company deemed relevant should attend and that the whole session would be over in 20 minutes. The stated problem was 'How can we gain business in alternative markets?' Anna then used a selection of CPS tools to help the group generate several ideas. She then helped them to build mind maps using Post-It notes and to display these on the boardroom wall. Every participant was then asked to contribute to clustering and shaping the mind map. They were then invited, one by one, to come up to the mind map with a sheet of green sticker dots and a sheet of blue sticker dots and to use them to indicate the ideas that were very good (green sticker dots) and those that were good and worthy of serious attention (blue sticker dots).

The session revealed several business opportunities including domestic water pumps, air purifiers, wheel clamps, hardened steel and aluminium road signs, heavy duty air compressors and hydraulic ram components. Afterwards Graham admitted it had been one of the most productive 20 minutes of his life.

The following week Graham was due to speak at a regional meeting of engineers and though he knew that they would all be sceptical he decided to introduce them to CPS in his 15 minute slot.

Task

How would you advise Graham to proceed? Write a brief memo suggesting the main points that Graham should get across.

References

Baron, J. (1988) *Thinking and Deciding*, Cambridge, Cambridge University Press.

Buzan, T. and Buzan, B. (1993) *The Mind-map Book*, London, BBC Books.

Delbecq, A.L., Van de Ven, A.H. and Gustafson, D.H. (1975) *Group Techniques for Program Planning*, Glenview, IL, Scott, Foresman.

Getzels, J.P. and Jackson, P.W. (1962) *Creativity and Intelligence*, New York, Wiley.

Goman, C.K. (1989) *Creative Thinking in Business*, London, Kogan Page.

Guilford, J.P. (1967) *The Nature of Human Intelligence*, New York, Mcgraw-Hill.

Guilford, J.P. (1986) *Creative Talents: Their Nature Uses and Development*, Buffalo, NY, Bearly.

Kolb, D. (1984) *Experiential Learning*, Englewood Cliffs, NJ, Prentice Hall.

Kreitner, R. (1980) *Management: A Problem-solving Process*, Boston, Houghton Mifflin.

Mednick, S. (2009) 'Be a better problem solver – Get more REM sleep', *Machine Design*, September, Vol. 81, Issue 13, p. 44.

Mitroff, I.I. (2008) 'Knowing: How we know is as important as what we know', *Journal of Business Strategy*, Vol. 29, Issue 3, pp. 13–22.

Okes, D. (2010) 'Common problems with basic problem solving', *Quality*, September, Vol. 49, Issue 9, pp. 36–40.

Rikards, T. (1974) *Problem Solving Through Creative Analysis*, Epping, Gower.

Rikards, T. (1990) *Creativity and Problem Solving at Work*, Aldershot, Gower.

Stevens, M.S. (1988) *Practical Problem Solving for Managers*, London, Kogan Page.

Sullivan, D.M. and Ford, C.M. (2010) 'The alignment of measures and constructs in organizational research: The case of testing measurement models of creativity', *Journal of Business & Psychology*, September, Vol. 25, Issue 3, pp. 505–21.

Tassoul, M. and Buijs, J. (2007) 'Clustering: An essential step from diverging to converging', *Creativity & Innovation Management*, March, Vol. 16, Issue 1, pp. 16–26.

Torrance, E.P. (1988) 'The nature of creativity as manifest in its testing', in R.J. Sternberg (ed.) *The Nature of Creativity: Contemporary Psychological Perspectives*, Cambridge, Cambridge University Press.

VanGundy, A.B. (1988) *Techniques of Structured Problem Solving*, 2nd edn, New York, VanNostrand Reinhold.

Appendix: Outline notes on a CPS toolbox used by AJM Management Development for over 15 years

CPS Stage 1: problem evaluation

Explore the problem statement

Having decided to call a CPS session, a creative facilitator should ensure that the problem to be addressed is clear and concise to all session attendees before moving on to the second stage of a CPS exercise (idea generation). A skilled facilitator will explore the original problem statement using tools such as *'Why?'*, *Kipling's Questions* and *Stakeholder analysis*. After a brief creative personal problem solving (CPPS) exercise the original problem statement usually gets revised. Our experience shows quite dramatically that it pays to address the real problem!

Problem evaluation tools

Below are some basic tools that should enable you to get going plus an additional three drawn from the *Synectics* collection (Gordon, 1961; Rikards, 1974). Try them out. In a subsequent CPS session use them in a different sequence.

- 'Why?' (VanGundy, 1988)
- Five Ws and H or Kipling's Questions (Rikards, 1990; VanGundy, 1988)
- Stakeholder analysis (Stevens, 1988)
- Wishful thinking (Rikards, 1974)

plus from the Synectics collection

- 'I wish'
- How-to . . .
- Concerns

'WHY?'

This is a simple but surprisingly powerful tool that enables creative problem-solving groups to define a problem at several levels of abstraction. The tool has four cycle steps:

1. Read the problem as originally defined.
2. Question why you want to do what is in the problem statement.
3. Redefine the answer in the form of a new problem statement.
4. Repeat question 2 to achieve another level of abstraction.

Then repeat as many times as is sensible. Then agree a new problem statement. Here is an example:

Question: Why do we want to go on holiday?
Answer: To get a break from work.
Redefine: In what ways might (IWWM) we get a break from work?

Question: Why do we want to get a break from work?
Answer: To relax, and recover from the strains of everyday work.
Redefine: IWMM we relax and recover?

Question: Why do we want to relax and recover?
Answer: To charge up our batteries to face the rest of the year at work.
Redefine: IWWM we charge up our batteries, etc.

FIVE Ws AND H (KIPLING'S QUESTIONS)

This is a powerful tool as it uses the main interrogatives of the English language: *Who? What? When? Why?* and *Where?* Rounded off with a *How?* question (VanGundy, 1988). Each member of the problem-solving group is asked to write down the six questions and then asked privately to answer them briefly:

- Who is involved in this matter? Who is interested in this issue?
- What is it all about? What is the matter?
- When did this occur? When must it be solved?
- Why did this happen?
- Where did this happen?
- How did this come about?

STAKEHOLDER ANALYSIS

With both personal and group CPS exercises both the problem and the potential outcomes are often of interest to other parties. Most problem evaluation sessions benefit by the inclusion of an analysis of the key publics involved. This can be achieved in a variety of ways so feel free to experiment. You might like to try the following sequence:

1. *Problem owner* states problem.
2. Individual or group carry out a *personal brainstorm.*
3. *Problem owner* or *facilitator* institutes a *round robin* and gathers in ideas.
4. *Problem owner* or *facilitator* collects information on a mind map or *force-field diagram.*

WISHFUL THINKING

This is a useful technique to assist groups to break out of the constraints imposed by conventional approaches to problem solving and work practices. There are five steps involved:

1. State the problem.
2. Now tell the group to imagine that anything is possible.
3. Ask them to state what they would like to happen.
4. Get them to relate this back to the problem statement.
5. If you need to, repeat steps 3 and 4.

SYNECTICS COLLECTION (GORDON, 1961)

Synectics is a registered trade mark. It is the brand name of an American firm of consultants who have developed their own style of CPS out of the original work on brainstorming carried out by Osborn (1957) in the 1930s (e.g. Stevens, 1988).

HOW TO . . .

The advantage of the format of this question and the way in which it is used is that it welcomes all suggestions irrespective of whether the group intends to adopt the suggested solution. Thus practical constraints do not deter thinking. Suppose that the group was faced with the problem of a cracked furnace. They might ask:

'How can we get the furnace going?'
'How can we stop it from causing so much trouble to our operations?'
'How can we get it properly relined?'
'How can we best project manage the job?'
'How can we get this done?'
'How can we get X to be more careful in the future?'

Facilitate the group to generate at least 20 questions and try for 30! Possible answers to these are generated by asking the group to respond to the prompt 'In how many ways can we . . . ?':

'Get the furnace going?'
'Stop it from causing so much trouble to our operations?'

'Get it properly relined?'
'Get it project managed?'
'Get it done quickly?'
'Get X to be more careful in the future?'

Try these questions on your problem statement and see what happens, but be careful to keep up the pace. The facilitator then gathers up the group's replies and assists it to redraft the problem statement. Then try *Why?*, *Kipling's Questions*.

CPS Stage 2: idea generation and development

Stuck in a rut?

Sometimes it is hard to generate imaginative ideas for progressing problems when groups find that tools such as conventional brainstorming, checklists and so on do not seem to produce any good results. When this occurs it can cause a facilitator to panic. To all intents and purposes the group is stuck in a rut. Fortunately, there is a group of CPS tools that can deal with this situation. They are the so-called right-brain tools.

Ask the group to look out of the window or round the room and then ask them to focus on a particular object. This often provides individuals with new insight by simply unblocking their right-brain thinking channels. Suitable tools to try here include *analogies*, *metaphors* and *reversal* to cut thought paths (which then become memory traces) in your mind. The ideas generated are then related/forced back to the problem definition. An interesting and frequently successful option is to take time out (an *excursion* in the Synectics terminology) from the problem situation and give your attention to something else. A short break or a brisk walk usually works wonders as they provide a means of breaking though the paralysis of analysis and set the mind free to look and connect. It is amazing how easily such new ideas and approaches can occur. On returning to the group room or after an *in situ* look and connect exercise it is often a good thing to conduct a round robin, to collect participants' selected images and then to transfer them as graphics to a new pictorial mind map. Then ask individuals to state what new ideas came from the forced fit part of the exercise, collect them up and place them on a conventional mind map. Then ask the group to study both mind maps and see what happens!

Wildest idea (Rikards, 1974)

This is another useful tool to use when groups get bogged down. It simply involves the facilitator introducing a new idea totally at random. For example, in a recent workshop in Durham, a group were looking at ways of introducing a creative management training programme to a local borough council headed by Elizabeth Fry. Faced with the seemingly impenetrable problem of how to sell it to the executive, the group found themselves stuck in a rut. At this point the facilitator responded by asking the group to brainstorm sausages! To show that he was serious he drew a picture of a string of sausages with a 'fry-up' featuring Elizabeth Fry the Local Investors in People Executive! This broke the ice with Elizabeth who realised that she needed to be part of an exercise that would release creative thinking in an informal way. Later the organisation signed up to a scheme with their local Training and Enterprise Council to apply creative thinking to a selection of complex council problems.

Should one wild idea not work then the facilitator can suggest another or call for some suggestions from the group. A variation on this tool that we have used successfully is to keep an odds and ends box. Produce this when the going gets tough and pull an item out at random and get one of the group to say to the rest 'Look what I've got!'

Analogies (Rikards,1974)

An alternative option to taking an excursion on the move is to take one from an armchair. Try to imagine the problem being explored in a different scenario:

- Place a writing pad (A4 ideal) and a sharp pencil to hand.
- Relax, breathe in and out slowly for a few seconds, then close your eyes for minute or so.
- Now think of your favourite hobby (e.g. fishing, gardening) or sport (cricket, golf, rugby, soccer, tennis) or your last summer holiday, or your last trip to London or a recent long-distance drive. Concentrate on your experience and attempt to picture the scene in as much detail as you can. Picture the sky, the background and the foreground, listen for any sound, see if you can detect any movement.
- Now open your eyes and summarise what you have 'seen' on your A4 pad, trying to use drawings, sketches and symbols as much as you can.
- Then relate the material summarised back to the original problem.

Cut and connect!

Try this one! Get a couple of old magazines and a pair of scissors and select five pictures to count out. Then relate back to the problem statement.

Checklists

The main attraction of the *right-brain* family of CPS tools is that they encourage you to see one set of stimuli you have experienced by means of another. It is an interactive process and will often inspire you. If you experience difficulties in using this group of tools you may like to try some *checklists*. They can be useful for individual CPS but can easily become monotonous if used in group sessions. Essentially they are stepping stones that can prove useful to define a path to approach a problem. It's *what* you do on each stepping stone that is important. They can be useful in the same way that a motorist, for example, may use a road atlas to find the way. Coping with what happens on the way is an entirely different proposition.

Attribute listing (Rikards, 1990; Stevens, 1988; Majaro, 1992)

This approach entails reducing the problem statement to its prime components and auditing the characteristics of each identified part. This can be extended through a number of sub-component rounds if required. The ultimate objective is to discover what is really needed to do the job and whether the existing components can be put together in another, more efficient, way that directly addresses the original problem. Experimenting with this tool we built a wooden caterpillar at Durham and a wooden mechanical wave machine that provided a useful creative *divertimento* for our CPS sessions. A more complex version of this technique, morphological analysis, is often used in the development of new products, services and systems. It is a powerful though time-consuming tool, and has resulted in some spectacular successes in high-technology industries (see Rikards, 1974; Majaro, 1992).

Scamper

This is a variation of Osborn's (1957) checklist rearranged by Eberle (1972) after Stevens (1988) (see also http://www.mindtools.com/pages/article/newCT_02.htm).

S   *Substitute*
    Who else? What else? Alternative inputs/outputs, people, places etc.
C   *Combine*
    Blend different approaches, ideas, use, cross-functional teams units, cost centres, plants.
A   *Adapt*
    What else is similar to this? What other ideas seem to fit this problem? What precedents are there? Who else had this problem recently?
M   *Magnify/minify*
    What needs to be added? Time, resources, product/service features, promotional messages etc. What needs to be reduced, saved, omitted, simplified etc.
P   *Put to other uses*
    How else could this product/service be used? Who else may want it? Where else might it be used?
E   *Eliminate/elaborate*
    What needs to be scrapped? How can this be made more user-friendly? How can things be simplified? What savings can be made? What delays can be eliminated? What needs to be stressed? What needs to be developed? Can we manage with existing supply/ distribution arrangements? Is something more elaborate required?
R   *Rearrange/reverse*
    What other ways can we find/develop to do this? How can we reverse known consequences?

5Ws and H or Kipling's Questions

Some of us first heard this on our mother's knee as we listened to her reading Kipling's famous children's poem:

> I keep six honest serving men
> (They taught me all I knew);
> Their names are *What* and *Why* and *When*
> And *How* and *Where* and *Who*.

This tool features the leading interrogatives of the English language. It is useful as it opens up a number of different aspects of a problem and ensures that CPS activity pays due regard to material and people, resources, delivery and time implications. Try it next time you get stuck.

Software packages

For those who like computer-based packages both *idea generating* and *mind mapping* softwares deserve a place in a basic CPS toolkit. However, as with most software packages, in the final analysis:

- Each problem is unique therefore it requires an original choice of CPS tools.
- Computers should serve in CPS sessions as a tool and should not be allowed to dominate the proceedings.
- Many people experience problems in correctly using the software and these can easily take over a CPS session.

Such packages are interesting to play with when you require a change (or perhaps are just feeling lazy) or run as an occasional backup exercise to an on-going CPS session. Sometimes switching between manual and computer CPS modes can be advantageous. Other things worth mentioning here include the use of presentation packages, such as Microsoft PowerPoint, that can display random arrangements of computer graphics as a source of right-brain activity provocations. Also the outline facilities on good-quality word processing packages such as Microsoft Word can be used effectively.

Focused total thinking

There is little doubt that we would be wise to use both left- and right-brain thinking (total thinking) to concentrate as much thinking power as we can on problems. However, in the West the learnt way is traditionally seen as being left-brain oriented and right-brain thinking is often regarded as being odd. This is a pity, as in reality we are meant to use both means of thinking. It is hoped that this text may play a small part in correcting this strange practice.

The art of harnessing both modes of thinking enables individuals to see problems in their proper perspective (context) and to find and select a suitable creative problem-solving track. Truly creative thought is the result of a subtle synthesis between left- and right-brain modes (*total thinking*). Bright ideas on their own are fine but usually disappoint unless they can be practically applied to a real personal or group problem. As Fritz (1989) elegantly describes it there are three stages in the creative process:

1. Conceiving what it is that you want – knowing what you want.
2. Knowing what exists at present – developing an accurate contextual perception.
3. Doing something about it – by invention, learning and adjusting *usual* responses.

The *visualisation* lobby argue vociferously that if you start out by visualising the outcome you are more likely to end up closer to it than if you rely predominantly on the traditional left-brain tools.

Imagineering

The deliberate selection of imagery tools to stimulate ideas has assumed the title of 'Imagineering' (Morgan, 1993). For ease of explanation the nine imagery tools included in the Introductory CPS Toolkit have been divided into three categories: passive, bridging and active; though, in practice, problem solvers often use all or a selection of the nine tools in combination.

All CPS exercises should begin with a quiet time of relaxation and gentle preparation. Too hasty an entry into either left- or right-brain thinking tends to result in an inharmonious (divergent) response to the *problem statement*. Good creative facilitators know that CPS takes time. Quick answers emanating from a codified rule-set are permissible if the conventional mind-sets fit the problem and the context in which it has occurred. In times of escalating change this is less and less likely to be the case. The whole mind needs to be focused on clearly defined problems, which calls for the active participation and co-ordination of both thinking modes. This takes a little time and therefore, to avoid the onset of early bias, individuals need to be aware of the tendency for 'spur of the moment panic' to override sounder options that will emerge from disciplined total thinking.

To counter the 'quick fix' tendency, we begin all our CPS sessions with a brief period (two to three minutes) of gentle relaxation. This entails sitting comfortably in a chair (or if you prefer lying horizontally) and seeking to reduce stress levels in the body by:

- Taking a few deep breaths – three or four is usually enough;
- Relaxing all your muscles – easing the tension out of your face, arms, legs, neck and torso;
- Closing your eyes and trying to imagine the tension flowing out of your body.

There are a number of good, respectable audio tapes that will assist if you prefer to be precisely guided by a commentator. Others will find their peace by just relaxing in their favourite chair with some soothing music playing in the background.

Sound is a powerful and emotive medium. So too is nature. Good recordings can capture the natural world in great clarity and depth. Many CPS sessions have been run with soothing music playing in the background. The following composers have been found to be particularly evocative:

- Beethoven – Symphony No 6 ('The Pastoral')
- Copland's 'El Salon Mexico'
- Grofe's 'Grand Canyon Suite'
- Hadyn – Symphonies 6 ('Morning'), 7 ('Afternoon') and 8 ('Evening'); 'Creation'
- Handel – 'Water Music', 'Fireworks' and 'Messiah'
- Mozart – Piano Concerto No 21 ('Elvira Madigan')
- Smetana – 'River Moldau'
- Vivaldi – 'The Four Seasons'

Compile you own list and share it with colleagues and friends.

If the creative facilitator is looking for some interesting CPS tracks it is useful from time to time to ask the group to record on paper (resorting to graphics and images wherever possible, but if the group finds this difficult, then word pictures are acceptable) what they hear in the background music. Then share this information with the group via tools such as *round robin*, *mind mapping* and so on.

BRIDGING APPROACHES I – GROUP

These tools are particularly useful in jogging the mind with right-brain stimuli into cutting and then exploring new memory traces. The main tools in this category are use of *metaphors*, *puns*, *multimedia* and *virtual reality* programmes.

BRIDGING APPROACHES II – METAPHORS

Metaphors (VanGundy, 1988) are a fascinating source of inspiration for a creative manager. We hear them virtually every day as sports commentators, politicians and ordinary folk employ them to make powerful points about groups: such expressions and quotations as 'first past the post'; 'their moves always break down in the box'; 'have we missed the boat?' List the metaphors that you habitually use when involved in group activity at work. If this is a difficult task, ask some of your work colleagues to help.

The use of metaphors is closely entwined with the use of analogies. What do you think is the difference between a metaphor and an analogy?

BRIDGING APPROACHES III – ANALOGY

Thinking through action sequences, such as catching a train, and then relating this back to the Problem Statement can provoke an array of useful ideas.

Problem owner:	IT Department
Problem statement:	Produce 'user-friendly' computer software manuals
Analogy:	Catching a train

Relating analogy to problem statement:

Event/issue	Software manual
Catch a train	Cut it down to one page
Get to station	Prioritise
Timetable	Five separate guides
Waiting	Question & answer page
Late train	Explore software enhancement
Frustration	Transparent pages
Easy, quick journey	Help sheets
Colour-coded timetable	Importance of spacing, layout, use of icons and alphabetical listings.

BRIDGING APPROACHES IV – THE ART OF PUNNING

Imagining an object and then punning for as long as you can keep it up can be a useful ice-breaker for a group CPS session. For example, show a picture of a tree and ask group members to talk about their day using 'tree puns'.

'I had to *bough* out of X's meeting today.'
'I got to the *root* of a tricky problem.'
'Did your boss *leaf* you alone today?'
'How can I *branch* out into something else?. . .I have got enough to do!'
'She expected me to do it all, *root and branch*.'

Whilst criticised by some – usually rather uncreative people – as a low form of wit, punning is a good warm-up exercise for creative managers as it lubricates the channels between the left- and right-brain thinking modes. Have a go!

ACTIVE APPROACHES I – COMPUTER-BASED METHODS

1. *Multimedia.* Now that modern technology has given us the opportunity to acquire relatively low-cost multimedia equipment, a modest investment will provide you with the opportunity to seek right-brain inspiration by *playing* with some suitable software. However, once again it is wise to consult a real expert (rather than a commercial one!) before parting with your money.
2. *Virtual reality.* Alternate reality is nothing new. We have all imagined something impossibly exciting such as driving a racing car or piloting a plane, or become totally absorbed in a good book, play or film. There seems to come a point in these experiences when fantasy takes over and we partially believe we have leapt into a new contextual reality. We are a character in a film. We are on the track at Monte Carlo. *Virtual reality*, or 'cyberspace', takes alternate reality a step further by introducing a computer system as a mediator, or imagination enhancer. A typical system incorporates one or two input devices (such as a joy stick, a steering wheel or a body harness), several forms of output (such as light, sound and pressure), and a powerful computer to process all the data. The net result is that many of your senses are duped into thinking that you are really in control as you grapple to keep a jet aircraft in the air and on course!

We have a selection of virtual reality software that we occasionally use in creative management courses to ring the changes and literally blow people into a new world, where they can shake off the shackles of the old and dream new dreams and dare to be creative! As the computer companies are working to perfect virtual reality systems, researchers in California are working on technologies that allow people to view their own virtual or subconscious reality – in other words, their dreams (see Foremski, 1994).

ACTIVE APPROACHES II – DRAWING

This tool switches the traditional emphasis from verbal to graphical skills; from left- to right-brain expression. Given a free hand to draw a problem on paper, individuals, either on their own or in groups, are presented with an entirely new perspective that avoids the tendency to get trapped in familiar verbal memory traces. Here is a small selection of some of the simpler tools that are particularly suitable for group CPS sessions.

1. *Picture.* This is a neat and 'user-friendly' tool that brings out key issues in a very powerful way. It is especially helpful when produced in a meeting or CPS session on a flipchart

and used by an individual to convey important information to a group. There are three stages:

Stage 1 Declare problem statement.
Stage 2 Draw picture on flipchart (mixing colour pens helps).
Stage 3 Discuss.

2. *Picture book* (VanGundy, 1988). This is a tool that is suitable for individual or group CPS exercises but is usually best when used in group sessions. There are five stages:

Stage 1 Produce a *conventional Problem Statement* and convert it into a simple picture format.
Stage 2 Generate ideas to progress the problem and express them in picture format.
Stage 3 Each individual chooses two or three ways to progress the problem (i.e. what needs to be done) and draws a picture illustrating each option using colour to emphasise important issues or aspects.
Stage 4 *Select* the most suitable progress picture for the *Problem Statement.* This is straightforward in the case of individuals. Groups have a two-phased task to complete during this stage:

(a) selection of suitable picture (after a showing of all the efforts of each individual in the group); and
(b) revision of selected picture (partial or complete) after reviewing each individual picture.

Stage 5 Draw the final solution as individuals would like to see it.

You do not have to be to be a gifted artist to produce an acceptable *picture book*; you can use simple diagrams and stick-people. Do the best that you can. With a bit of practise you will be pleasantly surprised by the results. It is advisable to complete Steps 1 and 2 sequentially. Then some prefer to complete Step 5 before Steps 3 and 4. Alternatively you you can opt to work progressively through the five stages. Experiment and see what suits you best. Some individuals, if they are bashful about the standard of their art, opt to revise their original drawings using standard computer clip art.

3. *Broad sheet.* This uses the same five stages as *picture book* but presents the 'story' using a computer desktop package as a broad sheet that features pictures and words. Best results are normally achieved if roughly three-quarters of a side of A4 is covered by graphics and one-quarter by words.

ACTIVE APPROACHES III – THERAPEUTIC ACTIVITIES

Guided imagery. A number of well-regarded short scenarios are available that should be sensitively read by an expert. There is a rich audio tape library available for sale. Do take expert advice before you spend your money either on commercial tapes or on the services of a guided imagery expert.

Selection. Generating a flow of ideas is an important process in any CPS exercise and quickly builds up creative momentum. To progress there comes a point, which is usually obvious to the individual or creative facilitator, when it is sensible to assess the ideas that have been generated in the light of the *problem statement* and to select the most promising ideas for adoption in the *realisation* stage. This reductionist stage can in complex exercises be a very lengthy phase of a CPS exercise. To help you to get started quickly the Introductory CPS Toolkit offers four good all purpose tools.

Colour code (VanGundy, 1988). For quick and easy selections you can try colour code. This involves simply giving each individual a supply of green and blue coloured stickers and asking them to select and then mark the best idea or ideas with a green sticker and the second best ideas with a blue sticker. Then the idea with the most green stickers emerges as the winner. This is a rough-and-ready tool but can be useful to gain a quick measure of group opinion.

Creative evaluation (VanGundy, 1988). This is a straightforward ranking tool that can be used after *colour code* and assigns numbers to the leading ideas as follows:

1.   Represents a simple idea (requires little time and money);
2.   Represents a hard idea (requires more time and money);
3.   Represents a difficult idea (requires the most time and money);

The idea categories are then referred to management for further evaluation.

Reporter. This is a quick converging tool that usually arouses a positive response. The creative facilitator (say after running colour code) simply informs the group that a journalist is arriving in a few minutes time (20 minutes seems to work particularly well) and needs to be given a one page summary of the selected options.

Advantage–disadvantage (VanGundy, 1988). After using *colour code* issue all participants in the group with a selection matrix and ask them to privately evaluate all the green ideas in the light of the constraints declared on the matrix. Table 5.2 presents an example of this tool in a group problem-solving exercise concerned with finding a suitable hotel for a one-day creative management workshop.

Participants were simply invited to assess each of the 'green' ideas in the light of the criteria and to respond by placing a tick or star in the appropriate column.

CPS Stage 3: realisation planning

Once a CPS exercise has generated a realistic option (*What* can sensibly be done) it is important before too much of the momentum and inevitable enthusiasm is lost that some action is planned to achieve the implementation (*How* to respond) that its adoption assumes. In instances where more than one option is generated it is often prudent to carry out a detailed *Realisation Planning* exercise for each option before inviting executive evaluation. This is because both the *What* and *How* aspects of the proposed solutions or responses to the initial challenge, issue or problem may need to be presented to decision-making management. It is prudent to spend some time thinking about arguments that may be raised in opposition to a

Table 5.2 Advantage/disadvantage assessment

Criteria	Advantages	Disadvantages
Location	*	
Ease of access	*	
Parking		*
Conference facilities	*	
Reputation of venue		*

suggested idea or set of options. Generally speaking, there are two broad factor sets to consider: those affecting the proposed problem solution and those surrounding the people who have an interest in the solution. There are many helpful tools but here are a couple to experiment with: *Advantage and disadvantage* and *Comfort zones*, which addresses the delicate subject of presenting to other people's mind-sets.

Advantage and disadvantage

This is a simple checklist approach to assist in the early identification of the likely support for and opposition to a proposal. The criteria adopted by individuals and groups are usually contextually determined but progress can generally be made by adopting Kipling's Questions (see Table 5.3).

Table 5.3 Advantage/disadvantage proposal checklist

Criteria	Advantages/support	Disadvantages/opposition
Who?		*
What?	*	
Why?		*
Where?		*
When?		*
How?	*	

Force field Analysis is a variation of this tool.

Comfort zones (Rikards, 1990)

All of us are influenced by both our own mind-sets and value systems as well as those of the organisation in which we operate. When proposals are being prepared for presentation to executive management, it is prudent to take into account the personal mind-sets of the individuals who are going to be vitally involved in the decision process. Some will be supportive, others tolerant and some possibly hostile. To be forewarned is to be forearmed.

References

Eberle, R. (1972) *Scamper: Games for Imagination Development*, New York, D.O.K. Press.

Foremski, T. (1994) 'Waking up to dream control', *Financial Times*, 22 February, London.

Fritz, A. (1989) *The Path of Least Resistance: Learning How to Become a Creative Force in Your Own Life*, New York, Ballantine.

Gordon, W. (1961) *Synetics*, New York, Harper.

Majaro, S. (1992) *Managing Ideas for Profit*, London, McGraw-Hill.

Morgan, G. (1993) *Imaginization*, London, Sage.

Osborn, A.F. (1957) *Applied Imagination*, New York, Scribners.

Rikards, T. (1974) *Problem Solving through Creative Analysis*, Epping, Gower.

Rikards, T. (1990) *Creativity and Problem-solving at Work*, Aldershot, Gower.

Stevens, M.S. (1988) *Practical Problem Solving for Managers*, London, Kogan Page.

VanGundy, A.B. (1988) *Techniques for Structured Problem Solving*, 2nd edn, New York, Van Nostrand Reinhold.

6 Cultivating a suitable environment for personal and group creativity

The world can only be grasped by action, not by contemplation. The hand is more important than the eye . . . The hand is the cutting edge of the mind.

(Jacob Bronowski)

The men of culture are the true apostles of equality.

(Matthew Arnold)

Cultivate simplicity.

(Charles Lamb)

Teamwork is the ability to work together toward a common vision. The ability to direct individual accomplishments toward organisational objectives. It is the fuel that allows common people to attain uncommon results.

(Andrew Carnegie)

Introduction

Learning the fundamental skills is one thing; putting them into regular practice is another that in most cases requires an attitude change. For an individual attention needs to be given to a number of contextual factors that are essential for the successful application and development of individual primary Gateway Personal Creativity tools. This empowers individuals; however, as most individuals work in groups (the collective group being an organisation) it is necessary to explore the operation of individuals working in teams (group dynamics). This provides a springboard to group empowerment by seeding and nurturing the establishment of sympathetic group culture.

The chapter contains a Group Creativity Audit to assess current status. The audit can be repeated after an agreed learning period (say three months) and should provide evidence of progress as long as individual, group and organisational mindsets do not compromise the learning and blunt achievements. Whilst much can be done at the individual and group levels to develop a new climate that encourages the application of creative thinking, action is also needed to fully exploit the potential of both individual and group creative problem solving at the organisational level. This is addressed in Chapter 14.

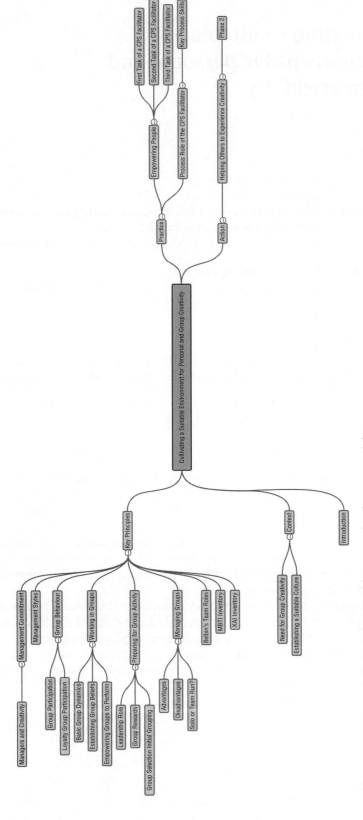

Figure 6.1 Seeking a suitable environment for personal and group creativity.

Context

Need for group creativity

Traditional management practice, whether casual or hierarchical, is not best suited to performing effectively and efficiently in current challenging business arenas. A tolerance of, and better still a positive encouragement to practise, business creativity skills requires both reskilling and rethinking management activity. Most individuals work directly or indirectly with other individuals and groups and need to be encouraged and empowered in their working environments. This chapter discusses some pointers to how managers can establish a climate that encourages business creativity in highly challenging business contexts.

Key principles

Management commitment

Managers and creativity

If managers are to make a real commitment to learning creativity techniques they need to welcome creative responses and then champion them. This will involve adopting a new approach and developing individual and personal relationships with their staff. The 'one manager, several staff members, one corporate relationship for all' strategy needs to become a process of the past. Whilst there always has been a body of very good managers in organisational life, many have chosen to play the detached corporate game. Not all car dealers are untrustworthy. The ones who are ruin things for those who are not. If individual members of staff are to open up and practice creative responses they will need to *trust* their managers.

Management styles

Table 6.1 Management styles

Behaviour trait	High	High/medium	Medium/low	Low
Approachable				
Honest				
Supportive				
Fair				
Open dealing				
Communicative				

This will depend not on the individual manager's perception of himself or herself but rather on staff's collective perception of the manager. Food for thought! If you are a manager respond, on a separate sheet of paper, to the brief questionnaire in Table 6.1 by ticking the appropriate column. Now turn to Appendix 6.1 and score your responses. Would you be happy for your staff to complete this questionnaire? Do you think that they would broadly agree with your perceptions of yourself?

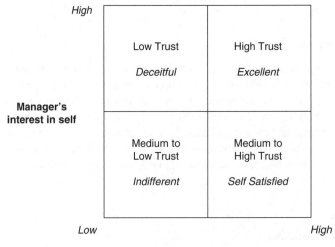

Figure 6.2 Manager's interests.
        Source: M.R.V. Goodman, Durham University.

Figure 6.2 presents a matrix that looks at individual staff and their manager's interests. The ideal situation is when the interest of the manager and the individual is high. This is the high-trust quadrant and will enable the manager to cultivate creative responses and excellence. The quadrant below, high/medium trust is when the individual is convinced of the manager's personal support but doubts if the manager really values the support of the individual. The quadrant to the left is where the interests of both are low. This produces mutual indifference. Finally, the quadrant above this is where the manager's interest is high and the individual member of staff's is low. This results in low, if any, trust as the individual assumes the worst.

Group behaviour

Group participation

Man is a social animal and thus most of what we do as individuals has an effect on other people. Similarly what other individuals and groups do has an effect on us, either consciously or unconsciously. We are all prone to modify our behaviour, whether we are in the company of a single individual or a group. The degree to which we modify our responses is directly related to what we believe the expected behaviour pattern is (the group *norm*) and the magnitude of the threat that we perceive in the social transaction. In the company of some people we are at ease whilst the company of others leaves us fidgety and nervous. Generally speaking behaviour breeds behaviour – how other people behave towards us determines the way that we behave towards them.

In the course of our everyday lives most of us belong to several different groups. Each of these groups assumes a collective individuality and personality, we choose whether or not to adapt our behaviour accordingly in our private lives we tune our responses very finely toward domestic stimuli and often feel quite at home in the social groups we choose. Social groups tend to be regarded as extensions of our family life and for most carry little perceived anxiety. Traditional professional groups, on the other hand, are usually regarded as being

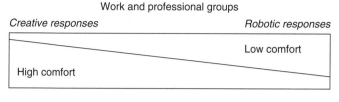

Figure 6.3 Group responses.

different as many are deeply suspicious of the culture of the 'rat race'. Thus our responses tend to be carefully considered and can become programmed to fit into the observed habits of the group. In other words the further we move from home or our close circle of friends into the world of the work place the more conditioned our behaviour becomes. This can and does place a damper on individual creativity as people seek the non-controversial comfort of the group viewpoint. Figure 6.3 shows how our individual responses change from unchecked spontaneity (high tendency for creativity) to controlled norms (low tendency for creativity) depending on the degree of 'ease' or comfort the group culture provides.

Gemeinschaft and *Gesellschaft* are ideal types of social or group organisation that were systematically elaborated by the German psychologist Ferdinand Tönnies in his influential work published in Leipzig in 1887 (see Wirth, 1937). Tönnies' conception of the nature of social systems is based on his distinction between the *Gemeinschaft* (communal society) and the *Gesellschaft* (associational society). In social organisations that typify the *Gemeinschaft* personal relationships are defined and regulated on the basis of traditional social rules. People have simple and direct face-to-face relations with each other that are determined by *Wesenwille* (natural will), that is, natural and spontaneously arising emotions and expressions of sentiment. In contrast *Gesellschaft* is the creation of *Kurwille* (rational will) and is typified by modern societies, with their large government bureaucracies and organisations. In the *Gesellschaft* rational self-interest and calculating conduct act to weaken the natural bonds and synergy of the *Gemeinschaft*.

Movement from *high comfort* individual behaviour to conditioned *low comfort* group behaviour is critically dependent on the level of trust expectations of individuals. If this is appreciably and consistently high, then individuals will tend to adopt common behaviour patterns and the group will function as a cohesive and united team. Everyone will pull together and the collective purpose (vision) of all will boost performance. The difference between a united and highly tuned rowing crew and an ill-at-ease one is obvious to all standing on the river bank. Close identity with a group or team generates a collective loyalty or supra individuality that in the right context can be highly creative. If this is missing in groups then the collective individuality loses its dynamism and simply becomes a label – individuals go through the motions. They play the notes but the tune is flat.

Loyalty and group participation

Individuals choose the degree to which they are prepared to relax in a group culture (i.e. within a set of recognised and accepted norms or behaviour patterns). When loyalty is high and the degree of participative membership is low (see Figure 6.2) individuals can be said to be displaying *dutiful adherence*. In this case the vision or purpose of the group is accepted but there is little enthusiasm for joining in to further the cause. This appears to be

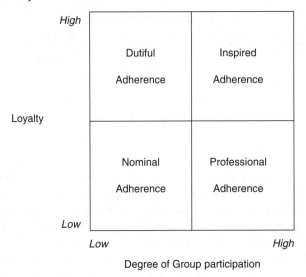

Figure 6.4 Degrees of group participation.

the behaviour pattern adopted by many towards such groups as local churches, charities and so forth. If both loyalty and degree of membership are low then individuals are practising *nominal adherence*. Such 'take it or leave it' attitudes rarely result in much creative output. This response is neatly captured by the words of President Kennedy who invited Americans in his inaugural speech to 'ask not what your country can do for you but rather what you can do for your country'. When group loyalty is low and group membership high, individuals will tend to see their inputs as being merely *professional adherence*. This behaviour pattern produces prescribed results characterised by a tendency to do just enough to meet expected job requirements but is often rule-bound and robotic. When the contextual stimuli are both complex and fast changing, professional groups need to display both a high degree of loyalty and participative membership. This we term *inspired adherence* and it can be seen in the daily work of many teachers, preachers, researchers and health and social workers whose loyalty to their clientele is often stronger than their loyalty to the organisation.

Working in groups

Individuals are managers in the sense that every day they have to take a host of decisions relating to what behavioural actions they are going to select in response to contextual stimuli. Managing group responses is a totally different matter. As most training films point out, individuals need to learn how to manage themselves before they seek to manage groups. Individuals who are poorly focused will only confuse themselves. If they are exposed to groups their confusion will be compounded. This inevitably leads to them becoming isolated in the group and often regarded with disrespect and scorn. Primitive attempts to pull rank to get their own way just result in inadequate and poorly supported group responses.

Every aspiring group manager should be aware of the basics of group dynamics before working with groups. Naive managers who just blunder in will cause severe damage to professional group relationships. They are like over-hasty drivers who attempt to change gear without first depressing the clutch. Similarly, power managers who attempt to get their own way by hoodwinking groups will soon be found out and then found lacking. The resultant damage this cowboy approach does to groups can be devastating and long lasting. Responsible group managers should pay heed to: establishing group beliefs; empowering groups to perform; encouraging group members to interact; and attempting to understand interactions and group belief systems.

Establishing group beliefs. The group must have a constructive purpose or vision. This needs to be effectively communicated to all group members. When groups are formed to look at problems that are complex and messy, wise managers invite group members to discuss the initial brief to achieve a consensus understanding of *what* is involved and *what progress options* can be explored.

Empowering groups to perform. Avoid threatening individuals or deliberately forming subgroups under the manager's control to check or thwart progress. Divide-and-rule policies are sometimes legitimate ploys but only in exceptional circumstances. Everyday use of such tactics is a trait of the guerrilla manager – a person who is easily recognised by a tendency to have an exaggerated opinion of his or her own talents that is not validated by the rank and file in the group.

Encouraging groups members to interact. Interaction is the mechanism that builds and sustains the belief system of a group. Interactions involve the mutual sharing of a situation between two or more people, so that each of them benefits from the experience and has his or her belief system strengthened by the encounter. Sensitive managers will be aware that interactions need not necessarily mean the same to all those who are involved. People are individuals and will have differing perceptions of the real meaning of what happened. Recognise this as a human trait and remember to summarise deliberations at regular intervals – in any case a good convergent creative problem-solving technique. As evidence of this, try asking individual members of a group one by one what they thought of their group meeting. You can expect a variety of answers!

Attempting to understand interactions and group belief systems. Responsible managers should endeavour to discover why one group clearly works more effectively than another that is apparently equally resourced. Why are the individuals who work in one section off-putting and difficult to talk to, while those in another section are happy and willing to help? Often it is because of the influence of one individual or a small subgroup of people who exert a strong influence on the rest of the group. This common occurrence is caused by the nature of the interaction within the group. Individuals who interact frequently tend to be the ones who influence the development of the group.

Preparing for group activity

Leadership role

Much has been written about the leadership role of the manager (Adair, 1983, 1985). If the intention is to focus the *total thinking* potential of the group, in the expectation of finding a suitable agreed solution to a messy problem, the role of leader assumes a special signifi-cance. In this instance the traditional military task-oriented command approach needs to give way to a softer, more subtle, steering role that enables the group to perform to high stand-ards. This is a highly skilled function that facilitates rather than dictates a response from the group. It is an enabling role that we describe as *creative facilitation*.

Group rewards

Man does not necessarily live by bread alone. Whilst the level of remuneration will always remain important to an individual it is not the only reward that most expect. If an individual can be afforded respect by group peers this acts as a powerful motivator. If managers join groups as team members and not as members of the corporate aristocracy this will generate *high comfort* behaviour in the group and is likely to encourage creative responses. Most individuals will warm to this 'all for one and one for all' approach (as it is often in marked contrast to the residual expected behaviour pattern of 'all for one and one for one') and gain a great deal of satisfaction from participating in the group. Soon the group will become a pseudo-private gathering that displays high levels of trust and appreciation of the contributions of its members. If managers can achieve this, and it may take some sustained action, then a real corporate family culture will develop and individual group members will positively identify with the group. The resultant mutual appreciation and respect is for many, a highly valued experience. This high level of mutual internal support will soon attract external attention and further enhance the kudos of group membership within the organisation.

- Inform them why they have been chosen for the exercise in question.
- Assure them that they are all equally valued. The *creative facilitator* could, perhaps, achieve this by adopting the slogan of Dumas's musketeers – 'one for all and all for one'.

Group selection and initial briefing

To minimise the potentially stultifying effect of deeply entrenched mindsets *creative facilitators* should, wherever possible, assemble unstructured groups. The choice of individual group members itself is a subtle task that balances technical expertise with cross-functional objectivity. Nominated individuals should then be invited to attend a briefing meeting that is designed to:

- Tell them how the *creative facilitator* will operate.
- Tell them what they can expect to get out of the process.

Managing groups

Every individual is a manager and regularly accepts and accomplishes a variety of tasks all on his or her own. Many may legitimately feel that they are the best person for an important job and opening up the matter to Group CPS is not a very attractive option, as it will lead to a lower performance standard and introduce the additional complexity of managing others. So does it always make sense to use groups?

Advantages

If a group is defined as consisting of more than one person, then clearly more than one mind can be focused on the problem, which should lead to a greater concentration of *total thinking*. This has real advantages if the problem is a messy one. In any case even under traditional management practice groups can potentially offer the following advantages to the lone manager:

- A group contains a mix of skills and experiences.
- A group has potential to generate more ideas than a lone individual.

- A group provides a division of task responsibility.
- Members can *bullet proof* each other's arguments, thus cutting down the risk of the adoption of faulty or suspect solutions.
- The stimulation that results from personal interaction can lead to improved ideas or solutions.

Disadvantages

Whilst there are obvious benefits to be obtained from working in groups it is interesting to note that even the smallest of groups – basic partnerships – often seem to generate operational difficulties. How many such difficult partnerships can you recall? Start your train of thought with Gilbert and Sullivan, Tim Rice and Sir Andrew Lloyd Webber and so on. Moreover, some groups have been found to be disastrous for the following reasons:

- Members were too similar in character and functional speciality.
- Group discussion was poorly managed and failed to harness the potential group strengths.
- There were too many members – ten to 12 is probably the optimum number.
- The group developed what Janis (1982) referred to as *group think* – 'a determination of mental efficiency, reality testing and moral judgement that results from in-group pressures'.
- There was a tendency for certain members to dominate group discussion.
- There was too great a tendency to wander off the point.
- There was poor use of CPS skills.
- There was an over hasty desire to find a solution at any cost.
- There was a failure to identify expertise lying within the group.
- There was a deliberate restriction of key information.

All these disadvantages can be directly addressed by a skilled *creative facilitator* as long as the organisational management are supportive. However, when pressed to achieve something quickly, especially if it involves a superior, many individuals seriously consider doing the job themselves. This can become such a strong personal behavioural norm that it can potentially threaten the acceptance of the group manager by his or her staff. A suspicion arises that their manager does not trust them with important tasks and assignments. As behaviour breeds behaviour this inevitably dampens enthusiasm and the standard of group performance.

Solo or team run?

Clearly it is impossible for group managers under pressure to do everything. Delegating authority for important tasks remains a difficult challenge for many managers. If the contextual stimuli are well known the solution to the problem is often straightforward and may simply entail asking a subordinate to follow a clearly defined problem-solving sequence. However, if the contextual stimuli are complex and changing rapidly, the problem under examination may be better addressed by a group. The decision to go it alone or to take the problem to a group is one of the most taxing that managers have to make. The key element here is mutual trust. If this is not evident then interactions will be severely limited in what they can accomplish. The interactive process of management becomes more difficult when the contextual stimuli are messy. This is often the time when managers need to open up to their staff. If their style in more stable times has been autocratic and characterised by their staff as mainly 'one for one' they will need to set about securing a 'one for all and all for one' style. As individuals take some convincing, this will take time. The problem is that time is just not available. If the underlying contextual stimuli are changing rapidly managing successfully may mean abandoning traditional mindsets and intricate management models and risking real-time action. Theory often lags behind practice. Indeed it often manifests itself as the codification of previous practice. Rapidly changing stimuli call for a new style of practice. We believe that this is the *creative management response.*

Belbin's team roles

In a study first published in the mid-1970s that addressed the subject of successful teams (the release of creativity in the group situation to provide a winning outcome), Belbin (1981) suggested that there were a number of finite and limited roles 'adopted naturally by the various personality-types found among managers' (Adair, 1987). These team roles are presented in Table 6.2. This inventory produces well-balanced teams and looks to the people-oriented Chairperson to keep the group together and moving in the right direction, the task-oriented Shaper to see that the job is achieved and the Plant to provide the creative spark. The other five roles are supportive ones once the people, task and idea inputs have been addressed.

These are, in turn, split into three role groups:

Action oriented,
People oriented,
Thought oriented.

1. Action oriented roles:

    • Shapers are dynamic and energetic – they tend to challenge teams to improve and to maintain focus and momentum.
    • Implementers are disciplined and task-oriented – they get things done through planning an implementable strategy.
    • Completers (or finishers) pay attention to detail and stick to deadlines to ensure a project is completed thoroughly and on time to the highest standards possible.

Table 6.2 The Belbin roles

Role	Description
Chairperson	Good with people
Shaper	Good at getting things done
Plant	Good at generating ideas
Resource investigator	Good at finding out what is needed
Monitor evaluator	Good at measuring progress and performance
Team worker	Good at supporting and helping the group
Implementer	Good at working for the organisation
Completer/finisher	Good at attending to detail to get the job done

2.   People oriented roles:

- Chairpersons take on the role of leader – they delegate tasks and guide team members to achieve specific goals.
- Team workers provide support to ensure effective team work – they are good negotiators who give priority to team cohesion.
- Resource investigators are enthusiastic team members and good networkers who explore options and negotiate for resources to help the team to accomplish its goals.

3.   Thought oriented roles:

- Plants are creative innovators who have good ideas but who prefer to work on their own.
- Monitors (or evaluators) critically assess and evaluate other peoples' ideas in an objective and impartial manner before taking decisions.
- Completer/Finishers are experts who are in possession of specialist knowledge which is required for the attainment of the group project or task

Although Belbin's model provides clearly stated roles for team members, what happens in real life is often more complex and messy as individuals' skills and attributes may overlap from one role to another. This may depend on context and team dynamics. Some team members may move easily from one role to another when the conditions which constitute the group change, such as when new members join the group or when a new group is formed.

Forming, storming, norming and performing

Another model of team development first developed by Tuckman in 1965 is the Forming, Storming, Norming and Performing model (see Bonebright, 2010). During the forming phase, people get to know each other, relationships and trust are built, and implicit or explicit rules are formulated. The four stages demonstrate how a team develops, faces up to challenges, gets down to action and delivers results. Another final phase is sometimes added. This is the Mourning or Adjourning stage, when the team goes through the process of disbanding. During this stage, personal conclusions are formed and steps may be taken to deal with the stress of splitting up the team, which is often a consequence of the project coming to an end.

One of the main advantages of utilising teams is the synergy which emerges as a result of the accumulation of the skills and attributes of all the team members. Team sports, such as football (soccer), where one player may be better at defence, another at attack and another at scoring goals, provides an interesting analogy. Although each player is assigned a specific role, the outcome of collaboration and the role assignment is based on individual strengths and is likely to lead to increased synergy and success.

Effective teams may provide valuable input to the innovation management process, particularly if attention is paid to the manner in which the team is constructed and to how it evolves and develops over time. Teams may, moreover, build, collaborate with and support internal and external sources of ideas, networks and relationships.

The MBTI inventory – Jung's personality typologies

The Swiss psychologist Carl Gustav Jung, though an early follower of Freud, advocated that behaviour was influenced by drives other than purely sexual ones. He studied the differences between people and developed a set of typologies that reflected whether individual personalities were characterised by a tendency toward introversion or extroversion. He described four basic scales (see Table 6.3):

> *Extroverts (E)* tend to look outward and focus on an outer world of people and things. Thus they prefer to communicate verbally rather than in writing and tend to prefer action and variety.
> *Introverts (I)*, on the other hand, prefer to focus more on their inner world and they can appear to be timid and shy.
> *Sensing (S)* types prefer to work with what is given and so appear as practical people that have an eye for detail and prefer proven methods.
> *Intuitive (N)* individuals can look beyond their senses and harness their imagination in order to see new possibilities and are not too bothered with points of detail.

For each of the four preference scales Jung identified two pairs of opposing preferences (making 16 personality types in total). *Thinking* types rely heavily on their powers of reason and are good at sizing up situations. *Feeling* types, on the other hand, pay an especial regard to the impact of their behaviour on others. *Judgers* have a strong liking for order, control and organisation. Lastly, *Perceivers* prefer to react and adapt to the moment and thus appear more flexible (see Myers-Briggs, 1987).

The 16 types described are not intended to be predictive but to assist individuals to recognise their own and others' gifts. The assessment procedure selects the highest score on each of the four scales as being the dominant characteristic of the individual. So, for example, a person who scores ten for extroversion and 13 for introversion would be classified by the MBTI inventory as being introverted. As with the KAI inventory (see Section 6.3.10), environmental factors can distort the results.

The KAI inventory

Kirton's KAI inventory (Kirton, 1987) seeks to assess an individual's an response styles in terms of their characteristic approaches to decision making. His *adaption-innovation theory* places individuals on a continuum from highly adaptive to highly innovative. Adaptive individuals

Table 6.3 Jung's personality typologies

Extroversion	Looking outward
Introversion	Looking inward
Sensing	Manipulating facts according to established procedures
Thinking	Applying logic and analysis in decision-making
Judging	Tendency to be organised and controlled
Intuition	Using imagination and refusing to be submerged by detail
Feeling	Reacting to personal preferences (own and others) and value sets
Perceiving	Tendency to be spontaneous and flexible

are seen as those who like to do things within the same personal, group and organisational standard practices or mindsets. They prefer not to rock the boat. They are less radical in their approach than innovators and so their failures tend to be less damaging to their reputation. They quite easily work with others. Innovators, on the other hand, approach problems from an entirely different perspective. They tend to escape from mindsets that surround the problem, the organisational environment, and look for inspiration by exploring the problem in another environmental setting. They reconstruct the problem and tend to produce less conventional solutions. They often find it difficult to work with others and many see them as being abrasive and insensitive.

The KAI continuum ranges from 46 (extreme adaptor) to 145 (extreme innovator) with a mean of 90. A difference of ten points between individuals can lead to communication difficulties. The inventory seeks to measure an individual's response to three subscales:

O   *Originality* which has a range from 13 to 65 and a mean of 39. Innovators with a high score tend to produce a proliferation of ideas, whether needed or not, and tend to adopt a radical style.
E   *Efficiency* which has a range from 7 to 35 and a mean of 21.
R   *Conformity* which has a range from 12 to 60.

The question remains, what is it measuring? The way individuals respond to the KAI inventory is influenced by the key stimuli that they experience in their total living environment (domestic and professional). As much of Kirton's work was researched within an organisational context the organisation itself will significantly affect the KAI score. Individuals will be more inclined to work within the accepted mindsets in tight cultures than they will be in freer environments. Whilst it is undeniable that the KAI inventory does reveal some interesting information about individuals it also says quite a lot about the organisations in which they work. High-trust managers, groups and organisations are more likely to encourage what Kirton terms innovative responses than restrictive cultures. It can therefore be difficult to determine what the characteristic style is. Is it that of the individual? That of the organisation? That of the individual within the organisation? There is a danger with the KAI inventory that organisations may see it as a way of classifying individuals according to their perceived level of creativity. Despite Kirton's efforts to prevent this – as he does argue that creativity can be exhibited at both ends of his continuum – many users of his inventory probably do associate *active creativity* with a high KAI score.

Practice

Empowering people

First task of a CPS facilitator

As Chapter 4 has set out to demonstrate, individuals need to step off the familiar stepping stones (memory traces) of their everyday lives and express a willingness to try a different path. The first task of a *creative facilitator* is to stimulate individuals to become curious about creative thinking. The *creative force* is omnipresent but not always obviously active in the behaviour of individuals. As individuals can choose their behaviour, they can choose to harness their natural creativity to any challenge in life. So it is a matter of choice to get going with the *force*, rather than specific *know-how,* and this choice factor is heavily dependent on dominant contextual factors such as climate or environment.

To foster creative thinking the championing individual needs to create a local climate in the work organisation that, first, upholds favourable psychological dimensions, as, for example, described in the research of Ekvall and Ekvall (1983) of the Swedish Council for Management and Work Life Issues in Stockholm:

- The need to issue a challenge to employees;
- To grant them the freedom, at least at regular intervals, to exercise their own initiative on problems – to do their own thing. This is a powerful motivator (see Amabile, 1983);
- To support CPS as a *bona fide* workplace activity.
- To trust individuals to deliver an answer or set of options to the 'what' problem without feeling that the method (the how) has to be proven beforehand. A purely cognitive explanation of creativity is not possible as its presence is critically dependent on contextual stimuli (see Garnham and Oakhill, 1994). Thus it cannot be modelled and repeated. It may, and usually does, throw light on complex issues, but it cannot be switched on and off like a lamp-post. It is not a standard single solution to a problem. A lamp-post is a static object with a single intensity light. Creativity is a spontaneous flash that can be regular or intermittent in frequency and can also vary in its illumination (obviousness) to others.
- To acknowledge that real-life stimuli are dynamic and so, therefore, should be the response patterns of individuals, groups and organisations. The construction of individual and organisational patterns, rules and mindsets that are too tight, in a bid to capture the cognitive understanding of control, is always a dangerous practice – particularly so in times of rapidly changing stimuli.
- The acceptance that playfulness is a legitimate creative trait and not a childish, gimmick activity.
- The openness both to permit and then debate the effectiveness of various CPS tools and techniques.
- The recognition that conflicts occur in groups, will need to be sensitively managed, but can be a powerful stimulant to creative activity.
- The realisation that quickly changing stimuli cannot always be accommodated by low risk responses. New challenges will always put pressure on precedent. New memory traces have to be fashioned.
- The realisation that teams can only function well in crises if there is mutual respect.

Second task of a CPS facilitator

Second, the aspiring creative facilitator needs to give careful attention to the visual climate or environment. This entails:

- Taking a positive lead – in the creation of a new climate;
- Getting oneself and others trained as *creative facilitators*;
- Seeing that a suitable room is available, that is light and airy, with uncluttered walls, an informal physical layout (chairs in circles rather than rows), good table tops, preferably brightly painted with some carefully chosen right-brain stimuli placed on shelves and walls (e.g. plants, interesting shapes, pictures, audio/visual facility etc.);
- Seeing that the room is well stocked with vital materials (such as, Blu-Tack, paper (A4, and it is useful to have a supply of A3 sheets too), marker pens, flip chart/s, Post-It notes, clipboards and notebooks) encouraging individuals and groups to use the room.

Third task of a CPS facilitator

Third, it is important for *would be* creative managers to take the plunge themselves and lead by example.

- Perhaps the first task here is to generate a supportive atmosphere in the established physical setting by purposefully signalling to your work groups that you really mean business. Convey that you have a genuine desire for the group to solve real problems and expect to see some action.
- Be prepared to give it a sustained go for at least a year and to meet and manage any carping criticism from other parts of the organisation.
- Encourage the formation of small groups (seven is about right) and balance the group members in terms of functional and general skill and length of service. Resist any early temptation to invite senior executives to attend. Wait until you have sorted out early teething troubles and then the group is ready to include senior management.
- Encourage all group members to contribute, by affirming right at the beginning that your philosophy is 'one for all and all for one'. Discourage any tendency for any one individual to assert too great an influence on the group. Keep the group together and resist the formation of splinter groups.
- Inform the group that you are looking for the interplay of three main roles in the meetings of the CGPS (Creative Group Problem Solving) Group:

    (a) A *problem owner*;
    (b) Up to five additional assistants or helpers; and
    (c) A *creative facilitator* – a responsibility you should be prepared to take on initially yourself – who is responsible for keeping the group on a creativity path and for introducing suitable CPS tools.

Process role of the CPS facilitator

Key process skills

The role of *creative facilitator* is a vital one and calls for a sound understanding of the basics of group dynamics and a familiarity with simple CPS tools and techniques. It is important to:

- Practice both divergent and convergent thinking modes. This is a subtle task that is necessary to activate both left- and right-brain thinking modes to achieve the potential benefits of the total thinking mode. If the group gets bogged down or stuck, then it is the responsibility of the creative facilitator to prompt some right-brained excursions to get the group back on track.
- Mix periods of heavy disciplined thinking with periods of light and zany thinking.
- Watch the quality of the group's performance. Be flexible. It is better to have several short bursts of energetic activity than to persevere with long sluggish sessions. With the best will in the world most people's performance starts to wane when they get tired and hungry.

- After each session ask each group member to write down on a Post-It note what they liked about the session and one thing that could be improved.
- End each session by thanking people for their involvement and announce the date and time of the next session.

Conflict in groups and teams

Conflict and tension may arise in teams, particularly in circumstances when strong personalities clash, when communication amongst team members is ineffective or when tasks assigned to individual team members are not sensitively distributed. Team leaders should be constantly aware of this and eliminate possible tension by exercising empathy and listening skills and encouraging participation.

Since conflict may arise as a result of divergent opinions, attitudes or decisions, team members may be trained in skills such as the Six Thinking Hats (de Bono, 2009) which allow for 'parallel thinking', a method which may be used for planning, decision making, generating ideas and conflict resolution. Training in mediation or in conflict resolution skills develops increased acceptance of individual differences, together with an appreciation of the richness of divergent opinions and personalities. Sometimes a decision to reach a compromise may be taken, and sometimes negotiation skills may be sufficient for the conflict to be resolved.

The team's perception of conflict may be challenged and shifted from a threat to an opportunity. Constructive conflict may give rise to a healthy competitive climate with outcomes which may surpass initial expectations. Achieving a balance between resolving conflict and drawing out positive competitive elements which may result from conflict is not an easy task. It is important for team members to recognise and deal with any destructive elements which may arise and to appreciate, respect and understand the value of diverse perspectives. Although conflict often arises as a result of differences of opinion, values or attitudes, diversity in the manner in which a team is constituted is one of the main factors which adds value to teams and may lead to the successful attainment of the assigned team goals.

Action

Group CPS Audit

Turn to Appendices 6.2 and 6.3 and complete the Group CPS Audit as an individual member of a group. Now ask all group participants to complete the audit and average out the scores.

Helping others to experience creativity

One to one (primary networking)

The previous chapter was designed to help the individual discover and experience creativity. Whilst native curiosity, persistence and a willingness to persevere will bring its reward at the individual level it can, nonetheless, be difficult for individuals to share their discoveries and experiences with others. This is a result of a complex set of factors including a degree of self-consciousness – not wanting to look silly to colleagues – and the personal approaches that all of us have to take in order to find and appreciate the *creative force* (Goman, 1989).

Unfortunately there is no common, foolproof, detailed map or set of procedures that all can follow. Whilst it is a matter of going from A to B – from a theoretical and *abstract regard* (most of us, even the most cynical admit that creativity exists) to an individual *experienced regard* (feeling the *creative force*) – the journey is different for all individuals. Whilst carefully trained facilitators can render assistance the ultimate discovery is truly a personal one.

Thus one individual cannot lead another by reason alone to a realisation of the potential of the creative *force majeure*. However, if a curious individual can temporarily suspend his or her personal prejudices and adopt an open, *inquiring regard*, then a successful outcome will result. Creativity passes many individuals by as it is very hard to describe in words. It is a natural force that convinces Doubting Thomases at a deeply personal level – that of inner trust and conviction. Sharing creativity cannot be achieved through words alone and it is a disservice to the cause for individuals to attempt this. Pious false charm turns people off as there is no argument to be won. The *force* exists; the issue is how to assist others to find it for themselves.

Research has clearly shown that the best way to assist enquirers is to facilitate their self-discovery by guiding them over a series of simple stepping stones. If the will is present for enquiring individuals to open up to the possibility of discovering something meaningful, then progress can be made. If the approach mentality is heavily tinged with doubt and obduracy the process of discovery will be long, possibly personally painful, and may never happen. The discovery you can make for yourself is free, exciting, quite natural and very much of the real world. It cannot be explained by logical thought. It is the free gift of the creator to all mankind.

Summary

This chapter has explored a number of ways that managers can cultivate a suitable working environment that encourages creativity. This usually requires the acceptance that effort has to be invested in learning and practising new skills. Realise that the only thing of real importance that leaders do is to create and manage culture. Decide to widen your business skill set by exploring creativity techniques.

Discussion questions

1. List the four individual/manager interest styles. Which style best characterises your impact on others?
2. Briefly explain what is meant by *Gemeinschaft* and *Gesellschaft.*
3. How would you empower a group to perform?
4. What are the three key tasks of a CPS facilitator?
5. Briefly describe the main process roles of a CPS facilitator.

Case exercise

Morning Star is an American company that ranks as the world's largest tomato processor. The company was founded in 1970 by Chris Rufer who was then an MBA student. In 2010 Morning Star generated revenues over $700 million. What makes the company particularly distinctive is that no-one working for it has a traditional boss. Employees negotiate their responsibilities with their peers; everyone can spend the company's money. Each employee is responsible for procuring the services and tools required to do his or her work. Chris views the traditional hierarchical power-command model of management as expensive, slow to react, prone to poor judgement and often demotivational to employees.

Task

Drawing on the material in this chapter, write some brief notes on how Morning Star might empower its people and create an environment where people can manage themselves effectively and efficiently.

References

Adair, J. (1983) *Effective Leadership*, London, Pan.
Adair, J. (1985) *Effective Decision-making*, London, Pan.
Amabile, T.M. (1983) *The Social Psychology of Creativity*, New York, Springer-Verlag.
Belbin, M. (1981) *Management Teams: Why They Succeed or Fail*, Oxford, Heinemann.
Bonebright, D.A. (2010) '40 years of storming: A historical review of Tuckman's model of small group development', *Human Resource Development International*, February, Vol. 13, Issue 1, pp. 111–20.
de Bono, E. (2009) *Six Thinking Hats*, London, Penguin.
Ekvall, G.A. and Ekvall, I. (1983) *Creating Organizational Climate: Construction and Validation of a Measuring Instrument*, Stockholm, F.A. Rodet.
Garnham, A. and Oakhill, J. (1994) *Thinking and Reasoning*, Oxford, Blackwell.
Goman, C.K. (1989) *Creative Thinking in Business*, London, Kogan Page.
Janis, I.L. (1982) *Groupthink*, Boston, Houghton Mifflin.
Kirton, M.J. (1987) *Adaption–Innovation Theory (KAI) – Manual*, Hatfield, Occupational Research Centre.
Kirton, M.J. (1989) *Adaptors and Innovators: Styles and Problem Solving*, London, Routledge.
Myers-Briggs (1987) *Type Indicator Report Form*, Palo Alto, CA, Consulting Psychologist's Press.
Wirth, L. (1937) 'The sociology of Ferdinand Tönnies', *American Sociological Review*, February, Vol. 2, Issue 1, pp. 9–25.

Appendices

1 Management traits

Table 6.4 Management traits assessment

Behaviour trait	High (score 4)	High/medium (score 3)	Medium/low (score 2)	Low (score 1)
Approachable				
Honest				
Supportive				
Fair				
Open dealing				
Communicative				
TOTAL				

The higher your TOTAL score the better! Do reflect on your individual behaviour trait score.

2 Group CPS Audit

Table 6.5 Group CPS Audit

Q		Never	Sometimes	Fairly often	Regularly
1	Are the group members at ease with one another?				
2	Do individual members participate?				
3	Does the group always know what it is supposed to achieve?				
4	Is the group closely facilitated?				
5	Is the group empowered to achieve?				
6	Do group members interact well with each other?				
7	Is their work acknowledged by a manager?				
8	Do group members socialise after work?				
9	Are their efforts visibly rewarded?				
10	Are they optimistic?				
11	Does the group generate many ideas of its own?				
12	Is the group membership well balanced?				
13	Can the group spirit be described as 'one for all and all for one'?				
14	Is the group's achievement predictable?				
15	Is the expertise in the group fully utilised?				
16	Is the group's work appreciated by the organisation?				
17	Has the group assumed an identity of its own?				
18	Does it use CPS tools and techniques?				
19	Is change welcomed?				
20	Does the group like meeting?				
21	Does the group use right-brain tools?				
22	Do group members work well together?				
23	Are group members highly motivated?				
24	Does the group reach decisions by consensus?				
25	Does the group deal with problems effectively and efficiently?				
26	Does the group get easily distracted?				
27	Does the group prefer to adapt the ideas of others?				
28	Does the group challenge rules if they think that they are silly?				
29	When the going gets tough does the group stick together?				
30	Does the group have a tendency to wander off the point?				

3 Assessing group performance

Instructions

Circle the Descriptor you selected (i.e. Never, Sometimes, Fairly Often or Regularly) in the table below.

Then add up your overall score and place it on the creativity spectrum.

Table 6.6 Assessing group CPS performance

Question	Never	Sometimes	Fairly Often	Regularly
1	1	2	3	4
2	1	2	3	4
3	1	2	3	4
4	4	3	2	1
5	1	2	3	3
6	1	2	3	4
7	1	2	3	4
8	1	2	3	4
9	1	2	3	4
10	1	2	3	4
11	1	2	3	4
12	1	2	3	4
13	1	2	3	4
14	4	3	2	1
15	1	2	3	4
16	1	2	3	4
17	1	2	3	4
18	1	2	3	4
19	1	2	3	4
20	1	2	3	4
21	1	2	3	4
22	1	2	3	4
23	1	2	3	4
24	1	2	3	4
25	1	2	3	4
26	4	3	2	1
27	4	3	2	1
28	1	2	3	4
29	4	3	2	1
30	4	3	2	1

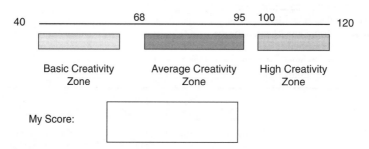

Figure 6.5 Group CPS performance continuum.

7 Overcoming resistance

Mindsets and paradigms

To know one's own limitations is the hallmark of competence.

(Dorothy L. Sayers)

'Assume' makes an 'ass' out of 'u' and 'me'.

(Anon)

If the doors of perception were cleansed everything would appear to man as it is: infinite. For Man has closed himself up, till he sees all things through narrow chinks of his cavern.

(William Blake)

At first people refuse to believe that a strange new thing can be done, then they begin to hope that it can be done, then they see it can be done – then it is done and all the world wonders why it was not done centuries before.

(Frances Hodgson Burnett, *The Secret Garden*, 1911)

Introduction

Many individuals, groups and organisations appreciate the need to adopt a fresh approach to meeting the complex challenges of modern buyers' markets. However, successfully converting this 'wish' to practical achievement is often frustrated and sometimes killed by the destructive power of individual, group and organisational mindsets and paradigms. Resistance to practising business creativity skills and to successfully managing innovation and entrepreneurial skills is common. Commitment to learning new methods of problem solving requires both a dedication and a time commitment. This chapter explores the destructive power of this resistance and explains how steps can be taken to overcome many of the frequently experienced creativity blockers.

Context

The power of mindsets and paradigms

As managers are placed under sustained pressure to perform in the rapidly changing wealth-creating environment, *how* they think in chaotic conditions is attracting increasing attention. This is determined by a complex pattern of mental input factors including personal, group and organisational influences. At the individual level thinking patterns that fashion behaviour are determined by four key *factor sets*: cultural, social, personal and psychological.

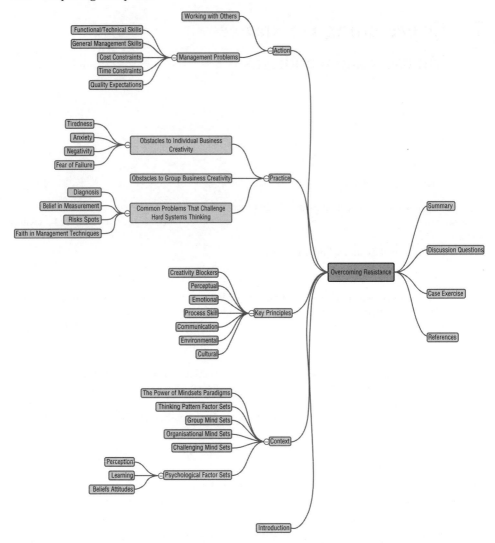

Figure 7.1 Exploring how to overcome mindsets and paradigms.

Thinking pattern factor sets

Cultural factor sets include the dominant cultural and social class factors that surround an individual from birth. *Social factor sets* encompass an array of influences such as preferred reference groups, family expectations, and so forth. *Personal factor sets* describe a complex collection of variables that shape individuals' thinking and value choices, such as age, lifestyle, economic status, personality and so on. *Psychological factor sets* address the key variables that determine individuals' perceptions, learning patterns, and the way that they acquire beliefs and attitudes. These *factor sets* integrate to form a complex system (*personal mindset*) that governs the general/habitual thinking patterns of individuals.

When individuals are viewed in group situations further complexity arises. *By definition a group is a collection of individuals all with their own unique collection of factor sets.*

Harmonising their behaviour is cognitively a highly complex task. The imposition of linear causality – for example, the belief that the way to get individuals to work together, is to stick them together, give them something to do and then determine their reward on how much they accomplish in a given period of time – is a mechanistic approach to management that will inevitably constrain individual performance. At its most extreme this reduces individuals to units of input, and unless they have private reasons for accepting this (because there is little if any alternative employment) most individuals will tend to go through the motions and do the minimum that is necessary to earn their bread. Others, though severely repressed by insensitive management, will for their own satisfaction – perhaps to stay sane – put in some extra effort to innovate somehow.

Group mindsets

A group of individuals is by definition a collection of individual mindsets. The cognitive and motor behaviour that people perform in the course of pursuing a goal can induce a mindset that persists to influence the strategy they use to attain very different goals in unrelated situations (Wyer and Xu, 2010). Individuals also change their behaviour patterns when they interact with others. Behaviour breeds behaviour. The degree to which behaviour choices are changed is governed by a complex set of factors that include perceived trust, motivation and so on. (Individuals tend to naturally release more creative effort at home than in the work place where the sensed group and/or organisational climate – contextual stimuli – makes them less at ease.) A new *group mindset* emerges that is separate from and additional to each individual's *personal mindset*. The nature of this is conditioned by the perceived level of trust in the group. In short, more personal trust produces more collective or group trust and potentially greater creativity.

Chapter 6 discussed the basics of group dynamics and the leading factors that commonly arrest group performance. Individuals can be encouraged to express themselves in groups and this is a key skill of an effective traditional manager. Sustained high group performance requires sensitive management skills that seek to enable or release it rather than impose it. If external stimuli make a group's task more and more difficult to achieve, then effective managers will know that they have a real problem. Months of sound management practice can dissipate into chaos, falling morale and disillusionment if a group manager is tempted to go for a quick (often linear) fix to appease some organisational authority. The credibility – and thus success – of an enabling manager can take months to achieve but can be lost in less than a minute. Group managers under pressure should be given open encouragement by their organisations to audit their own skills, and be given the opportunity to improve key competencies and to acquire new ones that are relevant to the prosecution of their responsibilities. They should not be required to perform in new and changing contextual situations by being expected to use management tools and techniques that were designed for quite different days. Nor should they be hindered by beliefs and attitudes that were formed to serve the needs of former times.

Organisational mindsets

So a manager who is responsible to his or her staff/group (is loyal) will have to find an approach that harmonises all the constituent mindsets. This is further complicated by his or her need to exercise responsibility to the organisation (Pina e Cunha *et al.*, 2001) which will possess yet another collection of mindsets. Managing effectively in a chaotic context will often put the the manager in a position where it is very difficult to win. The *organisational mindsets* may insist that things are done in certain ways because that is how they have always been done. To suggest anything different smacks of disloyalty. Most of us at some time or another have been reprimanded for an unconventional approach to a problem by the sharp retort, 'We don't do things that way here'. Organisations, like individuals, are jealous guardians of their beliefs and attitudes. Again individuals may dislike some organisational ways that perhaps owe their origin to sunnier days and over the years have become enshrined in the corporate mindsets. Frustration abounds when individuals realise that these organisational mindsets are blocking their efforts to solve today's complex problems. Then there are the work groups. These often present real problems as they tend to be caught between the individual and corporate mindsets.

To any manager, and especially a potential creative manager, warring mindsets pose a really difficult challenge. To make matters worse, mindsets are self-perpetuating and self-reinforcing mechanisms that are capable of flying high over current contexts whilst attempting to understand and manage them with the tools and techniques of the past (see Figure 7.2).

Challenging mindsets

It is therefore quite understandable for managers to spend much time agonising over how much they can challenge an organisational mindset if they honestly believe that it is restraining problem-solving activity. Some managers, in the belief that most problems are temporary and organisational mindsets are permanent, sacrifice the pressures of the contextual reality to those of history. In turbulent times these responses can severely damage individual and group morale and hence achievement levels.

Psychological factor sets

Some useful light can be thrown on understanding individual, group and organisational mindsets by taking a brief look at the psychological factor sets whilst, for the time being,

Figure 7.2 Assumptions becoming mindsets.
    Source: M.R.V. Goodman, Durham University.

treating the cultural, social and personal factor sets as hygiene factors (Herzberg, 1987). The key psychological factors are: perception; learning; and beliefs and attitudes.

Perception

When individuals and groups are exposed to external contextual stimuli they either accept that the stimuli are real and so seek to respond positively to the challenges this brings, or they modify this reality (under the influence of heavy mindsets). One modification is to distort the reality so that it becomes agreeable or comfortable. An alternative modification is to reject the current stimuli all together and to retain older, more comfortable, perceptions. Once individuals and groups have made their respective selections they need to collect and collate information that will assist them to interpret fully the meaning of the contextual factors and so be in a position to think about their positions. As individuals and groups tend to be closer to contextual reality than organisations they are often aware earlier of the need to move away from the *virtual reality* that many organisations display. This means that they are often ready to think about alternative courses of action before their organisations. So why try to change organisations from the top down? In essence an organisation is the shared view of its members and so can be seen as a single collective mind (Mitroff, 1984). The private response activities of individuals and groups will be characterised by changes in behaviour resulting from a careful consideration of the changing stimuli. This is the learning factor.

Learning

A willingness to modify and sometimes abandon old ways makes sense for private groups, for they are custodians of their own future. Stay in one place too long and the social world passes you by. Organisations, on the other hand, are frequently characterised by stronger mindsets and so seek to maintain the comfort of their *status quo* when everything else around them is changing rapidly. This stiff-upper-lip approach can be quite valid if the change dynamics are purely temporary and confidence expects the good old times to return soon. If the change dynamics are not temporary this failure to acknowledge the real state of the environment can be suicidal.

Beliefs and attitudes

Organisations can so envelop themselves with mindsets and paradigms that they effectively lose sight of their operating environment. Solid successes in previous times may well have led to the construction of immense bureaucracies whose job is often interpreted as being to maintain this *status quo* at all costs. Sometimes whole organisations can become the prisoner of myopic thinking and overzealous administrators. Forms, regulations, statistics and other measures are designed to keep the organisation happy. If powerful cliques feel that the real news is just unacceptable, then some will attempt to blow it away by altering the measuring system so that it says what they want it to say. This is an acute version of *distorted perception* but it is more common than many would like to admit.

Of course, there are many fine organisations that capture the wind of change and use it to create wealth, but, sadly, many fail to perceive accurately the seriousness of their contextual positions until very late in the day. No over harsh criticism of administrators is intended, for their services are required. However, they are needed to support management not to subsume it or to place it in chains. Administrators should serve organisations and not dominate them. Organisations that allow their administrations to escalate in the good times later discover that they are still employing large numbers of administrators when times become less prosperous. Some even continue to expand their administrative departments when operating conditions are waning.

Consultancy work has given first-hand awareness of many vastly inflated administrative empires that in some cases outnumber the productive headcounts in organisations. As operating environments become harsher, most organisations are faced with more and more complex problems that require more than basic *rational–analytical thinking* and the common tendency to over subscribe to *linear causality* models. Today's 'borderless world' is a complex place that is increasingly characterised by complex systems. To understand these systems, managers need to become acquainted with *systems thinking*. There is mounting evidence to suggest that *how* managers think about problems and their organisations is directly related to their ability to achieve responses (Senge, 1990). The next section provides an overview of *hard and soft systems thinking*.

Key principles

Creativity blockers

The key six blockages to personal creativity commonly identified in the literature (e.g. Osborn, 1963; Kreitner, 1980; Stevens, 1988) are as follows (see Figure 7.3):

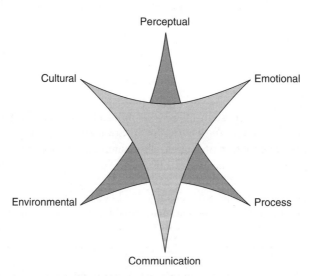

Figure 7.3 Common individual CPS blockages.
Source: M.R.V. Goodman, Durham University.

Perceptual blockages

These blockages arise from the way that we have learnt (instruction and experience) to adapt to the stimuli that surround us in the world as we see it. Habitual responses can lead us to miss other, perhaps contextually more suitable, responses. For example:

- Seeing only what we expect to see, failure to really understand contextual stimuli – driving in fog!
- Stereotyping – tendency to jump to conclusions too quickly.
- Eyes down – propensity to tunnel vision.
- Mistaking cause and effect – if there turns out not to be hotel room for an invited guest and we assume that it is the hotel's fault when in reality our secretary forgot to make a reservation, then our search for solutions will be misdirected. The fact that there is no room for our guest is an effect of the problem not the cause.

Emotional blockages

These blockages are evident when we deliberately suppress an idea or course of action because we perceive that it will be unpopular with our peer group and do not want to risk their scorn. Or, perhaps, when we come up with an idea that is different (such as, for example, an Imagineering approach) and we do not want to look ridiculous in the eyes of our fellows. For instance:

- Fear of making mistakes or looking silly.
- Racing away – rushing in too quickly may result in the wrong problem being solved or the right problem but with the wrong CPS approach.
- Playing it safe and avoiding anxiety – a common response in individuals who are uncertain of how much support they will receive from the group or organisation.
- Awaiting instruction – related to the above cause, and tending to be found in rule-bound organisations.
- Sloppy response – tends to be found in situations where the problem is routine and the overall motivation of the staff is low.

Process skill blockages

These are caused by a basic lack of technique. This can all too easily arise when we have been used to existing in fairly stable operational conditions where real problems and challenges are few and far between. For example:

- Lack of knowledge in problem-solving process.
- Lack of creative thinking – a reluctance to use creative thinking.
- Too heavy a reliance on left-brain skills – wanting to write the proof before the problem is solved.
- Snatching at the problem – failure to apply methodical convergent/divergent tracking points.
- Lack of sufficient contextual information, poor or the wrong *problem statement* and poor CPS ability.
- Lack of understanding of the facts – shooting in the dark.

Communication blockages

These occur when we are unable to communicate in a suitable style for our voice to be heard and understood by those charged with tackling the problem in question. Examples are as follows:

- Failure to couch the problem and its proposed solution in suitable terms. General management will not understand functional jargon. Not all concerned outside publics will understand the organisational 'speak'.
- Difficulty in explaining the position to others as the explanation is sometimes unconsciously cloaked in jargon and/or organisational 'speak'. The safe default in such situations is to explain the things in a style appropriate to an educated third party.
- Failure to justify recommendations.
- Failure to capture the attention of vital parties owing to weak presentation skills.
- Autocratic, argumentative styles that easily put people's backs up.

Environmental blockages

These often crop up to distract us from getting to grips with a problem and frequently result from unexpected or seasonal increases in our workload. For example:

- Management culture – the impact of the organisational mindsets.
- Comfort factors – poor facilities (everything from toilets to coffee and tea provision) can dampen enthusiasm and quality of response.
- Ambivalent attitude of key contact(s) in the organisation.
- Stress factors – the too frequent imposition of tight deadlines.
- Monotony – need-to-know management causes people to get bored.
- Absence or *kaizen* – people are more responsive if they know that they are expected to look continually for better ways of doing things.

Cultural blockages

This set of blockages impact on us through personal, group, organisational and national cultures. For example, some managers feel that the Creative Management style is too open and risky and may harbour the latent opinion that staff are to be instructed and not consulted! Instances are as follows:

- Religious acceptance of the *status quo*.
- Resistance to major change.
- Distrust of right-brain skills.
- Belief that humour is for private life only.
- Prejudiced suspicion that anything to do with *Imagineering* is definitely not management!
- Reluctance to work in teams – everyone-for-himself mentality does not foster co-operative effort.
- Lack of vision.
- Work environment.
- Socio-cultural factors.

- Emotional charge.
- Communication factors.
- Perception issues.
- Participation issues.

Practice

Obstacles to individual business creativity

After a creativity workshop in Durham, delegates were asked to brainstorm the main obstacles, as they saw them, to introducing creative personal problem solving (CPPS) into the lives of their colleagues at work. They were also asked to suggest ways that these obstacles might be overcome. Table 7.1 summarises the results.

Tiredness

Many exhibited a reluctance to put in the necessary time to learn a new skill. Home was seen as a place to relax and that did not include thinking about being creative! Work was identified with pressure, paper and politics that made people tire quickly and reduced their enthusiasm to attempt anything new. Invariably the workplace was seen as a mechanistic culture where some pulled the levers and the others 'did their bit'.

Anxiety

Experienced at work, this was often transferred after working hours to home life. Many found it difficult to relax away from work and free their minds to attempt anything new.

Negativity

The harsh economic climate of the North East led many to adopt a pessimistic outlook on life. Often frustration with the performance of 'the management' or the euphemistic 'they' seemed to produce a pronounced negative culture.

Fear of failure

Occurred frequently and was cited by individuals working in both large and small organisations. Many in this group did not realise that it was possible to practise creativity at home in a safe environment (Storm and Angello, 2010; Kennedy, 2011).

Table 7.1 Individual CPS blockages

Obstacle	Antidote
1. Tiredness	Get a good night's sleep
2. Anxiety	Relax
3. Negativity	Be positive
4. Fear of failure	Trust your intuition
5. Fear of standing out from the crowd	Stand your ground
6. Fear of challenging the rules	Rules should help, not hinder
7. Fear of emotional things	Realise that total thinking makes sense
8. Myopia	Wake up!

Obstacles to group business creativity

Some weeks after the workshop in Durham, another set of delegates on a creativity workshop were asked to indicate what they saw as the main blockages to introducing CPS successfully. Table 7.2 summarises the results. By comparison, blockages commonly identified in the literature on CPS – basically stemming from a poor understanding of how to manage groups – are summarised in Table 7.3.

Table 7.2 CPS difficulties: an empirical sounding

Obstacle	Antidote
1. Negative attitudes	Quietly get on and try some CPS tools and techniques without going overboard to explain the *how* involved and produce some good results.
2. Politics	Stand your ground; argue to be judged on results – seeing, rather than telling, encourages believing.
3. Fear of exposing poor teamwork of other groups	Operate tactfully. Tackle problems – resist any temptation to evangelise the CPS cause in the organisation.
4. Myopia	Tactfully explain contextual factors affecting the problem situation to all group participants.
5. Concern over choosing the right problem to obtain a recognised success	Start simply – select progressable issues.
6. Low creativity	Need for instruction and guidance of a creative facilitator.
7. Lack of trust	Do your best to earn it.
8. Poor problem-solving ability	Introduce and demonstrate some basic tools.
9. Unclear aims	Try to clarify.
10. Reward structure viewed as unfair	Show your appreciation and seek to influence the system.

Table 7.3 CPS difficulties identified in the literature

Obstacle	Antidote
Lack of vision	Inform group of what is involved and seek their collective ownership of it.
Poor participation	Encourage individuals to contribute – provide a safe environment. Avoid power driving the group.
Poor interaction	Get the group to talk amongst themselves as well as to you. Promote a 'one for all and all for one' philosophy.
Lack of trust	Up to the facilitator to dispel.
Poor reward	Up to the facilitator to use imagination – successful group behaviour has to be recognised in some way. Remember that man does not live by bread alone.
Starting too soon	Facilitator needs to impose restraint and ensure that the group does not rush in too quickly.
Confused operation	Facilitator needs to ensure that the group converges and diverges at suitable intervals.
Tendency to argue	Facilitator needs to resist the formation of pre-conceived solutions to group blindness – a preference to operate in a predictable form irrespective of the problem and contextual environment.

Common problems that challenge the effectiveness of hard systems thinking

Diagnosis

A tenet that is open to question, especially in times of accelerating change, is that individuals, groups and organisations are able to diagnose key problems correctly. Frequently it is organisations, rather than groups or individuals, that have the greatest difficulty in obtaining accurate problem diagnoses as their collective thinking can be confused and distorted by their corporate milieu of mindsets. Some organisations like to believe that they never really have serious problems for these only confront other, and in their eyes usually badly run, organisations. This mindset has variations, such as a strong confidence in the power of *rational–analytical thinking* to solve almost anything, and the belief that all problems have happened before so may confidently be considered as temporary irritants that will soon be gone.

Belief in measurement

Another drawback in turbulent times is the tenet that all goals, decisions and important issues can be quantified and measured. This positivist contention has prompted many organisations to invest in sophisticated IT systems to produce vast wads of information. Whilst this has made many corporations 'feel good' it has also left many of them struggling to get to grips with all the data that their mainframe and networks provide. However, many organisational activities, such as operational and tactical matters, where the situations are clearly structured, can be capably handled by *hard systems thinking*.

Risk spots

Even in the best of times most organisations have *risk hot spots* in their operations that seem to continually resist the efforts of hard systems to control. Here chaos reigns and life is uncomfortable. In these cases reality is reality and attempts to rationalise and programme these *hot spots* inevitably lead to disappointment and frustration. Some organisations find that their mindsets blind their vision so causing them to function in an imagined or *virtual reality*. When this occurs frustration mounts, as the chaos continues and managers tend to apportion blame for poor performance levels on the contextual factors. In stable times, when most of the organisation is functioning well (in equilibrium) the *hot spots*, though still irritating, can be carried along by the general positive momentum of the organisation. As fundamental changes in contextual stimuli cause chaos in the base operations and as the *hot spots* become more and more unstable, many managers must feel that life is very unfair. In this situation *soft system thinking* may be the most appropriate course of action.

Faith in management techniques

Finally, the belief that organisations can be steered into the future by traditional management techniques alone is a critical assumption especially in times of accelerating contextual change. Mechanistic planning is fine where the probability of being able to forecast the future accurately is high; when the reverse is the case managers need to form a clear picture of what makes sense in the new context.

Action

Working with others

Most would agree that the potential output of several minds is greater than that of a single mind. Working with others obviously seems to make sense. However, in the often frantic activity of an average day, many managers probably attempt to progress far too many problems under their own steam. Opening problems up to others makes sense, but is there time to call the necessary meetings? Or might there be some latent reluctance to do so, as the organisational culture may view that it is the manager's job to solve problems?

When this occurs in organisations it tends to make individual managers reluctant to separate the *what* from the *how* in problem-solving activity. Some managers may even perceive working with others as a sign of weakness, preferring to take everything on themselves and working long and arduous hours. Such managerial supermen and women can find it very difficult to share problems with others, even though they may appreciate the logic of harnessing the talents of colleagues. Coping with pressure is a constant process for busy managers. As the problems come faster and faster and as the complexities increase, many managers must feel that they are running in order to stay in one spot. There inevitably comes a point when sheer workload convinces them to actively contemplate involving others.

Viewing management problems

Management problems can usually be viewed in the light of five key issues:

1. Functional/technical skills
2. General management processing skills
3. Cost constraints
4. Time constraints
5. Quality expectations.

Most managers have a sound perspective on their functional/technical ability and experience has equipped many with know-how in relation to cost and time constraints. As their operational environment becomes more and more chaotic so greater emphasis needs to be placed on the realisation of the skill potential contained within groups and organisations. This contextual pressure is challenging many individual management styles and is promoting the cause for effective team working.

Whilst managers usually value talking to others about functional and technical skills, there is frequently a marked resistance to seek the thoughts of others on problem-processing matters. The management *how* is often seen as a very private affair. There are immense gains to be made by opening up problems to groups. As the pressures on managers to perform to high standards in difficult conditions intensify, so many, hitherto private, managers will steel themselves to explore the dynamics of team working. Apart from organisational mindsets the major factor restraining many managers is probably a deep concern about losing control. There is no doubt that whilst opening up problems to others is beneficial and, if handled correctly, a creative joy, people can be difficult too. Individuals regularly need to check their interpersonal skills as it so easy gradually to slip back into an autocratic style in the heat of the moment. Then, as behaviour breeds behaviour, suspicions gain ground and the essential band of trust is damaged. Most team workers will allow the captain to have the occasional private moment and still respect his or her role. If this becomes the regular mode of behaviour, however, teams will soon collapse in a regrettable climate of mutual suspicion and fear. Effective managers have to win through thick and thin. Collaborative team spirit is essential and of especial importance to CEOs (Ibarra and Hansen, 2011).

Fostering good group relations is not easy. It means giving people space to express themselves. It means not being too judgmental too early and too negative in any criticism that you may make. It means being responsible to all your individuals, to groups and to the organisation. It means promoting a 'one for all and all for one' climate in place of an 'all for one and one for one' approach. It means playing a considered and honourable political game when pressures threaten individual, group or organisational relationships. Politics was intended to be an honourable pursuit; it has only become an object of popular scorn because it has been conducted irresponsibly for private gain. However, private gain can be achieved both by responsible means as well as irresponsible means. The latter is unlikely to foster the growth of group creativity, the former will and, in the process, make a real hero of the manager.

So, many managers who are determined to become *creative managers* can expect to be apprehensive to begin with and need to be bold enough to re-examine their interpersonal skills and practical understanding of group dynamics. Apart from any individual contemplation that managers may care to make, a good way of sparking business creativity is to examine organisational mindsets, to call a meeting of key staff away from the work place and explain to them just why it is sensible to try something new (Capozzi *et al.*, 2011). This is the value of a strong contextual approach. Different conditions require a different approach. Every sports person knows that and most others soon appreciate it too. Once the contextual argument has been put concerned individuals should then open up to new problem solving initiatives. Then as soon as possible demonstrate some CPS action. Help from a fully trained creative facilitator is invaluable at this stage. Be careful of the temptation to do too much too soon.

Once underway, talk about experiences with various CPS tools and techniques amongst colleagues. Find others who are also in the process of getting to grips with CPS and compare notes. Set up a networking system to share knowledge and experience in the use of the CPS tools and techniques. This can be done using a variety of means including face-to-face meetings, email, and social networking (e.g. Facebook, LinkedIn and Twitter).

Summary

Both organisations and management theory seem obsessed with creativity and a fixation with the new is accompanied by just as strong a rejection of that which is different. Muhr (2010) turns to the moral philosophy of Emmanuel Levinas (1981) to address this paradox and argues that profound novelty can only be accomplished in ethical encounters that nourish trust and confidence. Good managers do not attempt to manage creativity, they manage for creativity, by providing a working environment and culture that allows creativity to flourish. This challenges all managers 'to bring paradoxes, conflicts, and dilemmas out in the open, so that collectively we can be more intelligent than we can be individually' (Senge, 1990). Finally, as Gosling and Mintzberg (2003) argue, 'imagine the mind-sets as threads and the manager as weaver. Effective performance means weaving each mind-set over and under the others to create a fine, sturdy cloth'.

Discussion questions

1. Briefly describe the thinking pattern factor sets.
2. Why do managers, whether individual, group or CEOs, have to be wary of assumptions in current buyers' markets?
3. How can consideration of psychological factor sets assist managers to overcome the resistance of employees to new ways of thinking?
4. What are the leading blockages to individual creative thinking?
5. What are the leading blockages to group creative thinking?
6. Briefly discuss the common problems that challenge the effectiveness of hard systems thinking in times of discontinuous change.
7. Name the five key issues that help to address management problems.

Case exercise

GD and Partners is a long-established family firm providing Audit, Tax and Advisory services primarily for SMEs in the South West of the UK. The firm has 20 branches plus a headquarters office in Bath. The top management are remote and family dominated. In the last five years profits have declined steadily and the firm is expected to make a loss at the end of their next tax year. The current CEO, Graham Dooley, though possessing a sound financial brain, is a bad people mixer. He has a massive ego and rules the partnership in a strict Dickensian manner.

The firm is short of people as the long-serving partners and staff have seen out their time and retired and most have not been replaced by fresh blood. As a result the offices are understaffed and have lost a considerable amount of previously loyal clients. David Dooley, Graham's son, had been told that he will assume the position of CEO when his father retires in three months' time.

David plans to totally revolutionise the way things are done when he assumes control and has gained his father's blessing. He thought that he would start by establishing a new vision, mission and set of company values. He was determined GD should continue as a partnership and wanted all the partners and staff to work together to develop a new collaborative way of doing things. After careful consideration he decided to run an away day in a comfortable hotel in a village near Bath. His father did not attend in order not to act as a distraction.

A CPS facilitator was obtained to lead the day and all employees were asked to take part. David opened the day by stating his desire to adopt a new *modus operandi*. The facilitator worked hard in the morning sessions but was continually frustrated by the reluctance of people to take part with any degree of enthusiasm. He sought out David during the lunch break to raise his concerns. Several of the older members of staff were loath to get involved with soft systems approaches and held that real business was all about honed hard systems thinking. In contrast many younger members were keen to take part but were disturbed by the attitudes of the older people. A third group of people were quite keen to give the new approach a go but felt the hostility of their older colleagues.

David was determined that the day would be a success and asked the CPS facilitator to summarise the main problems as he saw them. The result was truly shocking. The morning session had been full of a tendency for the 'old guard' to argue their preconceived points of view; to poorly participate and as a result place a dampener on the interaction of the others during the morning session. This, in the eyes of the facilitator, was evidence of a general lack of trust.

David decided to seize the initiative at the start of the first afternoon session. He gave participants an upbeat talk on his plans for the future of GD and was pleased that he had taken the precaution of asking a senior partner of the retailer John Lewis to address his people.

Task

Imagine that you had been asked to make some recommendations to David during the lunch break to effectively deal with the resistance of many of his staff to take part in CPS activity.

Draft a short note for him with what you consider he should do about the problems reported by the CPS facilitator.

References

Capozzi, M.M., Dye, R. and Howe, A. (2011) 'Sparking creativity in teams: An executive's guide', *McKinsey Quarterly*, April, pp. 74–81.

Gosling, J. and Mintzberg, H. (2003) 'The five minds of a manager', *Harvard Business Review*, November, Vol. 81, Issue 11, pp. 54–63.

Herzberg, F.I. (1987) 'One more time: How do you motivate employees?', *Harvard Business Review*, September/October, Vol. 65, Issue 5, pp. 109–20.

Ibarra, H. and Hansen, M.T. (2011) 'Are you a collaborative leader?', *Harvard Business Review*, Kindle edition, July.

Kennedy, D. (2011) 'Moving beyond uncertainty: Overcoming our resistance to change', *Leader to Leader*, September, Issue 62, pp. 17–21.

Kreitner, R. (1980) *Management A Problem-solving Process*, Boston, Houghton Mifflin.

Levinas, E. (1981) *Otherwise than Being, or, Beyond Essence*, Pittsburgh, PA, Duquesne University Press (translated by A. Lingis).

Mitroff, I.I. (1984) *Stakeholders of the Organizational Mind*, San Francisco, Jossey-Bass.

Muhr, S.L. (2010) 'Ethical interruption and the creative process: A reflection on the new', *Culture & Organization*, March, Vol. 16, Issue 1, pp. 73–86.

Osborn, A.E. (1963) *Applied Imagination*, New York, Scribner.

Pina e Cunha, M., da Cunha, J.V. and Kamoche, K. (2001) 'The age of emergence: Toward a new organizational mindset', *SAM Advanced Management Journal*, Summer, Vol. 66, Issue 3, pp. 25–31.

Senge, P. (1990) *The Fifth Discipline*, New York, Doubleday.

Stevens, M.S. (1988) *Practical Problem Solving for Managers*, London, Kogan Page.

Storm, B.C. and Angello, G. (2010) 'Overcoming fixation: Creative problem solving and retrieval-induced forgetting psychological science', *Psychological Science*, September, Vol. 21, Issue 9, pp. 1263–5.

Wyer, R.S. and Xu, A.J. (2010) 'The role of behavioral mind-sets in goal-directed activity: Conceptual underpinnings and empirical evidence', *Journal of Consumer Psychology*, April, Vol. 20, Issue 2, pp. 107–25.

Part III

Innovation from theory to practice

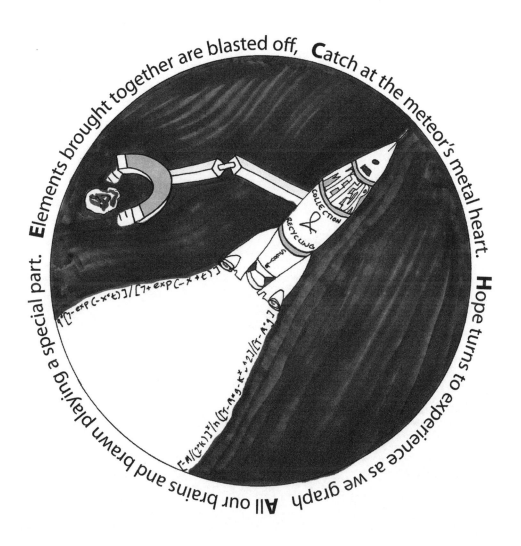

8 Key innovation principles

The innovator makes enemies of all those who prospered under the old order and only luke-warm support is forthcoming from those who would prosper under the new.

(Machievelli, *The Prince*, 1513)

But innovation comes from people meeting up in the hallways or calling each other at 10:30 at night with a new idea, or because they realized something that shoots holes in how we've been thinking about a problem.

(Steve Jobs, visionary and inventor)

Introduction

Although the concepts of creativity and innovation are, to some extent, interlinked a distinction should be made between them. Creativity (see Chapter 4) involves the generation of ideas which are original. Innovation involves the development and implementation of the ideas which are considered to be of value. These ideas can relate to an organisation's product, process or service and enable it to deliver distinct customer-perceived value. Innovation involves action, strategy and convergent thinking. It takes a linear and logical path, as it involves taking decisions about the future goals and destiny of an organisation. Organisations need to take innovation seriously if ideas that are considered to add value are to be implemented. Creative ideas feed the innovation process.

Innovation management facilitates creativity by the successful activation of a number of processes which also assist an organisation to gain a competitive advantage. It requires the implementation of a process together with a serious consideration of strategy, problem solving and decision making. It is only through managing the innovation process that organisations can create a culture and climate that are conducive to the generation, communication and evaluation of new ideas. The realisation of appropriate and feasible ideas through innovation management may be driven by either vision or knowledge.

It is no longer wise for organisations to ignore the possibilities for improvement that innovation provides (Gurteen, 1998). Organisational innovation management uses creative ideas which have been generated within an organisation to develop new products and processes. This chapter links the theories outlined in previous chapters to the fostering of effective strategic management, continuous improvement, added value, increased R&D and the encouragement of an entrepreneurial spirit.

Figure 8.1 Exploring innovation: key principles.

Context

The management of innovation is a process that is vital for success in today's competitive global scenario. However, it is a stiff challenge for many organisations as it is fraught with change issues, uncertainity and risk and usually requires considerable disturbance to the current *modus operandi* (Jones-Bliss and Kapetanovic, 2009). The physical working environment is important, as people tend to spend more time at their workplace than anywhere else during their lives. It reflects the standard, 'image' or 'brand' which the organisation wishes to present to staff, customers and suppliers. Both the organisational culture (including the goals, mission and vision of the organisation) and the climate (the physical and psychological environment) play a key role in this regard. Innovative organisations focus on creating and sustaining a culture and a climate which feature regular communication, and generate trust and thus work satisfaction.

Innovation is essential for success

There may be a number of reasons for an organisation to decide to take innovation seriously. The most obvious is crisis management, where survival is key. However, this does not usually lead to outcomes which add to the competitiveness of an organisation. For this to happen, a strategic plan needs to be implemented ensuring the participation of both top management and all staff. Harnessing and utilising the ideas of all employees and creating open channels of communication at all levels, both vertically and horizontally, is essential for success. This will encourage a climate where creativity may be nurtured and where the mindsets of all employees are primed towards innovation.

Training in creativity techniques is one way to harness the creative potential of employees. However, this should be sustained over time and should not simply be conducted as a *one-off* event without any follow up or additional strategies in place. Training on its own, often undertaken as a 'quick-fix', usually disappoints.

Once ideas have been generated, they need to be communicated and evaluated to indicate their relevance to the organisation's goals. The introduction of an idea management system harnesses creative ideas and selects the best for implementation. An idea management system involves a number of activities which include meetings (either face-to-face or virtual), an intranet where ideas are uploaded and discussed through a forum, and a traditional paper-based 'suggestion scheme'. All of these activities require trust and for all communications to be treated with respect. Ideas should then be relayed to those, generally at a higher level of the hierarchy (or located in a department set up for the purpose), who are in a position to evaluate and select the ideas which are considered to add value, improve effectiveness and efficiency and increase the competitive edge of an organisation.

Principles

Harvesting creative ideas

Both creativity and innovation are key drivers for the success of any organisation. There are several ways in which the ideas that are generated within an organisation may be harvested. Nowadays most successful idea management schemes tend to use information technology systems such as the organisation's intranet. Rewards may be monetary (cash gifts etc.), recognition (an award or a mention in an internal publication) or 'in kind' (vouchers perhaps). An individual or a team may be the recipient of a reward, depending on the manner in which innovation is managed or on how the idea was initially submitted. Research has demonstrated that non-monetary rewards are generally appreciated more than cash gifts or bonuses (Amabile, 1996). Recognition is important as it is one of the key motivating factors which enable innovation to be sustained within an organisation.

Innovation champions

The establishment of an innovation network within an organisation is an ambitious programme that requires careful planning and systematic implementation in order to function successfully. It involves establishing a carefully planned programme of work headed by a 'visionary' or 'champion' whose task is to plan, direct, enthuse and control the process of encouraging and developing innovation. Key employees should be trained in creativity techniques and in the management of innovation. Innovation networks can then begin to function. Larger organisations could consider the introduction of a Director of Innovation who would be the person responsible for the entire innovation process and to whom all innovation champions would report.

Essential factors to maintain and sustain an innovation management programme include:

- A visionary or champion who gets things started;
- An energetic manager or director who visibly supports and oversees the on-going implementation, development and maintenance of the programme;
- Sincere commitment from relevant sections of the organisation (top management, human resources, finance, etc.).

Other relevant factors include:

- Flexibility: such an initiative should not remain static but should develop according to the context, culture and sensitivity of the organisation;
- On-going development: by means of self-reflection and self-evaluation on the part of the champion and innovation network leaders in order to evaluate, constructively criticise, provide feedback and modify strategies for continuous improvement;
- Motivation: on the part of both champion and innovation network leaders who model good thinking;
- Sustaining a creative climate: where mutual trust, open communication channels and self-confidence are fostered and where risk taking and creative initiatives are encouraged.

An organisation that manages to incorporate creativity and innovation into a holistic framework will be successful. This can only happen at the instigation of top management and must commence with the formulation and adoption of a visionary planning process that includes a commitment towards innovation networks.

Radical and incremental innovation

Organisational innovation may occur either on a small scale (*incremental innovation*) or as a dramatic 'paradigm shift' (*radical innovation*) which challenges and changes the current way of doing things. Both strategies offer advantages, although it should be clear from the start that incremental innovation involves the use of fewer resources and hence is less risky than radical innovation.

Incremental innovation exploits existing forms, products, services or technologies. It either improves something that already exists or it may reconfigure an existing form or technology to serve some other purpose. Software upgrades which claim to fix problems in PCs or laptops are an example of incremental innovation.

Radical innovation involves the introduction of something that is new to the world and a departure from existing technology or methods. It is sometimes called 'breakthrough innovation' and 'discontinuous innovation'. 'Disruptive technology' is sometimes used to describe a technical innovation that has the potential to upset an organisation's (or the industry's) existing business model. Disruptive technologies tend to displace existing technology and precipitate the decline of organisations whose business models are based on them. They may even result in the creation of new markets. Digital imaging technology used for cameras, for example, represents a radical departure from the chemically coated film technology that became synonymous with Kodak. Smart phones are now also used for taking photos and may eventually displace digital cameras.

Radical innovation has one or more of the following characteristics (Leifer *et al.*, 2000):

- An entirely new set of performance features;
- Improvements in known performance features of five times or greater;
- A 30 per cent or greater reduction in cost.

This implies that radical innovation has the potential to change the basis of competition. Radical ideas are always present in R&I (Research and Innovation) laboratories or in the minds of scientists or entrepreneurs. They usually take a long time to germinate and develop. Their appearance is both infrequent and generally unpredictable, although developments in new digital technology appear to result in a faster time period for the implementation of some radical innovations. Radical innovation has the potential to change the basis of competition in favour of the innovator. The use of typewriters is one example. Manual typewriters were replaced by electric typewriters which, in turn, signalled the end for all manual typewriters in the office market and gave electric models a commanding share of the office market for decades. Electric typewriters have now been replaced by PCs and laptops which risk being replaced by tablets such as the iPad and smart phones.

Despite the advantages of radical innovation, it presents organisations with a number of serious challenges. Projects may be risky, expensive and usually take many years before tangible results are achieved. For radical innovation to be successful, organisations must have the patience and budgets to support long timelines. The problems associated with risk, expense and long timelines may encourage organisations to pursue incremental innovation. Radical technological innovations may prove to be the exception here. The time to market is generally briefer, particularly when the innovation is concerned with 'intangibles' such as knowledge or software.

Handled systematically, incremental innovation may provide organisations with a steady stream of new, improved and varied products, processes or services which are essential for sustainability and competitiveness (Robinson and Schroeder, 2004). Organisations considering the implementation of incremental innovations must however be cautious about the following:

- *Avoid adding too many features or functions:* pressed by market demands for new versions of a product or service, designers may tend to add features even though few customers may require them (e.g. televisions, music systems, computer software). This practice may irritate users and may result in the creation of a new market for more simple and elegant innovations.
- *Do not invest all resources and efforts on incremental innovation:* although incremental innovation is less risky and produces results faster, it will not bridge current and future generations in technology. Only radical innovation can alter the competitive game in one's favour. A balance between the pursuit of incremental and radical innovations is important, particularly in an environment where change occurs at a fast rate, particularly where technology is concerned.

Organisations should ensure that both radical and incremental innovation operate together as much as possible. The introduction of a successful radical innovation is often followed by a period of incremental innovation, which improves its performance, irons out 'glitches' or extends its application.

Process, service and product innovation

People are accustomed to thinking of innovation in terms of physical, manufactured goods such as computer chips, flat-screen displays, fuel cells, smart phones, furniture, automobiles or night vision equipment. *Process and service innovations* are important in the competitive life of organisations. Technology supports a number of process improvements through the use of such things as social networking sites, online gaming sites and online payment systems and internet banking sites.

Service is an area where innovation plays a key role as customers' expectations need to be seriously addressed. Retention of customers in today's global and competitive environment is not an easy task and customers appreciate excellent service which leads to increased loyalty and less wastage of resources. Online bookstores are one example of service innovation, as are ATMs (automated teller machines), electronic scanners and automated tills at supermarkets. Service innovation sometimes produces winning business models. A good example is the service offered by low cost (no frills) airlines which provided 'first in' airlines with a competitive advantage over the traditional airlines.

It is important to direct attention to the *process* that supports each and every service innovation and to think carefully about every stage that goes into the development and delivery of the service. Each stage could be improved (incrementally), combined or replaced entirely (radically), by something *better, faster and cheaper.* The SCAMPER Checklist Tool (Substitute, Combine, Adapt, Modify, Put to another use, Eliminate and Reverse – see Appendix 5.1) may be used for this purpose.

Process and product innovation go hand in hand. A breakthrough product often fails to gain market acceptance until a low-cost process for manufacturing it at acceptable quality levels is created.

Systems thinking and innovation

There are occasions when innovation management tends to focus on a specific segment within a system in an attempt to instigate change, resolve a problem or add value. The consequences of interventions, however, often impact on the larger organisation and may, in addition, create ripple effects which affect customers or suppliers. In order to counteract such a narrow focus, systems thinking moves beyond a narrow focus on just a segment of the organisation. It views the relationships amongst each of the parts of an organisation, with particular focus on the interrelationships and with overlaps within and outside the organisation.

Jay Forrester of MIT first laid the foundation for systems thinking in 1958. A system may be defined as a group of components that interact, are interrelated and which may appear to be independent, but which together form a complex and unified whole. An organisation is one example of a system due to its being composed of parts which are interrelated, independent and which interact with each other. Each system possesses goals and purposes which are related to a larger system. Successful outcomes require the presence of all of the system's parts which must be arranged in a specific way for it to operate successfully. Systems are dynamic and respond to feedback by making adjustments based on the feedback received, subsequently maintaining stability.

Systems thinking recognises the need for testing new ideas in relation to social systems and the importance of understanding and making social systems more explicit. This contrasts with traditional analytical thinking, where focus is generally directed towards breaking down the component parts of a system and with focusing only on the areas where analysis is required. Systems thinking does the opposite by focusing on how each element within a system interacts with the other parts of the system. This method is particularly useful when dealing with the dynamically complex nature of social systems and the manner in which interactions occur. Feedback from both internal and external sources is drawn into the picture as an expanded view of a complex situation, together with all its intricacies, is composed.

The use of systems thinking may be valuable for organisations in a number of situations, not only when problems which are not obvious must be tackled, but also in the following circumstances:

- Organisations may face very complex problems and systems thinking may help those concerned to move beyond their own narrow perspective and to view the bigger picture in all its complexity.
- Some problems which organisations face may recur in spite of attempts to resolve them; other attempts to resolve problems may create a worse situation, and systems thinking may be usefully applied in such cases.
- Decisions may affect not only the section within the organisation towards which they are directed, but also the broader environment, and systems thinking enables organisations to include these factors (concerning, for example, the natural or the competitive environment) in the picture.

The broad picture which systems thinking offers moves beyond a view of specific events or segments towards a perspective which includes internal and external forces, their relationships with each other, the sub-systems involved and internal and external patterns, cycles and structures. Systems thinking enables the identification of the main cause of problems within a system and its holistic perspective allows for an identification of the area where change is required to resolve the problems, together with an identification of the appropriate solution. 'Leverage points' are the areas towards which change is directed and which 'leverage' improvement throughout the system by means of a ripple effect. The graphic depiction of a situation which systems thinking tools present may be computer simulated or it may consist of flow diagrams or graphs which include causal loops, feedback mechanisms and other dynamic interactions and interrelationships.

Senge, one of the advocates of systems thinking, recommends the use of system maps in his seminal book *The Fifth Discipline: The Art and Practice of the Learning Organisation* (1990). These consist of diagrams which include the key elements of the system, together with the manner in which these elements interact. His argument is that a better appreciation of systems thinking will lead to more appropriate and effective action in organisations that adopt this method.

Time is a precious resource, therefore efforts are often focused towards short-term solutions to problems that arise. When short-term interventions are viewed from a systems thinking perspective, significant long-term consequences may emerge. Short-term budget cuts, for example, may have long-term consequences which may prove to be detrimental to the organisation's competitiveness. Senge concludes that: 'The systems viewpoint is generally oriented toward the long term view. That's why delays and feedback loops are so important. In the short term, you can often ignore them; they're inconsequential. They only come back to haunt you in the long term' (Senge, 1990).

There are various tools available for conducting systems thinking within an organisation, each of which brings into the picture all the interrelated parts of the system which are relevant.

The tools include graphical representations of the system with connectors and feedback loops, graphical images (which demonstrate behaviour over time), flow diagrams or simulations. Each tool has the advantage of clearly communicating how a system functions, where the interconnections and feedback loops are located, the overall process and outcomes and whether there are any connections or blockages which require adjustment or action. The system as a whole always includes more than merely the sum of its parts, particularly as there is a change of perspective since, rather than looking at a system from the inside looking outwards, it is viewed holistically from the outside looking in.

Senge lists five disciplines for the learning organisation:

1.   Personal mastery
2.   Mental models
3.   Building a shared vision
4.   Team learning
5.   Systems thinking.

The final 'discipline', systems thinking, is the culmination of the other four.

Senge's learning organisation is closely linked to systems thinking. He defines learning organisations as 'organizations where people continually expand their capacity to create the results they truly desire, where new and expansive patterns of thinking are nurtured, where collective aspiration is set free, and where people are continually learning to see the whole together'. His five disciplines are 'concerned with a shift of mind from seeing parts to seeing wholes, from seeing people as helpless reactors to seeing them as active participants in shaping their reality, from reacting to the present to creating the future'.

Just as other tools require practice in order to build up skill in their use, tools related to systems thinking applied to organisations require professional training, time, patience and use. Senge's approach, which focuses on connections and relationships and which advocates a shift from 'product' to 'process', exhibits some similarities to network dynamics, a phenomenon which today's digital age accentuates. Although the methods of systems thinking are mainly directed towards practitioners in organisations, adopting it successfully requires a significant amount of time and effort. Support, motivation and follow-up training, together with the identification of 'champions', are necessary for a successful outcome.

Innovation bottlenecks

Effective innovation management may often encounter a number of obstacles and a prior understanding of those which arise in implementing innovation practices is essential. Strategies can then be designed to diminish the effects of the obstacles that are encountered. Some of the main barriers to organisational innovation are :

- The process of changing an organisation's climatee
- Lack of time to think
- Bureaucracy
- Structure
- Poor lateral communication
- External talent
- Financial constraints
- Limiting paradigms

- Inappropriate mental modes
- Limitations of traditional teaching and training.

One of the most difficult challenges is *the process of changing a climate* or corporate attitudes. This requires an imaginative, consistent, persistent and integrated programme of work aimed at modifying people's personal attitudes towards risk taking and sustaining flexible mindframes. Organisations that take innovation seriously should emphasise the importance of developing an all-embracing *climate* where ideas can be *generated, communicated, evaluated* and *implemented.*

Lack of 'time to think'. Managers generally do not allow subordinates to waste their time on non-productive activities. Creativity requires a certain amount of time to think and the absence of slack can act as a barrier to the successful implementation of the whole innovation process. Organisations that allow employees a certain level of slack are in a better position to generate ideas and identify valuable innovations. Organisations that deliberately allow for slack may be extremely successful with their innovations. Google, for example, reputedly allows its employees to spend 80 per cent of their time on core projects and 20 per cent on innovation activities related to their personal interests and passions, much of which results in efforts towards increased innovation.

Bureaucracy. Although bureaucracy is important in organisations as it creates necessary controls, organisations sometimes introduce bureaucracy under the misguided notion that it is a way of ensuring administrative effectiveness and productivity. One cannot expect employees to generate ideas directed against procedures that are accepted as unchanging. Management may take steps to neutralise the effect of bureaucracy such as: (a) eliminating irrelevant or inexplicable forms of bureaucracy; (b) 'promoting' the overriding role of innovation at all levels (specific instructions which explain the circumstances in which creative behaviour must override administrative rules must be clearly outlined); and (c) periodically reviewing the reasons behind bureaucratic procedures.

Structure. Small organisations seldom have major organisational problems. They may function extremely well without a formal structure. The manager knows precisely what is going on and can respond to needs or take decisions in a pragmatic way. Provided the manager has the right attitude towards other people's ideas, the organisation can benefit from a relaxed and informal flow of ideas and the implementation of innovations. Some large organisations restructure their hierarchy in an attempt to create better communication channels and subsequently increase the potential for innovation. This is often done by dividing the organisation into smaller autonomous divisions. It is important to keep in mind the fact that structural changes should not be authorised until (a) the impact of such changes has been thoroughly explored; and (b) strategic planning is in place to mitigate the possible undesirable impact of any changes to organisational structure.

Poor lateral communication. Communication is a key element for the successful implementation of an idea management system in an organisation. Effective communication in an organisation implies both cooperation and purpose with the aim of achieving a successful outcome. Open channels of communication mitigate against the possibility of insecurity, suspicion and lack of motivation, particularly where innovation and the change which it brings in its wake are concerned. Factors which may obstruct lateral communication include: (a) manipulative practices on the part of management such as holding back information, excessive secrecy or reluctance to communicate; (b) conflicting objectives amongst departments or sections within the organisation; (c) difference of attitudes, values and beliefs which give rise to incompatibility where communication is concerned; and (d) inadequate training which is essential for staff to become better aware (and better understand) the value of innovation and its practices for the organisation.

External 'talent'. A serious barrier to the development of a climate in which innovation can be successfully managed is the notion that progress may only be achieved through the importation of external talent. This tends to give rise to a feeling of humiliation, insecurity and a subsequent lack of confidence and it may give rise to a lack of motivation in those individuals who feel they should have had the opportunity to be considered for a particular position which is offered to a person external to the organisation. Another possible conse-quence is the adoption of a 'status quo' attitude where employees may feel it is safer not to take the initiative since any newcomer may just be a flash in the pan to be eventually replaced by another.

Financial constraints. It is well known that financial departments are never very forth-coming when resources are required, particularly for innovative projects. Some individuals may take offence at having their 'brilliant' ideas evaluated in financial terms. Innovation requires an element of financial risk and those who control the organisation's finances should recognise the advantages of innovation: to do things *differently, better, cheaper or more aesthetically, for the well-being of the organisation.* Having people from finance breathing down the necks of 'creatives' within an organisation is not very conducive to successful innovation, which requires the support of all the resources which may be required.

Limiting paradigms. This involves a mental 'lock-in', a way of thinking which is directed in favour of established and well known ways of doing things and which includes theories, values and beliefs. Paradigms are similar to mindsets or worldviews. Paradigms may often operate at a subconscious level and cannot always be easily brought to awareness. It is as a result of paradigms or mindsets that new ideas or new systems are often initially rejected. It is only human to rationalise our actions and to avoid the discomfort which innovative change may bring about. Paradigms may block the innovation process through constraints that limit thoughts, beliefs, perceptions and action.

Inappropriate mental models. This barrier is closely related to the previous one. Mental models operate at a conscious level and include fixed ideas on how, for example, business models, such as a specific revenue model, should operate. This gives rise to inflexibility as there is the mistaken assumption that the models by which the organisation operates are the best, regardless of context. We are, however, living in a scenario where models may shift like sand and where new business models, for example, are being applied in efforts to make organisations increasingly sustainable from a social, economic and environmental perspec-tive. Although existing mental models may have worked in the past, there is no guarantee that they will continue to do so. Adapting mental models in an attempt to make them more agile, flexible and adaptive to complexity and change is therefore necessary.

Limitations of traditional teaching and training. Traditional methods of teaching and training are no longer applicable in today's scenario where young people (often known as Gen Y or 'digital natives') are raised on fast interactive multiplayer online games and where they generally require a series of challenges in order for their imagination to be fired and their motivation to be increased. Baby boomers (those born around the 1950s) also need to move beyond traditional methods of training; if they stick to tried and tested routines they risk being totally ineffectual. Communication plays a key role in teaching and training, how-ever it is to be acknowledged that the best way to learn is not through theory, explanations or mere understanding – rather, it is through experience that transferrable skill sets may be built. There is no point in, for example, reading a manual if you wish to learn how to drive a

Formula One racing car or play tennis. The only way to build such a skill is through experience, through trial and error and through regular practice.

Identifying the barriers which create bottlenecks and which act to inhibit the implementation of innovation management systems is the first step to overcoming them. Once they are identified, a strategy may be formulated and steps taken for the barriers to be challenged and eliminated.

Practice

It is evident that NGOs (non-governmental organisations), charities, state funded entities and public organisations operate in an environment that differs from that of private organisations. The latter generally focus on profitability in a context where competitive forces play a key role, which does not generally apply to the former. Although not much has to date been published on innovation related to NGOs, charities, state funded entities and public organisations, it is relevant to discuss the role which innovation may play (or has the potential to play) and the differences in focus that emerge in these types of organisation.

Innovation in non-governmental organisations (NGOs)

An NGO may generally be defined as 'an independent voluntary association of people acting together on a continuous basis, for some common purpose, other than achieving government office, making money or illegal activities'. NGOs generally operate as 'non-profit' organisations although they may at times organise fund raising or revenue generating activities to sustain their activities. Private voluntary organisations are often viewed under the 'umbrella' of NGOs, particularly if they are focused on goals which do not involve either profit or direct participation in governmental politics.

NGOs may be involved in a number of areas, many of which are directed at either influencing public policy or operating specific projects on issues related to, for example, the environment, animal welfare, disaster relief, or human rights. They generally operate in a democratic manner by enrolling members and periodically electing representatives to manage their affairs, which may operate on a local or global level. Amnesty International, Greenpeace and the Worldwide Fund for Nature are three examples of well known global NGOs. Some NGOs collaborate on particular issues and may join forces, when and if necessary, in an attempt to increase pressure, organise protests or raise awareness. NGOs are today acknowledged as key players in democratic societies as they may provide a 'voice' for minorities, create legitimate opposition in particular areas or instigate democratic debate on controversial issues.

It is in the interest of governments and private organisations to create alliances whenever possible with NGOs, particularly with those that operate in similar areas of interest. This may ensure greater responsibility concerning ethical issues and lead towards an increase in democratic dialogue, which has the potential to result in better outcomes for all concerned, both when the NGO is involved with campaigning and when the NGO is involved in specific projects.

Innovation in charities

Charities are generally considered to be non-profit organisations, independent from government, run by volunteers, often with a distinctive legal position and tax status, dedicated to improving the welfare of others. Charities are regulated in a number of countries and require registration. This leads to their having to follow a strict set of legal and financial procedures which may increase regulation and bureaucracy but which allows for increased trust, transparency and higher standards of operation. Although there is some overlap between NGOs and charities, since both operate as non-profit organisations, charities focus on philanthropic goals with activities generally directed towards the public interest or the common good with clear perceived benefits for humanity.

Trust is a key factor where charity fundraising is concerned as door-to-door or street-based cash collections may be viewed with suspicion and be considered as inconvenient, disruptive and disconnected from the benefits or goals which the charity is attempting to achieve.

Charities often function with limited resources and it is often the case that volunteers take on various roles at which they may not be experts. To combat this charities could pool resources such as office space, technology and expertise in an attempt to improve efficiency. Charities could, moreover, network with social entrepreneurs in related areas of interest in order to maximise awareness and create positive change.

Many of the factors concerning NGOs and innovation could be relevant for charities in their attempts to raise funds, increase the pool of donors, improve their image in the media, campaign for their cause, organise events, operate effectively and regulate their affairs in a transparent and efficient manner.

Innovation in state funded entities

State funded entities contribute to innovation through research, funding programmes and the implementation of government policy related to innovation. Government may fund entities to promote research that is theoretical and not necessarily related to market forces, the latter being generally undertaken by private research institutions or R&I laboratories in private organisations. Research involves the scholarly work required for the creation of new knowledge.

The research undertaken may, however, eventually have applications for commercial gain and this may be achieved through the creation of alliances with strategic partners. This is one way to overcome the restraints that may occur with private funding of research, where confidentiality is often imposed due to fear of competition from rival organisations, and may lead towards more collaborative initiatives where both private organisations and government funded entities such as university or research laboratories share information and knowledge.

Risk taking may also play a role in the reluctance of private organisations to conduct research on topics concerning health issues, particularly those which are prevalent in third world countries. Research projects that lack market potential may therefore be more suitable for state funded entities where risk related to market forces does not play a key role in the selection of research focus areas.

Various state funded institutions offer the possibility of funding innovative research projects. These include the National Science Foundation in the USA and the European Commission. The latter regularly issue calls for projects on specific topics to be funded and these generally require the participation of universities, research institutes and, at times, private organisations. Dissemination of the knowledge acquired as a result of research and collaboration plays a key role in the success of European projects selected for funding under the various calls, with the subsequent publication of reports, journal articles and books which are publicly available.

Cross-border collaboration is another important issue where project funding by the European Commission (EC) is concerned. The resulting co-creation of knowledge by individuals from different cultures and countries can deliver innovative ideas with potential for eventual commercial possibilities. One disadvantage of these EC-funded projects is that research generally ends once the project comes to an end, although applying for research funding for a new project is always a possibility.

Research projects are considered to be an integral part of what is called the 'knowledge cycle' which is defined as 'knowledge acquisition, assimilation and development' (Ho, 2007). Innovative opportunities arise as 'knowledge development may lead to creating or discovering new knowledge/technology or creating new value by applying knowledge/technology to societal or business challenges. The knowledge development stage is where value is created, in other words, innovation' (Ho, 2007).

Knowledge could be considered as a commodity which may be traded in today's knowledge economy. However, too much focus on the commercialisation of university generated research may threaten academic autonomy if it involves limitations on the free exchange of ideas and if academics risk being in situations where a conflict of interest may arise. One advantage of university generated research is that it has the potential to provide support for knowledge transfer and innovation. The formation of networks, alliances and consortia allows universities to build on their strengths, to pool resources and to draw on the mutual support in areas in which they may not possess the required expertise. This could offer one avenue to combat the difficulties experienced by academics in small nations or communities with regard to publishing research in recognised and accredited journals, often due to language constraints.

University research may play a role in bridging the apparent incompatibility that may arise between commercialisation and sustainability. Two examples of this relate to sustainable energy and health issues, both of which have benefited from academic research. It is interesting to note that some authors dispute the role that innovation plays in universities. In a discussion on innovation policy, Fagerberg (2009) distinguishes between science and innovation which, he claims, are often considered by policy makers as similar activities.

Although policy measures for commercial organisations and universities may differ, more attention should be paid to the potential bridge that may be created between them and to the possibilities which arise due to university research results tackling issues which may not be considered commercially or sustainably relevant in the short term. Organisations have to, and will continue to, build on the solid basis provided by university research, the results of which are generally publicly available. Moreover, innovation is essential for universities to deal with changing times where resources are sparce and where technology is having a strong impact on students and faculty.

Innovation in public organisations

Some authors provide a broad definition of government to include all publicly funded organisations. In a working paper published by NESTA and authored by the LSE Policy Group, governments are defined as 'central departments, agencies and non-departmental public bodies; devolved governments in Scotland, Wales and Northern Ireland; regional development agencies and London governance bodies; local authorities; universities and FE colleges; health trusts and authorities; and police authorities – basically all bodies operating within the conventionally recognized public sector' (LSE Policy Group, 2008).

The report quotes Mulgan (2006), who defines public sector innovation as being about:

> new ideas that work at creating public value. The ideas have to be at least in part new (rather than improvements); they have to be taken up (rather than just being good ideas); and they have to be useful. By this definition, innovation overlaps with, but is different from, creativity and entrepreneurship.

Competitive forces do not operate in the same manner in the public sector as they do in private organizations. As a consequence, the LSE Policy Group (2008) observes that 'for government organizations, survival rates are high and average organizational lives are long'.

The factors which play a role in innovation in the public sector include structure, policies related to human relations and the area in which the organisation or sector operates. These should be considered along with increased accountability factors which public entities deal with related to the taxpayer, the opposition and the media.

The goals pursued are many and varied:

> government programmes often involve multiple goals being pursued at once, including some key but expensive considerations that involve treating all citizens equally and providing universal service under the rule of law, covering all areas of the country, fully consulting stakeholders or social partners, protecting citizens' rights and providing redress in administrative processes via complaints and appeals systems, and so on.
>
> (LSE Policy Group, 2008)

The research conducted by the LSE Policy Group (2008) in the UK demonstrates that several factors make innovation systematically more likely to occur in national agencies or large-scale public authorities in central regions. Patterns of promotion tend to create a drift of talented staff to higher-tier agencies, because the public sector uses more fixed-scale award systems, making it harder to earn high salaries in smaller sub-national bodies. The development of public sector ICT has for decades shown a strong pattern where organisations at higher tiers and in more central regions have more modern systems.

One of the recommendations of this working paper is that 'For government agencies to be genuinely innovative, they must signal this stance to their staff (and perhaps customers) in their core organizational practices, demonstrating that innovative staff will be promoted or otherwise rewarded' (LSE Policy Group, 2008). Moreover:

> to do better organisations need to positively expect managers and policy-level staffs to push through changes, take feasible risks and run some pilots that fail. Shifting away from people running individual 'desks' towards project teams working with changing problem solving foci may also encourage more innovations.
>
> (LSE Policy Group, 2008)

Government procurement plays a key role where innovation is concerned as governments could be considered as 'lead users' capable of making substantial purchases. When properly managed, innovative procurement can have a positive effect on innovation related to technological advancement, it may define product quality and standards and may lead to increased interoperability. Through placing orders for large quantities of products, governments may be instrumental in encouraging innovation by influencing the suppliers that are selected to deliver the goods. Large orders could act as an incentive for suppliers to focus on more innovative products or services due to the financial benefits that occur as a consequence of being awarded tenders for the supply of large quantities of a particular product or service. This could provide incentives for increased private investment in R&I, particularly since governments have the power to set standards and to certify technologies as being reliable and promising.

Public–private partnerships and consortia are another means of influencing and incentivising efforts directed towards innovation and addressing market failures. The downside of this is the allocation of large infrastructure projects to those who may be considered as political allies, a tactic which risks generating resentment and lack of motivation on the part of the organisations that may be left out of the funding allocation process.

Technological innovation

The development of technology is a key element for successful innovation. New and improved technologies are developed and diffused for widespread use through the activity of various agents in the process of technological innovation. Public policy is one form of governmental intervention which encourages and promotes technological innovation. Barber (2009) identifies three elements which form the basis of the rationale for innovation policy:

1. Identification of some aspect of national (or regional) innovation performance which is regarded as unsatisfactory or some future worthwhile objective or strategy whose achievement is threatened;
2. Identification of a defect in the working of market forces, or in the functioning of the innovation system, that seems likely to prevent the weakness in performance from being corrected or worthwhile objective being realised at least within a reasonable timescale;
3. Some form of public support or intervention which will eliminate or offset the defect at a cost which is (expected to be) less than the benefits thus realised.

Barber claims that all three elements must be present for the justification of innovation policy 'ex-ante' or before it is implemented, besides also being successful after the event.

Barber also links technological innovation to national innovation systems (NIS). Drawing on research conducted by Professor Chris Freeman, Barber defines an NIS as a 'network of institutions in the public and private sectors whose activities and interactions initiate, import, modify and diffuse new technologies *in the country concerned*' (Barber, 2009).

Other factors besides technology are involved in this process. These include the activities of firms, the operation of markets, the system of training and education, the science and public research system, public procurement, taxation, networks, institutions and infrastructure, the business environment generally and the functioning of capital markets. This makes it important for public authorities to establish innovation-friendly policies. Flexibility is also important: 'because the processes of innovation and technology development change over time the boundaries between the private and public sectors may need to shift also' (Barber, 2009).

Both top-down and bottom-up approaches should be utilised if a national innovation system is to be successful. Intellegence gathering plays a role in this process. This may be linked to the setting up of Technological Innovation Systems where the creation of clusters could be considered (Carlsson and Stankiewicz, 1991).

There is no doubt that innovation is a complex and long drawn out process which does not always relate to technology. Fagerberg (2009), who holds this view, provides an interesting link between innovation and users, suppliers and competitors, and away from science and technology. Fagerberg finds that diffusion plays a key role in the innovation process and this should be considered when policy is drafted.

Due to the fact that most countries in the West are characterised by the presence of a large public sector, Fagerberg suggests that the public sector must play a key role in innovation diffusion in order for an innovation system to be effective. A tolerance for failure among both the general public and policy makers would play a key role in this scenario, since there is no guarantee of success for innovation and risk is always present. Technological innovations enable the process of diffusion due to there being so much dependence on communication by means of digital technology today.

Frustrated by what he saw as insufficient attention paid to innovation and that its academic status was not reflected in the executive world, James Dyson launched a £1.4 million professorship at Cambridge University in 2011.

Action

Increased competitiveness and efficiency

Innovation management in organisations is today a key priority as it adds value and increases competitiveness and profitability. Three concepts which motivate organisations to be innovative result from their seeking to be both effective (provide what is wanted) and efficient (with due regard to cost of provision):

1. The delivery of cheaper goods, services or products (less expensive and better quality for the consumer);
2. More efficient processes (fewer resources required);
3. Aesthetically pleasing goods or services (desirable image, user-friendliness for consumer, adds value to the product or service offered).

Organisations need to understand the motivation that lies behind the adoption of innovation management. The three rationales for organisational innovation listed above are linked. Increased efficiency is one key concept, as efficiency leads to reduced costs and possibly fewer stages in the process or a reduced number of components in a product.

Cost has always been an important consideration. This may be related to the cost of producing a product or service which is, in turn, related to the cost which the customer incurs when utilising or purchasing a product or service. Both efficiency and cost play a key role where competitive advantage and market share are concerned.

Porter and competitive advantage

M.E. Porter's views on competitive advantage (1980, 1985) are still influential today, even though they have been criticised for being over simplistic. Experience has, moreover, demonstrated that, contrary to what Porter claimed, it is today practically impossible for an organisation to build competitive advantage which cannot be copied by the competition, particularly due to lower-cost technology and employee mobility.

Innovative organisations may prefer to focus on developing a flexible workforce and on recognising opportunities to increase competitiveness as they arise. Sustainable competitive advantage is what Porter's ideas claim to offer, therefore revisiting Porter's ideas is relevant and organisations may find it valuable to recognise the importance of the three strategies which he identified:

- Cost leadership
- Differentiation
- Market segmentation (or focus).

Summary

Creativity is necessary but in itself is not sufficient to deliver innovation. Creativity can generate ideas but innovation is needed to process these into forms that can benefit people. Creativity and the potential for its expression is present in all people. Managing creatively in an organisation requires top management to commit to developing a climate and a culture which encourage the free flow of ideas. Similarly, innovation needs strong support from senior management to develop these ideas effectively and efficiently. The appointment of innovation champions greatly assists in this respect.

Innovation can be incremental or radical and most organisations will find that a bespoke mix of the two approaches is best. Potential innovations usually involve a subtle mix of product, process and service elements. Both hard and soft systems thinking is generally required and a major skill of innovation management is to combine these two approaches successfully, deal with process bottlenecks and actively develop and exploit relevant technology. The chapter has discussed issues concerning the practice of innovation processes in NGOs, charities, state funded entities and public organisations.

Discussion questions

1. What role does creativity play in the innovation process?
2. Briefly explain the role of an 'innovation champion'.
3. How can contributing staff be recognised?
4. Explain the difference between incremental and radical innovation.
5. What is meant by systems thinking? How does it assist personnel responsible for innovation management?
6. Name (and if you can, provide examples of) innovation initiatives in public sector organisations.
7. What are the three elements that form the basis of Barber's innovation policy?
8. Briefly critique Porter's beliefs about innovation.

Case exercise

ZIPCAR (www.zipcar.com) is an organisation that has adopted an innovative model of service. There are over 9,000 Zipcars available in different countries including the USA and UK. Its market is individuals, organisations and university campuses. ZIPCAR is used by people who generally use public transport or who do not wish to own a car. Reservations are made online or by means of a smart phone. Payment is based on time and mileage.

The service which ZIPCAR offers provides a convenient alternative to car ownership. It offers its members affordable access to vehicles for short-term use. After making a reservation, the member finds a ZIPCAR at a location close by and unlocks the vehicle with a Zipcard. This service is useful and appealing for those who wish to use a car for occasional trips, either to get away from the city or to transport bulky objects after a shopping spree. The car is later delivered to a convenient ZIPCAR location.

Task

Imagine that you have been asked to advise ZIPCAR on how they can apply innovation management to developing and introducing a bicycle service in a major European city of your choice.

References

Amabile, T.M. (1996) *Creativity in Context*, Boulder, CO, Westview Press.
Barber, J. (2009) 'Setting the scene', Position Paper for 6CP Workshop: New Economic Ground for Innovation Policy, Bilbao 13–14 September. http://www.6cp.net/downloads/Position%20papers%206CP%20Bilbao%2014%20September.pdf, accessed 20/02/11.
Carlsson, B. and Stankiewicz, R. (1991) 'On the nature, function, and composition of technological systems', *Journal of Evolutionary Economics*, Vol. 1, pp. 93–118.
Fagerberg, J. (2009) 'New foundations for innovation policy: Research directions'. http://www.6cp.net/downloads/Position%20papers%206CP%20Bilbao%2014%20September.pdf, accessed 20/02/11.
Forrester, J. (1958) 'Industrial dynamics – A major breakthrough for decision makers', *Harvard Business Review*, Vol. 35, No. 4, pp. 37–66.
Gurteen, D. (1998) 'Knowledge, creativity and innovation', *Journal of Knowledge Management*, September, Vol. 2, Number 1. http://www.gurteen.com/gurteen/gurteen.nsf/id/kci-article, accessed 01/12/10.
Ho, D. (2007) 'Research, innovation and knowledge management: The ICT factor', Commissioned paper for the UNESCO Forum on Higher Education, Research and Knowledge, Paris, UNESCO. http://portal.unesco.org/education/en/files/55811/12015104365Ho_final_versionEN.pdf/Ho_final%2BversionEN.pdf, accessed 13/04/12.
Jones-Bliss, B. and Kapetanovic, K. (2009) 'Keeping focus: The importance of innovation in an economic downturn', CBS Interactive Business Network Resource Library, October. http://findarticles.com/p/articles/mi_hb3147/is_8_47/ai_n41268107/?tag=rbxcra.2.a.44, accessed 21/12/11.
Leifer, R., McDermott, C.M., O'Connor, G.C., Peters, L.S., Rice, M.P. and Veryzer, R.W. (2000) *Radical Innovation: How Mature Companies can Outsmart Upstarts*, Boston, MA, Harvard Business School Press.
LSE Policy Group (2008) 'Innovation in government organisations, public sector agencies and public service NGOs', NESTA, UK. Innovation Index Working Paper, Draft, September. http://nestain-novation.ning.com/forum/topics/2132323:Topic:1669, accessed 22/12/11.
Mulgan, G.J. (2006) *Social Innovation*, London, Young Foundation.
Porter, M.E. (1980) *Competitive Strategy: Techniques for Analysing Industry and Competitors*, New York, Free Press.
Porter, M.E. (1985) *Competitive Advantage*, New York, Free Press.
Robinson, A.G. and Schroeder, D.M. (2004) *Ideas Are Free: How the Idea Revolution is Liberating People and Transforming Organizations*, San Francisco, Berrett-Koehler Publishers.
Senge, P. (1990) *The Fifth Discipline: The Art and Practice of the Learning Organisation*, London, Random House.

9 Support networks and systems

Observe how system into system runs.
(Alexander Pope, 'An Essay on Man', 1733)

Introduction

No organisation operates in isolation in today's global and competitive business environment as numerous actors or agents are involved in its innovation processes and activities (Drucker, 1999; Svetina and Prodan, 2008; Barber, 2009). This chapter discusses the importance of harnessing the brain power of human resources, suppliers, clients and stakeholders to enhance and improve the innovation process within an organisation. Flexible thinking, agility, intelligence and trust are key elements in this regard. The benefits of a holistic view of organisations validates the important role of networks, systems, interconnections and feedback loops in harnessing creativity and fostering excellence where organisational innovation is concerned.

Context

No organisation is an 'island'

Few people choose to live in isolation. Collaboration and cooperation are key skills which we are encouraged to develop from an early age. These skills enable us to exchange ideas, network with others, develop communities and support systems, and learn from others. No individual possesses all the necessary resources to be an expert on everything. Pioneers, gurus, geniuses and superstars usually collaborate with others in pursuit of success. New individual ideas are not often created in a vacuum. They often result from information, knowledge or experience obtained from an environment which is external to the individual or through a process of collaboration and co-creation.

The same applies to organisations. Although they may harness the ideas of their employees, there are other people and systems that interact with the organisation on a regular basis. They can provide a source of support, collaboration and co-creation where information, knowledge and ideas are concerned. The brainpower and ideas of suppliers, consumers and stakeholders involved or interested in the organisation (or its products or services), such as lead users, beta testers or networkers, should be harnessed as these could provide a valuable input. *Crowdsourcing* is a relatively recent concept and fosters the involvement of external talent in both ideation and innovation processes (see Section 9.3.3).

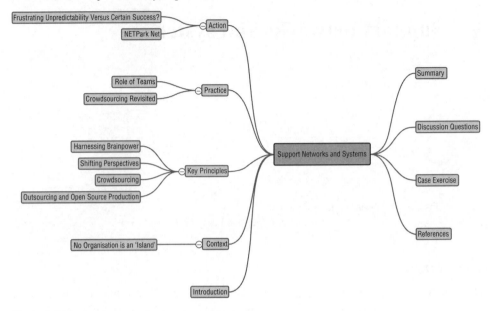

Figure 9.1 Exploring support networks and systems.

Key principles

Harnessing brainpower

Traditionally organisations tended to utilise the brainpower of their staff and R&I divisions. Following a trend which led organisations towards mergers, acquisitions and, where necessary, outsourcing or subcontracting, there now appears to be a strong tendency to move towards what is often known as 'customer centred innovation'. Other stakeholders such as user innovators, lead users and suppliers can also contribute to this process.

Human resources

Current trends should not result in the elimination of models which have been tested over time and proven to be successful. Sources which are internal to the organisation are readily available and employees at all levels should be involved in the ideation process. Issues related to motivation, communication, trust, reward and confidentiality need to be covered within the organisation for staff brainpower to be adequately harnessed. An idea management system (see Chapter 8) facilitates this process. Attention should also be paid to the climate and culture of the organisation (see Chapter 11) which play a key role in motivating employees to participate in the innovation process. Organisations need to tap into the creativity of their employees and to motivate them to use their creative skills and to contribute their ideas and suggestions to the right people.

Customers

Many organisations tend to rely heavily on internal human resources. External resources may, however, prove to be an excellent source for innovation and utilising this resource may prove to be faster and more cost-effective than relying solely on internal resources. Successful organisations that take innovation seriously consider customers to be an excellent source of ideas. This is especially the case when the market has moved on from the traditional 'supply–demand' model towards what is often known as 'customer centred innovation' in which it is imperative to meet customer perception of value solutions. A.G. Lafley, former CEO of Procter & Gamble (2000–2009), defined innovation as everyone's job, and he placed customers' needs at the forefront where innovation is concerned, transforming P&G into one of the world's most innovative organisations (Jones-Bliss and Kapetanovic, 2009). Von Hippel *et al.* (2011) claim that consumers should no longer be considered as 'passive recipients' of products.

Research conducted in three countries demonstrated that consumers tend to create and modify products. So organisations should collaborate with consumers and take their product innovations seriously, building on them and learning more about customer needs. The research, which discusses the adoption of user-generated innovation by organisations, concludes that 'product prototyping and initial testing done in-house by their [organisations'] own staff is very costly. Users bear those initial costs. Thus allowing companies to save money and raise their success ratio by focusing on product concepts that consumers have already prototyped and that are, to some extent, already market-tested' (von Hippel *et al.*, 2011).

Collaboration with 'user-innovators' is beneficial and it may lead to a virtuous cycle that could lower costs and lead to additional successful innovations if organisations offer user innovators 'the best innovation cost–reward ratio' (von Hippel *et al.*, 2011). This could motivate user-innovators who may be spoilt for choice of products on which to focus their efforts, as organisations may be in competition with one another to gain their attention and input.

Organisations can increase the attractiveness of their products for user-innovators in a number of ways and some of the most popular involve:

- Supporting user-innovation through the creation of interfaces including websites for the sharing of information and to facilitate co-creation;
- Exploring the 'wants' of user-innovators in exchange for their ideas being adopted by organisations;
- Acknowledging the use of user-innovations when they are commercially produced, that is, give the innovator credit (von Hippel *et al.*, 2011).

Attempts should be made to create a 'win–win' situation and this requires a clear communication strategy where the benefits and key motivating or reward factors are clearly outlined. Feedback and acknowledgement are essential and these constitute indispensible motivating factors for user-innovators and customers, whose contribution should be factored into any attempt to implement the innovation process.

Suppliers

Collaboration with suppliers too is a useful way to harness external brainpower and ideas. Good relationships with suppliers must be built and this involves trust-building and the creation of strategic networks and alliances. Organisations that effectively collaborate with suppliers and involve them in the ideation process can achieve increased competitive advantage. Suppliers are generally selected depending on their offering the lowest cost and the highest customer-perceived value. Supplier value could be increased due to supplier contribution to the innovation process, a contribution that could result in a win–win situation for both parties. Supply chains can be managed to achieve cost efficiency and high levels of customer-perceived value as well as playing an important role in ideation and innovation initiatives.

A win–win situation may be created through:

- The creation of trustful collaborative relationships;
- The involvement of suppliers in the innovation process, particularly where procurement and product development are concerned;
- The open communication and sharing of relevant information, particularly concerning planning, specifications and resources, in a timely manner;
- The awareness that collaboration acts to reduce costs and improve quality, which increases the competitiveness of both customers and suppliers and leads to increased business in a virtuous cycle.

The involvement of suppliers in product development has the potential to reap a number of benefits. Suppliers may contribute ideas concerning design which are valuable due to their expertise and knowledge of what is available or feasible, particularly from an engineering or technological perspective. The success of a new product/service market offering would result in increased productivity and profitability for both parties. Collaboration allows for the transfer of knowledge whereby suppliers may inform customers of new possibilities that may be launched on the market, which could be used to improve the market offering. Through effective and open communication practices, suppliers' innovation potential may be unleashed as they are aware of the needs of their customers and could work towards the satisfaction of those needs through the trustful collaborative relationship that has been established. This will, in turn, lead to increased collaboration and to more business opportunities.

Organisations may, however, hinder the contribution of suppliers to the innovation process if:

- They are too demanding when it comes to specifications which need to be met;
- They request urgent specifications with impossible deadlines;
- Their requests to suppliers to reduce costs are too demanding;
- They communicate conflicting objectives to suppliers.

The benefits of collaboration with suppliers include shorter product development cycles, lower costs and improved customer-perceived quality.

Idea scouts and idea connectors

'Idea scouts', who scan the web, and 'idea connectors', who are skilled networkers, play an important role by bringing new externally generated ideas to the attention of the right managers in organisations (Whelan *et al.*, 2011).

Successful organisations recognise the importance of idea brokers and identify the right people to take on these roles. Innovation brokerage can be successful and strategically implemented in organisations that foster open communication channels, seek high levels of trust and regularly scan the external environment. Such organisations also develop networks and cultivate networking skills. This fosters a cultivated and inquisitive mindset that is excited about ideation and innovation. Innovation brokerage may be successfully exploited through open innovation, through the creation of internal and external networks and through the creation of specific posts for idea scouts and idea connectors.

Shifting perspectives

Organisational innovation and change processes are key drivers of competitive advantage. An understanding of innovation in organisations incorporates perspectives that include issues such as institutional change and the related dynamics that emerge from this evolutionary process. This is not always a simple or straightforward process. Radical innovation, for example, brings elements of change into the organisation. Changes resulting from new management practices may affect the organisation's structure, the manner in which the product or service is processed or the climate or culture within the organisation. Radical innovations related to process or product usually require changes in the organisational structure.

Whereas structural stability was the norm in the past, in today's business environment innovation and change management require both flexibility and a more organic and agile organisational structure (Chen, 2008). Change may be required due to either internal or external forces or in most cases a combination of both (see Table 9.1).

Innovation may require the adoption of leading-edge technologies and processes as organisations strive to maintain their competitive edge. As a consequence, employees generally need to acquire new skills or knowledge to adopt the new technologies and processes. Current major challenges include the availability of low-cost production in other regions of the world and/or the emergence of new technologies which may displace existing organisations with a well established hold in a market. Today's globalised environment requires innovative organisations to deal with challenges from competition, low-cost production countries and/or new technology. These include:

- Changes to the organisational structure which allow for expansion into foreign markets;
- Changes to enable the ability to understand, operate in and adapt to different cultures;
- Changes related to increased political, social and ethical demands, expectations and standards.

Stacey's views on management and leadership provide valuable insights into the dynamics of change today. Drawing on the science of uncertainty and complexity, Stacey controversally maintains that 'management and leadership are not sciences but fundamentally social phenomena' (2009). According to Stacey, managers feel threatened by complexity and uncertainty which challenges their power and authority as it no longer allows them to control others or to deal with issues in an 'objective', 'rational' or 'linear' manner. This implies that problem solving or managing change can no longer be approached through the mechanistic application of methods. It is no longer appropriate to continue on the basis of 'business as usual'.

Table 9.1 Internal and external forces

Internal forces	External forces
Strategic forces	Competitive forces
Organisational development forces	Economic forces
Demographic and social forces	Legal and political forces
Ethical forces	Global forces

Source: Chen, 2008.

Managers cannot deal with change and control the future of their organisations independently of the dynamic processes and communicative interactions that surround them. Current assumptions need to be challenged, including those which relate to cause and effect. Causality is 'transformative', as the future is constructed through a process of local interaction. This process maintains and transforms individual and collective identities and ideologies. It shifts the focus of power relations that play a key role, where organisational change is concerned, to a more collective level. Change, according to Stacey, is not a result of managers' individual decisions, but of this dynamic communicative process. Managing change, which is a complex process of transformation, therefore requires challenging current assumptions, seeking a better understanding of communicative interaction and its relation to the emergent organisational outcomes.

Crowdsourcing

Crowdsourcing is a term coined by Howe in 2006 in *Wired Magazine* and has become both a buzz word and a concept often applied by innovative organisations to obtain ideas from external sources (Howe, 2006). Toyota's well known logo, which consists of three interlocked oval shapes, is the result of a crowdsourcing competition in 1936. The iconic Sydney Opera House is the result of another crowdsourcing competition (in 1955). Following a competition, Crash the Super Bowl, launched by Doritos and PepsiMAX in February 2011, six winning adverts were each awarded a substantial amount of money. These adverts were broadcast during the USA's Super Bowl event. Consumers voted for four of the six adverts, while executives from Doritos and PepsiMAX each selected an additional winner to represent their brands. New digital media has widely extended the possibilities which crowdsourcing offers to both individuals and organisations. Some well known examples of successful crowdsourcing include Wikipedia, iStockphoto, Digg, Threadless and other initiatives that use collective resources through networks. This process is sometimes referred to as 'collective intelligence'.

Crowdsourcing has often been criticised, particularly when it targets non-experts or people who are not well versed in particular topics, as it utilises the input of anyone who may be motivated to contribute ideas related to a particular issue, task, problem or question. There is debate, moreover, about whether the 'crowds' in crowdsourcing can actually exhibit 'wisdom'. There has been criticism, for example, concerning the accuracy of Wikipedia or other user-generated content on the internet.

Some advantages of crowdsourcing include the following:

- Low cost;
- Payment is often by results or there may be none at all;
- Rapid process with relatively fast results;
- Possibility to tap extensive talent – a broader range than exists in one organisation;
- Input involves tapping into potential or actual customers' needs, desires or visions;
- Brand building through a sense of collaboration;
- Willingness of people to participate and to share ideas, locally and even more, globally;
- Satisfaction obtained through working with a relatively large number of people;
- Eliminates financial barriers to participation when organised online;
- Anonymity (when applicable) or 'remote' participation increases depth of participation as people tend to reveal more when participating remotely and not face-to-face;

- May generate better results than if outsourced or internally commissioned;
- Allows for a broad range of problems related to a variety of disciplines;
- Customer support – allows for peer-to-peer collaboration and for the resolving of customers' problems by other customers.

Some of the disadvantages of crowdsourcing include the following:

- Results may not always be of good quality;
- Crowdsourcing may be used to exploit others by sourcing low cost or free labour;
- Large-scale projects may be difficult to manage and time consuming;
- Some crowdsourced projects may require additional input and therefore incur added costs;
- Risk of too few participants, lack of interest or motivation;
- Language barriers;
- Lack of trust due to there being no contracts or non-disclosure agreements;
- Possibility of malicious or unethical input by participants.

New digital technology and the possibilities it offers for communities to form and to collaborate has provided new opportunities for crowdsourcing. Large organisations often use web-based platforms to solve problems and generate new ideas. P&G connect + develop is a web-based open innovation platform where the needs and assets of the organisation are communicated to 'the crowd' who are afforded the possibility of uploading their innovation. The site claims that 'more than 50 percent of product initiatives at Procter & Gamble involve significant collaboration with outside innovators' (https://secure3.verticali.net/pg-connection-portal/ctx/noauth/PortalHome.do). Threadless, a web-based organisation that produces T-shirts, employs no designers and depends entirely on crowdsourcing to create its products. These are always sold out as the T-shirts reflect precisely what the organisation's customers would like to purchase.

Outsourcing and open source production

Outsourcing is to be distinguished from crowdsourcing. The latter makes use of an undefined public (sometimes called 'the wisdom of the crowd'), while the former is allocated to a specific individual or organisation. Open source production is different from crowdsourcing and is a collaborative activity in which a group of people with similar interests work together to develop and to promote public access to an end product. This allows anyone to contribute, to build on what has already been constructed and to modify, copy or redistribute the product (or process) as they wish. Examples include open source software (such as Linux and Ubuntu), open source teaching (or instruction) and open source publishing (such as DEMOS publications).

Practice

The role of teams

Whilst ideas can be generated by individuals working alone, generally speaking, it is best to accomplish this in groups. Once ideas have been gathered and sorted into those which seem to be most appropriate in relation to the problem stated, the ideation phase morphs into the innovation action phase. This may require setting up a project management or project implementation team. The manner in which teams function has a profound effect on the performance of an organisation, particularly where innovation is concerned. Some teams may be officially set up to meet a particular goal or objective, others may be a more informal grouping of people who need to collaborate with each other in order to be effective. The manner in which people within organisations act, interact, network and function, as part of a formal or informal team, is of crucial importance to innovation management.

Teams may be temporary or permanent and team meetings may be either face-to-face or virtual. New technology which includes tools such as virtual world platforms, video conferencing or simple text-based 'chat' have made it possible to harness the creativity of virtual teams. A virtual mode of interaction for teams saves time, money and other resources such as a physical working space for a team to meet. It also allows for the possibility of team members to work from locations which suit them – such as at home or while travelling – due to the widespread diffusion of broadband internet access. This phenomenon has given rise to the production of a plethora of lightweight electronic devices such as the iPad and other tablets.

There are obvious advantages to utilising virtual teams, such as the possibility of engaging experts for the task, regardless of their geographical location. Attention should be paid to the manner in which the virtual relationship is assessed, as it may, for example, lack a physical image and this may be replaced with a graphical image or an avatar. When a team conducts virtual meetings, the physical characteristics of each individual are played down and although it is not always easy to deal with people when there are no non-verbal signals, more attention may be focused on the actual messages which are communicated. An individual's 'image' may sometimes prove to be 'distracting' in real-life situations.

A number of questions arise with virtual communication and virtual team building which it is necessary to address in organisations that utilise 'teleworkers'. Some managers may be uncomfortable with managing people who they do not meet on a regular basis or they may not possess the skills required to do so. Trust is another issue to be considered. Efficiency and effective supervision may raise further concerns. These may all be overcome through training to develop skills in building virtual relationships and in learning how to motivate people through regular communication and effective feedback mechanisms.

Online meetings may prove to be a great vehicle for creating team spirit amongst people at a virtual level. Although the means at the manager's disposal may vary, once trust and effective communication strategies have been established, the process need not vary very much from regular face-to-face relationship building. Young people in particular, such as Gen Y, are even more effective at creating such strategies due to their having been born into the digital age and their constant use of platforms such as social networking sites and chat to communicate with family, friends and acquaintances. This is one reason why they are sometimes referred to as 'digital natives'.

Consideration should, when feasible, be given to the composition of a team with a view to including a variety of personalities, attributes and skills to enable it to function in an optimal manner. Teams with diverse attributes and backgrounds are reputed to possess more potential for synergy. This implies that their output could possibly be greater than the sum of their parts.

Team leadership is another key concept. Some teams require assigned leaders who mentor and guide team members. Others may possess a more informal structure, although individual personalities may function in such a way as to enable particular leadership skills to emerge. Roles in teams may be strategically assigned to each individual member or they may be informally assumed. When tasks are assigned according to individual personality traits and strengths, each member may be in a better position to contribute and individual strengths may be developed that boost team performance.

Both the context within which the team operates and the tasks it is assigned to complete influence the manner in which the team operates. A relationship management style and an acknowledgement that individual behaviour and participation depend on team dynamics are essential for a team to achieve a successful outcome.

Conflict in teams

Conflict and tension may arise in teams, particularly in circumstances when strong personalities clash, when communication amongst team members is ineffective or when tasks assigned to individual team members are not evenly distributed, with some team members taking on the attitude of 'free-riders'. Team leaders should be constantly aware of this possibility and pay attention to resolving such conflicts and to eliminating tension by means of empathy, listening skills and democratic participation.

Since conflict may arise as a result of divergent opinions, attitudes or decisions, team members may be trained in skills such as the Six Thinking Hats (de Bono, 2009) which allow for 'parallel thinking', a method which may be used for planning, decision making, generating ideas and conflict resolution. Training in mediation or in conflict resolution develops increased acceptance of individual differences, together with an appreciation of the richness of divergent opinions and personalities. At times a decision to reach a compromise may be taken, at others negotiation skills may be sufficient for the conflict to be resolved.

The team's perception of conflict may be challenged and shifted from a threat to an opportunity. Constructive conflict may give rise to a healthy competitive climate with outcomes which may surpass initial expectations. Although attaining a balance between resolving conflict and drawing out the positive competitive elements which may arise as a result of conflict is not a simple task, it is important for team members to recognise and deal with any destructive elements which may arise and to appreciate, respect and understand the value of diverse perspectives. Although conflict often arises as a result of differences of opinion, values or attitudes, diversity in the manner in which a team is constituted is one of the main factors which adds value to teams and which may lead to the successful attainment of the assigned team goals.

Crowdsourcing revisited

After gaining steady attention in the business press over the past few years, crowdsourcing found itself catapulted onto the front pages when the UK's new coalition government turned to the online community for ideas about its future programme. It now seems to be reaching some kind of critical mass: from reports that Microsoft crowdsourced the making of Office 2010, to the UK Prime Minister asking civil servants for money-saving ideas via the Government's Spending Challenge.

As we have seen, one of the first businesses to acknowledge the potential of crowdsourcing was Procter & Gamble, with CEO Alan Lafley announcing in 2000 that he wanted more than half of the company's innovation to come from outside of the organisation – a remarkable challenge given that this is an organisation with $80bn of revenue and 7,000 researchers, but one that has been achieved via a variety of crowdsourcing mechanisms including technology brokers who actively go out and look for ideas.

IBM has put similar emphasis on crowdsourcing, despite being home to 3,000 researchers and six Nobel Prize winners. Its alphaWorks initiative, for instance, is used as an alternative to beta testing, releasing products while they are still in development to a select community of customers who can play with them and provide feedback, involving these customers in the innovation process. Dell's IdeaStorm is another well documented success, enabling customers to have input into the innovation process – most notably when Dell released a Linux-based laptop due to the weight of demand from IdeaStorm.

Essential crowdsourcing tools

Crowdsourcing gurus Dawson and Bynghall (2011) have highlighted six tools to boost organisational innovations:

1. *Distributed innovation platforms.* Platforms to support innovation processes that cross organisational boundaries (or take place entirely outside an organisation).
2. *Idea platforms.* Used within a company context to gather, filter and source ideas. Examples include web app IdeaScale and mystarbucksidea.com.
3. *Innovation prizes.* Innovation prizes are challenges designed to catalyse new thinking and ingenuity, such as Electrolux's Design Lab.
4. *Content markets.* Content markets are platforms where people submit their content for people to purchase. Threadless, for instance, allows people to submit designs for T-shirts, with the community voting for the best ones to be made into actual T-shirts which can then be ordered.
5. *Prediction markets.* Prediction markets bring together many opinions to predict the future, often based on 'stockmarket-type' mechanisms, which provide a value of a particular prediction. Google uses prediction markets, using its employees to predict which of its innovations and new projects are most likely to be successful.
6. *Competition platforms.* Provide expertise in areas such as fashion and graphic design, domain name ideas, company names and viral marketing.

In a world driven by innovation, those companies that can successfully tap the power of crowds to drive 'open innovation' will have an immense advantage over those that rely on internal ideas and skills. Dell, Starbucks, Procter & Gamble, Google and Netflix are among the many leaders that have embraced innovation from crowds.

Action

Frustrating unpredictability versus certain success?

Einstein is said to have claimed that 'creativity is 99 per cent perspiration and one per cent inspiration'. This statement could be interpreted in many ways, one implication being that creativity may lead to unpredictability and to frustration. The failure rate of start-up enterprises is high. Repeated failure could lead to frustration. Innovations are not always successful. Since innovation involves change, the process may instigate fear and a sense of frustrating unpredictability. To be successful organisations need to recognise opportunities and to build their capabilities to make the pursuit of growth through innovation more predictable.

Some managers perceive innovation as a process which involves frustrating unpredictability as it involves a great deal of time and financial investment, and the quality of ideas generated may not always be as good as expected. Innovation may prove to be a disruptive process. Christensen (2003) coined the phrase 'disruptive innovation' to describe a process in which a product or service emerges and displaces established competitors. Examples include smart phones and mobile phones displacing fixed line telephony, music and movie download processes replacing CDs and DVDs, online bookstores and retail websites displacing brick and mortar retail outlets and personal computers (tablets and laptops) displacing other media devices including television. Is it possible to predict a demand for something new? Skibsted and Hansen (2011) put forward the pessimistic and controversial claim that 'The demand for something fundamentally new is completely unpredictable'. Their ideas, which are mainly related to branding and design, go against all the recommendations that this chapter proposes, that is, the usefulness of external sources, including customers, lead users and suppliers, for successful innovation.

One way to deal with this, according to Skibsted and Hansen, is to hire the most creative people, to constantly launch new products (some of which may 'stick') and to speed up time to market. They view successful creativity and innovation as a chaotic, unpredictable and frustrating process which is 'the result of extraordinary efforts and visions of a few extremely talented people'. Inspiration, in their view, is an individual experience, and user-led innovation would prove to be boring for creatives within the organisation, does not provide for radical innovation and only leads to more of the same rather than to differentiation from the products of competitors.

It is unfortunate that the arguments which they put forward are based on a number of assumptions which are not justified or on statements which appear to be misguided such as 'The user-centered process is created as linear rational process for innovation and that's why it's so popular among managers'. User-centred processes may be linear and rational, but they do not necessarily have to be that way, as organisations such as Procter & Gamble and InnoCentive, an online open innovation, crowdsourcing and innovation brokerage facility, have demonstrated.

Successful user-generated innovation is today visible in a number of areas, some examples of which have been discussed in the previous sections. Other examples include:

- The creation of applications for smart phones and tablets;
- The use of beta testers and open source for software development;
- Downloading music and movies;
- Lego's involving its lead customers in a Mindstorms User Panel for a year to co-design the next generation Mindstorms NXT product;
- CNN iReport which solicits users to generate content and to upload their photos, videos and stories.

Organisations should identify the communities, systems and support networks with which they are involved and use their brainpower as a force to proactively plan for change. They should also identify and utilise internal creative talent. Organisations should view change with optimism as an opportunity. In this way they will manage planned change and innovation to achieve strategic and competitive advantage with a greater probability of success leading to profitable growth.

NETPark Net

NETPark Net in the UK currently has 294 businesses and 444 members collaborating via 19,458 activities in 13 groups. The NETPark opportunities system helps businesses source profitable tenders and new customer opportunities whether they are a growing SMEs, large, blue-chip companies or public bodies. Through the NETPark Net innovation support network and its online platform a virtual science park is available to help companies accelerate growth, improve productivity and become more innovative.

Summary

In today's globalized economy, where supply chains are distributed all around the globe and specialized research institutions are scattered in numerous locations, there is no reason to believe that a firm will find the precise knowledge needed in its innovation process within the local environment. Accordingly, firms search for the necessary knowledge elsewhere and often look for appropriate innovation partners irrespective of the geographic space.

(Svetina & Prodan, 2008)

Discussion questions

1. Why are organisations increasingly looking externally for innovative ideas?
2. How are organisations seeking to improve the attractiveness of their products for user-innovators?
3. How might 'win–win' situations be created with suppliers?
4. What do 'idea scouts' and 'idea connectors' do?
5. What are the major forces responsible for internal and external change?
6. What is crowdsourcing and what are its major advantages?
7. 'Virtual teams are always better for progressing innovations'. Discuss.

Case exercise

PSL Limited has created a formulation that offers a range of benefits, not just as a sports recovery drink but potentially as a platform for other nutraceutical opportunities. The unique drink not only reduces the 'sugar drop' experienced by athletes and commonly described as 'hitting the wall', but the base that's been developed can be used as the foundation for a range of different products that can provide health benefits for the heart, joints and other parts of the body. The company has now completed successful pilot studies of fuelSAQ™ and tested the product using professional sports people and elite athletes, under the direction of the world-renowned sports training company, SAQ International Limited.

Professional cricketers were among those who tested the product, and the results showed that their fatigue was reduced over several hours by between 21 and 49 per cent in tests, when compared to a placebo ('dummy') drink. In addition energy levels were maintained over a long period when consuming fuelSAQ™. PSL and and SAQ will now use the results and positive feedback from these and other athletes who have trialled the product, to support promotion of fuelSAQ™ to third parties via a distribution, acquisition or out-licensing deal, or to market the drink directly through its own niche channels, including online via www.fuelSAQ.com.

The unique selling point of the product, compared to currently available sports drinks, is its multicomponent formulation that provides several benefits in a single serving, according to Michael Horton, PSL's managing director. The drink contains a rapid-acting stimulant and a slow release carbohydrate component which has a longer-lasting energy profile compared to conventional sugars and which also avoids spikes in plasma insulin.

The formulation also comprises a protein hydrolysate that has been demonstrated in clinical trials to accelerate recovery from exercise and increase physical performance. There is a potential market of around 27 million people in the UK who regularly buy health and sports drinks to help them through busy schedules and fitness regimes. The global potential for this product is huge.

Task

Imagine that PSL have retained you as a consultant and have asked you to prepare a short memo that clearly advises the company how to harness crowdsourcing to fully exploit the global potential for their innovative sports recovery drink.

References

Barber, J. (2009) 'Setting the scene', Position Paper for 6CP Workshop: New Economic Ground for Innovation Policy, Bilbao 13–14 September. http://www.6cp.net/downloads/Position%20papers%206CP%20Bilbao%2014%20September.pdf, accessed 20/12/11.

Chen, M. (2008) 'Organisational change and innovation', *Amateur Management Review*, 1 September. http://amrjournal.blogspot.com/2008/09/organisational-change-and-innovation.html, accessed 26/12/11.

Christensen, C.M. (2003) *The Innovator's Dilemma: The Revolutionary Book that Will Change the Way You Do Business*, London, Harper Paperbacks.

Dawson, R.C. and Bynghall, S. (2011) *Getting Results from Crowds: The Definitive Guide To Using Crowd Sourcing to Grow Your business*, San Francisco, Advanced Human Technologies. See also http://rossdawson.com/

de Bono, E. (2009) *Six Thinking Hats*, London, Penguin Books.

Drucker, P.F. (1999) *Management: Tasks, Responsibilities, Practices*, London, Taylor & Francis.

Howe, J. (2006) 'The rise of crowdsourcing', *Wired Magazine*, June, Issue 14. http://www.wired.com/wired/archive/14.06/crowds.html, accessed 30/11/11.

Jones-Bliss, B. and Kapetanovic, K. (2009) 'Keeping focus: The importance of innovation in an economic downturn', *CBS Interactive Business Network Resource Library*, October. http://findarticles.com/p/articles/mi_hb3147/is_8_47/ai_n41268107/?tag=rbxcra.2.a.44, accessed 26/12/11.

Skibsted, J.M. and Hansen, R.B. (2011) 'User-led innovation can't create breakthroughs: Just ask Apple and Ikea', http://www.fastcodesign.com/1663220/user-led-innovation-cant-create-breakthroughs-just-ask-apple-and-ikea, accessed 02/01/12.

Stacey, R.D. (2009) *Complexity and Organizational Reality*, London, Routledge.

Svetina, A.C. and Prodan, I. (2008) 'How internal and external sources of knowledge contribute to firms' innovation performance', *Managing Global Transitions*, Fall, Vol. 6, Issue 3, pp. 277–99.

von Hippel, E., Ogawa, S. and de Jong, J.P.J. (2011) 'The age of the consumer-innovator', *MIT Sloan Management Review*, 2 September. http://sloanreview.mit.edu/the-magazine/2011-fall/53105/the-age-of-the-consumer-innovator/, accessed 26/12/11.

Whelan, E., Parise, S., de Valk, J. and Aalbers, R. (2011) 'Creating employee networks that deliver open innovation', *MIT Sloan Management Review*, September. http://sloanreview.mit.edu/the-magazine/2011-fall/53108/creating-employee-networks-that-deliver-open-innovation/, accessed 26/12/11.

Websites

Crowdsourcing – Meetup – a resource for mobilising crowds and organising events and meetings: http://www.meetup.com/

DEMOS publications: http://www.demos.co.uk/publications
digg: http://digg.com/
Innocentive: http://www.innocentive.com
iStockphoto: http://www.istockphoto.com/
KTM second life ideation quest: http://www.youtube.com/watch?v=urIrLzFxPz0
Linux: https://www.linux.com
P&G connect + develop: https://secure3.verticali.net/pg-connection-portal/ctx/noauth/PortalHome.do
Systems Thinking, an introduction: http://www.systems-thinking.org/intst/int.htm
Systems Thinking, Systems Tools and Chaos Theory: http://managementhelp.org/systems/index.htm#anchor234567
Threadless: http://www.threadless.com/
Ubuntu: www.ubuntu.com
Wikipedia: http://en.wikipedia.org/wiki/Main_Page

10 Applied innovation in organisations

He that will not apply new remedies must expect new evils; for time is the greatest innovator.

(Francis Bacon)

Through the unknown we will find the new.

(Charles Baudelaire, *Les Fleurs du Mal*, 1857)

Introduction

It is only through the efficient and effective management of innovation that the creative ideas which are generated and harnessed from internal and external sources may be implemented when found to be feasible and valuable. Management play a key role in the successful application of the innovation process. This chapter discusses the manner in which innovation may be applied in organisations with different structures. It explores the advantages and disadvantages of open source applications, comparing them to proprietary solutions such as patents, copyright and intellectual property (IP). The chapter provides a number of models which organisations could utilise to increase their potential for applied innovation. It concludes with a discussion on how the transfer of knowledge and technology is achieved, drawing out the implications related to innovation that arise from this process.

Context

The innovation process

The word *innovation* is derived from the Latin *innovare* which translates as 'to make new, alter' and defined by the *Concise Oxford Dictionary* as being concerned with bringing in new methods and ideas. These can be absolutely new in the sense that they have never been aired or practised before or new to a particular organisation. The innovation can refer to a new system, device, policy, programme or customer-perceived value offering (product/ service). Innovation is a key driver for added value, increased competitiveness, growth and profitability. The successful and effective application of an innovation process involves designing and cultivating a climate and culture that are conducive to innovation (see Chapter 11).

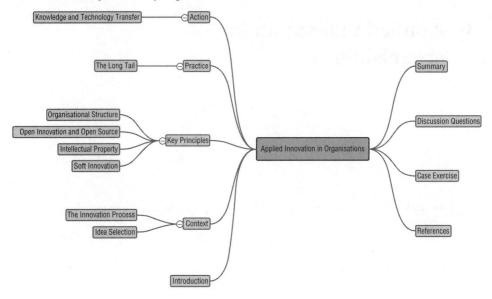

Figure 10.1 Applying innovation in organisations.

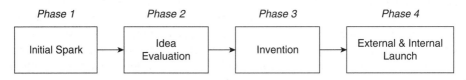

Figure 10.2 The innovation process phases.
          Source: M.R.V. Goodman, Durham University.

Phase 1: the initial spark of creative activity

Phase 1 of an innovation process features two inspirational creative acts:

1. Generation of ideas.
2. Selection of the best idea/s to progress to address either a clearly expressed need, for example a transparent baby's potty to answer every parent's question – 'have you been yet?' Or the sudden realisation that an idea generated by chance is the perfect answer to a problem, as in, for example, the case of non-drip paint.

Phase 2: idea evaluation

Phase 2 is concerned with testing a selected idea to decide whether it is advisable to invest more time and resources to develop it further into a proposal. The key questions are:

*   *Effectiveness* – does the idea meet a need for which there is or is likely to be a demand?
*   *Relevance* – does the idea lie within the compass of the company or organisational strategy?
*   *Know-how* – does the idea fit the company/organisation's business and technical competencies?

- *Efficiency* – is it sensible for the organisation to invest resources to further develop the idea and is it likely to offer a competitive advantage?

If the answers to these questions are positive the innovation process enters Phase 3.

Phase 3: invention

Phase 3 is concerned with developing the selected idea into a form that can be implemented, that is, a new customer-perceived value package offered to pre-researched customers or introduced within the parent organisation – for example a new administrative procedure.

Phase 4: external and internal launch

This phase covers the external introduction of the fully developed idea, that is, new product roll out. In the case of internal introductions the idea is practically adopted.

Phase 1 is essentially about the practical expression of creativity. Phases 2, 3 and 4 are essentially about innovation. Creativity also plays a critical part as the idea progresses from an original spark to a final entity.

Idea selection

Sometimes successful innovations result from serendipity as an organisation hits the jackpot with little regard to sound practice. This is said to have been the case with the decision to launch the original Walkman. The Sony CEO had a hunch it was a winner. In most cases however, it is prudent to pay considerable attention to picking the right ideas to move into the innovation phases. Two well-known filter models are The Idea Funnel and Stage-Gate systems.

The Idea Funnel

Ideas that emerge successfully from Phase 1 should be screened to reveal those with the greatest potential and with an acceptable degree of risk. It may sound negative at first but it is sensible policy for organisations to isolate and kill all the ideas that are unlikely to pass all

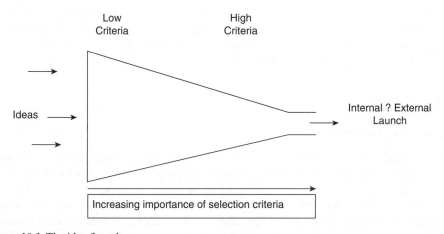

Figure 10.3 The idea funnel.
      Source: M.R.V. Goodman, Durham University.

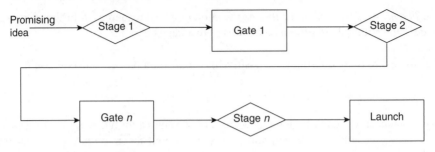

Figure 10.4 A simple Stage-Gate system.
            Source: M.R.V. Goodman, Durham University.

the innovation phases. Though sometimes brutal this releases time and resources for the promising ideas.

The Idea Funnel has a wide entrance to receive ideas that successfully complete *Phase 1*. The ideas are then subjected to periodic test criteria and only those that pass move toward the neck of the funnel, toward *Phase 4* launch programmes. The Idea Funnel is perhaps a simple model however – there is a danger that it could result in many embarrassing and/or expensive innovation failures as the model is critically dependent on the quality of the decisions taken at each check-point in the funnel.

Stage-Gate model

The model (after Grönlund *et al.*, 2010) which was traditionally applied in manufacturing industries, segments the innovation process into sequential stages. The model consists of an alternating series of development periods and assessment 'gates' that evaluate the chances of an idea passing through all four phases of an innovation programme to final implementation. Some have claimed that the model is too simplistic and linear for today's business environment. The Idea Funnel and Stage-Gate models are only as good as the decisions that are made (Sethi and Iqbal, 2008). Use of modern systems thinking can greatly strengthen the quality of the 'go, no-go' decision deliberations as the basic model does enable the incorporation of IT and dynamic elements, such as learning, strategy, iteration, feedback, agility, flexibility and adjustments. Metrics for evaluation, agility, flexibility, feedback and adjustment should and can be incorporated into the innovation process regardless of the model which is selected. The successful application of an innovation process builds on the unique capabilities of an organisation and on its strengths.

Key principles

Organisational structure

Organisational innovation occurs as a result of the interaction between strategy and culture. Culture leads to stability and continuity whilst strategy is necessary to achieve innovative direction and radical change. The current structure of any organisation evolves from the dynamism exerted by a number of forces. These include its history, strategy, diversity of products (or services), logistics and operational design. When considering changes to the organisational structure, top management should keep in mind that drastic changes should not be made to the structure of an organisation unless they are the result of a well considered management-of-change programme. Managers should first consider fostering incremental structures that can be adapted into the existing structure and which facilitate the innovation process.

Attention should be paid to issues discussed in Chapter 9 – no organisation is an 'island' and organisations operate within systems and communities. This implies that organisations should be viewed from a holistic perspective – as social systems that act and interact with both internal and external forces. Environmental and social factors, together with organisational factors, need to be taken into account when considering the possibility of incremental or radical changes. Organisational culture and climate are crucial intervening variables that affect any interaction between strategy and structure.

The contextual disturbances in the business world since the 1990s, driven by new technologies, fast-changing markets, global competition and financial crises (see Chapter 1), have provided the stimulus for many organisations to change their shape. The traditional hierarchical and functional command-and-control model was too inflexible to meet the new challenges facing business. Hierarchies have often spawned large costs rather than improved innovative performance. In a fast-changing business world they tend to slow down decision making as every major decision has to be filtered through the organisational hierarchy. The obvious conclusion drawn by many organisations is that hierarchical layers need to be reduced and companies that strongly encourage innovation (such as 3M) have evolved a flatter shape and have placed the onus on project teams and cross functional working. IT has been and continues to be a major force as it enable managers to communicate as never before.

Although various types of organisational structure may be identified, a distinction is generally made between mechanistic and organic structures. The former generally operate under stable conditions in a rigid manner through a centralised control system. Authority is exercised in a strictly hierarchial manner. The latter are more agile, flexible, adaptable and loosely defined, with increased delegation of decision making. Flat organisations possess fewer hierarchial levels and are generally preferred as communication flows more easily from one level to another and across sections, departments or divisions (vertically and horizontally – e.g. Morning Star and Semco cases, see Chapter 6, Section 6.8 and Chapter 14, Section 14.8, respectively). Flat organisations may operate either organically or mechanically. In the latter case, they may be subject to strict levels of authority and control which may restrict the emergence of the right climate for innovation.

Some of the factors that should be considered when examining whether the structure of an organisation is conducive to innovation include:

- A two-way flow of information and communication, both vertically (from one level to the next) and horizontally (between individuals, teams, sections, departments and divisions);
- The allocation of a specific person (or persons) or a department (or team) in large organisations, whose task it is to deal with matters related to idea generation, motivation, feedback, assessment, reward, decision making and the management of the innovation process (some large organisations appoint a Director of Innovation at the top level of the hierarchy);
- A two-way flow of information and communication from the person (team or department) that is assigned the tasks outlined in the previous factor and key decision makers who have the authority to give the green light to ideas selected for implementation;

- The creation of networks or links to sources external to the organisation for the harnessing of ideas and the exploration of possibilities concerning collaboration or outsourcing;
- The creation of awareness of the importance of external sources for idea generation and collaboration throughout the organisation, with particular focus on sustaining customer satisfaction and customer retention, and attention being directed to the interface between the organisation and relevant external stakeholders;
- The awareness that R&I is relevant in all sections, departments or business units and that all employees, regardless of their level within the organisation, should be involved in this process;
- The fostering of agility which allows for the setting up of teams which collaborate in new product development and in implementing new products or services;
- Fluidity among the sections, departments or divisions to avoid possible 'silos' and to create awareness of the importance of each organisational function, thus avoiding the possibility of any one section, department or division pulling away from the rest to foster its own interests, as opposed to the interests of the organisation as a whole.

Today's organisations having to deal with a rapid rate of change may require the creation of an interchangeable and flexible structure which combines both stability and agility. It may be necessary for organisations to shift their structure from one form to another at different stages of the innovation process. Adaptability and flexibility are generally required at the idea-generation stage, while stability is generally required at the implementation stage.

Organisation performance is related to several factors, including the organisation's mission, vision, strategy and innovation orientation. An innovation orientation describes an organisation's degree of innovativeness. Research has shown that an innovation orientation is related to overall organisational performance (Dobni, 2010). High innovating firms are at the top of the league and provide excellent customer satisfaction, bottom line growth and profitability. There is a corresponding positive relationship between return on investment and innovation orientation. Organisations possessing low innovation orientations have lower performance and enterprise values.

Open innovation and open source

The adoption of a successful innovation process also involves the cultivation of trust, the smooth flow of communication and collaboration with external sources. Outsiders such as customers, suppliers, networks and other stakeholders are all useful sources of new ideas. The discussion about consequences (especially the interfirm cooperation in R&I) dates back at least to the 1960s. *Open innovation* is a term promoted by Chesbrough (2003), who defined it as 'a paradigm that assumes that firms can and should use external ideas as well as internal ideas, and internal and external paths to market, as the firms look to advance their technology'. The outcomes that emerge from the adoption of open innovation may be proprietary and protected by means of copyright or patents (see Section 10.3.3), or they may be released into the public domain.

There is a distinction to be made between open source and open innovation, although the two terms are not mutually exclusive. As the discussion on IBM later in this chapter demonstrates, organisations may, for various reasons, decide to donate their patents to an open source community. *Open source* is a term which refers to software development which is redistributed freely. It may be commercialised or it may be combined with proprietary knowledge. Concepts that are central to open source software include:

- Elements of interaction may occur between open source software and proprietary software;
- Organisations that focus on proprietary software often contribute to open source development;
- Open source software and proprietary software are not mutually exclusive, they should be viewed as a continuum.

Organisations that focus on technology may benefit from the use of open source software. This has the potential to act as an intermediary for innovation through collaboration with open source software development communities. It is a particularly effective driver of innovation since software is 'intangible', it may be infinitely reproduced (at no additional expense) and it is freely shared and available at no cost.

The terms 'the cathedral and the bazaar' are sometimes used to describe the process through which software is developed (Raymond, 2001). The bazaar is a metaphor used to describe the open source software approach, while the cathedral represents the traditional method where a group of experts is assigned the task of designing and developing software.

The impact of open source software on economic development and the resulting implications for management include the following considerations:

- The adoption of a mix of open and proprietary software varies depending on the organisation's context and circumstances, with larger organisations more likely to engage (but not to specialise) in open source activity than smaller organisations.
- A cost–benefit analysis should be conducted when considering the costs and benefits of open source and proprietary software.
- The national level of economic development has an effect on the initial cost of the software and on costs that involve technology switching, interoperability, support and upgrades.
- Users of software tend to mix open source and proprietary software, since one product is not likely to satisfy all users. Before choices are made, target markets should be identified, together with potential consumer needs.

IBM is one example of a large organisation that combines open source and proprietary software. In 2005, IBM granted the use of 500 patents to open source software developers (McDougall, 2005). However, it claimed that it would enforce other patents which it had registered, which provided it with a competitive advantage. The intention behind this release was to create a 'patent commons' through which software developers could access code and programming techniques. IBM would potentially be in a position to build on the innovations which emerged from the open source software community.

It is interesting to note the motivating factors behind open source software development. This is generally conducted by individual programmers on a voluntary basis with no financial benefits for those involved. The motivating factors include:

- Peer recognition;
- Satisfaction obtained from achieving success through engagement with challenging tasks;

- Career benefits, such as being 'head-hunted';
- Access to research funds for software development.

The motivating factors are generally related to intrinsic or long-term benefits. Due to the fact that immediate financial reward is not applicable to open source software development, one requirement for success and survival is a low implementation cost, particularly when it competes with proprietary software. The competition between Windows and Ubuntu, two operating systems, are an example of this. The former is a proprietary system, the latter came about as a result of open source software development.

Open source software development operates in a similar way to crowdsourcing (see Chapter 9, Section 9.3.3). The main difference is that the crowd involved in open source software development consists of a dedicated community of volunteers who are not interested in financial gain, who are experts in a particular area, and who are willing to openly share the results of their efforts.

Proprietary knowledge is generally protected by copyright and patents. Both open source and proprietary software development are important for technological innovation. Collaboration (through the adoption or combination of both models) and competition (to attain a large user-base and market) result in an increase in investment (time and effort on the one part, and financial investment on the other) and to the potential of radical innovation.

Collaboration with open source software communities presents an interesting example of how open innovation can transform technology. It demonstrates the manner in which organisations can avail themselves of the opportunity to combine external and internal innovations in order to capitalise on technological possibilities and to add value to the product or service they offer to the market. Open innovation, including open source collaboration, does not simply involve a shift in the production of intellectual property by organisations. It transforms the manner in which organisations use and manage their intellectual property.

Intellectual property

The WIPO (World Intellectual Property Organisation) defines intellectual property (IP) as 'creations of the mind: inventions; literary and artistic works; and symbols, names and images used in commerce'. It provides two categories of IP:

1. *Industrial property*. Patents for inventions, trademarks, industrial designs and geographical indications.
2. *Copyright*. Literary works (such as novels, poems and plays), films, music, artistic works (e.g. drawings, paintings, photographs and sculptures) and architectural design. Rights include those of performing artists in their performances, producers of phonograms in their recordings, and broadcasters in their radio and television programmes.

Innovation managers need to be sure that they are familiar with the WIPO definitions of patents, trademarks and copyright. Before any hasty initiatives it is sound advice to clear all IP issues with the organisation's legal staff or with an outside law firm. The following outline key IP definitions and key WIPO dictates:

Box 1 Key IP definitions

Patents provide protection to inventions, generally for a period of 20 years, and are defined as 'an exclusive right granted for an invention – a product or process that provides a new way of doing something, or that offers a new technical solution to a problem' (WIPO, n.d.).

Trademarks are defined as 'a distinctive sign that identifies certain goods or services produced or provided by an individual or a company' (WIPO, n.d.).

Copyright involves the enacting of copyright laws which 'grant authors, artists and other creators protection for their literary and artistic creations, generally referred to as "works"' (WIPO, n.d.).

Box 2 Key WIPO dictates

Two treaties which are administered by WIPO cover IP rights. These are the Paris Convention for the Protection of Industrial Property (1883) and the Berne Convention for the Protection of Literary and Artistic Works (1886). Treaties allow the creators of IP to benefit from their work and protect the interests of those who own IP.

WIPO maintains that IP should be protected for:

- The progress and well-being of humanity [which] rest on its capacity to create and invent new works in the areas of technology and culture.
- The legal protection of new creations [which] encourages the commitment of additional resources for further innovation.
- The promotion and protection of intellectual property [which] spurs economic growth, creates new jobs and industries, and enhances the quality and enjoyment of life (WIPO, n.d.).

WIPO further claims that this system allows IP to act as a catalyst for economic development and social and cultural well-being, striking a balance between public interest and innovators, 'providing an environment in which creativity and invention can flourish, for the benefit of all' (WIPO, n.d.).

Patents

Patents are considered to be one of the key *drivers of technology diffusion*. A criticism that is sometimes directed at patents is that proprietary knowledge limits access to data, as opposed to open source models. Proprietary knowledge cannot be used by anyone who may wish to further develop the knowledge or invention on which it is based, unless he or she is prepared to buy the licence, which may not be feasible from a financial perspective. This may occur in the case of emerging technology with possibilities for innovative spin-offs or expansion. Inventors who may be motived to effect evolutionary innovations on a protected product are likely to be discouraged.

Patents are important for new technology oriented organisations that possess few assets besides intellectual property. These organisations may attract venture capital as a result of their patents, or they may licence their patents to other organisations. Boldrin *et al.* (2008) discuss an interesting historical case, the invention of the steam engine, in which they claim that patents hindered innovation. They claim that Boulton and Watt's patenting of the condenser of the steam engine enabled them to control its development and kept competitors at bay.

Boldrin *et al.* (2008) view both the steam engine innovations and open source software as examples of open source collaborative innovation:

> When the Boulton and Watt monopoly expired in 1800 steam engines were used only to pump water out of mines. The innovation of widely usable steam engines was the product of the efforts of Joel Lean and dozens of other equally anonymous Cornwall mining captains and engineers. It is equally a tribute to their steady innovation without making use of patents.

They conclude that open source collaboration leads to increased innovation.

Patents may have a negative effect on competition and on the diffusion of innovation. Patent holders may, moreover, limit the volume of sales by setting the market price higher than the competitive price. The Organisation for Economic Cooperation and Development (OECD) regularly compiles statistical data concerning patents to report trends (OECD, 2011). Part of the process involves tracking patenting related to sectors and nations and assessing the contribution of patents to the development of key technologies, such as biotechnology and ICT. OECD reports claim that the quality of patents has decreased over the past two decades and that this affects innovation. The main industrial sectors for which patents are registered, according to the OECD (2011) report, are biotechnology, nanotechnology, ICT, pharmaceuticals and the environment. New enterprises contribute to the patent process, as the report states that 'During 2007–9 firms less than five years old filing at least one patent application represented on average 25% of all patenting firms, and generated 10% of patent applications'.

The OECD report observes that patents are considered as an essential means to protect competitive advantage in the pharmaceutical sector due to high innovation costs, and that they are used by start-ups and university spin-offs in the biomedical field since these consider IP as a key asset to raise capital for further development. The following considerations are relevant for organisations that wish to successfully manage their IP strategy:

- Optimising the protection that patenting and IP provides, such as procuring patents for valuable innovations, defending ownership, protecting proprietary knowledge from competing technology and harnessing legal rights when required;
- Extracting the maximum amount of value from IP through the identification of opportunities for licensing and novel applications;
- Aligning the management of IP strategy with the core objectives of the organisation, including the future vision, resources and key strengths.

Each organisation possesses its own unique attributes such as size, structure, positioning, market, leadership style and support for innovation. Whether an organisation decides to opt for protection for its proprietary knowledge or whether it prefers an open source model depends to a great extent on these attributes and on the current context in the sector and environment in which it operates.

The 'soft' side of innovation

Most of the research on innovation, including the data published by OECD, tends to assume that innovation is functional, scientific and technological. The focus is mainly on products, services and processes with strong technological influences. This view neglects an important aspect of innovation, often called soft innovation.

A report by the UK's National Endowment for Science, Technology and the Arts (NESTA) defines 'soft innovation' as 'a concept that reflects changes of an aesthetic nature. Such changes are considered significant if they are economically important' (2009). These involve 'changes in goods and services that primarily impact on sensory or intellectual perception and aesthetic appeal rather than functional performance. Soft innovation mainly concerns product innovation and, with that, product differentiation' (2009). Soft innovations include books, movies, theatre productions, no frills airlines and cosmetic surgery.

The NESTA (2009) report identifies two main types of soft innovation:

- Changes in products in the creative industries which include new books and new movies;
- Aesthetic innovation in products or services that are functional in nature such as new furniture or a new car model.

A relationship between soft and technological innovation is possible since production in the creative industries and aesthetic innovation may depend on the introduction of new technology.

Soft innovation may involve an innovation with lower quality but at a reduced cost, such as the service which no frills airlines offer.

Traditional measures used to assess the extent of innovation in organisations, including R&I and patenting activity, focus mainly on innovation related to science and technology, excluding aesthetic or soft innovation. Alternative tools for evaluation and assessment are necessary to obtain the real picture concerning the role which innovation plays in organisations and in the economy.

The NESTA (2009) report claims that there are high rates of soft innovation in the creative industries, but that soft innovation is also to be found in other industries including pharmaceuticals and the food industry. This generally concerns innovations which impact on sensory perception through products which cater for different people's tastes and aesthetic preferences, including new ways of selling existing products, such as the use of a more aesthetically pleasing design for product packaging. One example which the report cities is aspirin, which 'may be branded or generic; there are soluble and children's versions; it may come in low or high doses as tablets, capsules or caplets; it may be mixed with other painkillers. That there is such variety is an indicator of soft innovation insofar as these products are differentiated, at least partly, by aesthetic characteristics' (NESTA, 2009).

Although patents are not possible where soft innovation is concerned, other forms of intellectual protection may be used, such as copyright, design protection or registered trademarks, although these are not considered to be the main tools used to protect intellectual property. Trade confidentiality and lead times are generally preferred, according to NESTA's research (2009).

NESTA (2009) claims that by ignoring soft innovations and their impact on the economy, the true picture concerning innovation activity does not emerge. Soft innovations may be dependent on technological innovations in the production or transportation processes. An example of this, cited in the NESTA report, is the growth of large supermarkets, which is 'at least in part based on IT advances in logistics, electronic funds transfer, refrigeration technology and plant breeding'.

Risk and uncertainty are generally prevalent where innovation is concerned and soft innovation is not immune to these forces. Costs are incurred before the product or service is put on the market for both soft and technological innovation, and there is no way to predict either success or potential financial returns in advance.

NESTA's (2009) report claims to be based on a draft of research conducted by Stoneman which was eventually published in 2010. Stoneman (2010) discusses the economic impact of soft innovation together with its other impacts and implications. He argues that soft innovation, which is of an aesthetic (design) or intellectual nature, has been largely ignored in research on innovation which is prevalent in economics. A consideration and acceptance of soft innovation demonstrates that innovation is more widespread than was previously thought, and is visible in forms which are different from those which are generally considered in statistical and other reports.

The research reported by NESTA (2009) argues in favour of establishing some form of metric to assess the economic impact of soft innovation, otherwise, the current picture is incomplete since these aspects are not taken into consideration, and too much emphasis is directed towards innovation related to science and technology. NESTA admits that its aim is to disseminate information on the importance of soft innovation, the manner in which its effects may be economically assessed and the fact that it merits more attention that it was given in the past.

Godin (2004) provides another view of soft innovation, although it possesses similarities to the concept described in the preceding paragraphs. He defines 'soft innovation' as 'clever, insightful, useful small ideas that just about anyone in an organisation can think up. Soft innovations can make your product into a Purple Cow, they can make it remarkable.'

Godin's use of the metaphor 'purple cow' is interesting. A normal cow would not attract much attention, under normal circumstances, but a purple cow would as it possesses remarkable qualities which generate a great deal of buzz. When applied to products or services, buzz about the manner in which they are aesthetically remarkable would add to their desirability and, consequently, allow them to achieve a larger share of the market. Godin advocates the use of idea champions to promote innovation. He maintains that 'Finding a Free Prize isn't the difficult part. The difficult part is getting the rest of the organisation to embrace it. The only way that can possibly occur is if someone becomes a champion for the idea'. The identification of possibilities for soft innovation is one way for organisations to increase their impact on the market and their competitive advantage with subsequent economic growth.

Godin's 'free prize' adds value to an idea which enables it to transcend its utility and turns it into an object which is desirable, remarkable and worth paying extra for. A 'free prize' does not satisfy any needs, rather, it satisfies 'wants' by providing the consumer with something 'extra'. Remarkable products or services generate debate and discussion even when their innovative features are additional to the core benefit which the product offers. Examples provided by Godin are frequent flyer miles, yogurt sold in a tube (does not require a spoon), selling watches for fun or for status (not merely as time pieces) and tooth whitening strips. Remarkable products don't simply include a free prize. The prize transforms them so much that the product category finds new life.

Godin proposes his own method, 'edgecraft', as one way in which soft innovations may be identified. This process involves identifying an 'edge' or an aspect that has made a product or service in another industry remarkable, and moving as far as possible towards that edge. He makes a number of suggestions for 'available edges' which he says are aspects which may be added, subtracted or done to an available product or service. These include a consideration of:

- Packaging (adding a free prize, making the packaging itself the free prize, adding more to the packaging, stripping away the packaging or making the product remarkable as a result of the packaging);
- Technology (cutting edge or yesterday's technology which is cheap today);
- Design (which has the potential to alter the user experience and to be quickly diffused as it makes people notice it and talk about it).

Successful innovation need not always be a complicated, expensive and time consuming process. Soft innovation may be applied to most products and services to add value to them through an appreciation of the dynamics at play in user experience. This includes the possible application of additional aesthetic features which consumers may find remarkable and which stand out in a remarkable manner from the competition. Soft innovation allows for increased competitiveness and increased economic growth through the identification of aspects which have the potential to make a product or service remarkable, without the expense or expertise required for technological innovation. If a product or service is not a 'purple cow', it risks becoming invisible.

Practice

The long tail

The term long tail refers to the statistical property that a larger share of population rests within the tail of a probability distribution than observed under a 'normal' or Gaussian distribution. It is based on an essay by Shirky written in 2003. In a discussion on web blogs and their audience, Shirky used the term to refer to 'the long tail of weblogs with few readers' which, he claimed, 'will become [merely] conversational [amongst a small group of close friends]' (Shirky, 2003). Shirkey distinguished between 'blogs-as-mainstream-media' (high volume), blogs-as-dinner-conversation (low volume, turning the blog into a conversation among friends) and the 'Blogging Classic' (moderate volume). The long tail of weblogs which Shirky referred to ran into millions with 'only a handful of links going into them' as opposed to blogs with high volume which were 'a relative handful' and which had 'many links going into them' (Shirky, 2003).

Anderson popularised the term 'the long tail' in an article in *Wired* in October 2004. This was later elaborated in a book, published in 2006. It refers to the strategy of selling a large number of small quantities of unique products which has an effect on the economic success of an organisation. This strategy generally applies to technological oriented organisations such as Amazon.com, eBay, iTunes, Google and Netflix, which have the potential to successfully sell small volumes of items to consumers (as opposed to only selling large volumes of a smaller number of popular items). The total sales of the small volumes are called 'the long tail'. The manner in which organisations are successful at capitalising on this model comes about through appropriate distribution and inventory processing which is often totally automated. The products may be 'real' and tangible, such as books or DVDs, or virtual, such as downloads for music or movies. For this model to be successful, the organisation should have a large amount of consumers and low inventory and distribution costs.

The concept of the *long tail* is of interest to online business and is generally used to refer to web-based services which include new digital media, micro finance, crowdsourcing, social networking, viral marketing and user-generated innovation. The main lesson to be learnt from Anderson's long tail is that products which are either low in demand or which have a small volume of sales may create a market share that could exceed products in high demand, if the distribution channel and customer base is large enough. Anderson (2006) states that:

> The theory of the Long Tail can be boiled down to this: Our culture and economy are increasingly shifting away from a focus on a relatively small number of hits (mainstream products and markets) at the head of the demand curve, and moving toward a huge number of niches in the tail.

Through the opportunities offered by technology, particularly the internet and the sales and distribution opportunities it provides, a potential market may be created which innovative organisations may successfully tap.

This concept moves beyond traditional retailing where the focus was on sales of large numbers of a few items in order to maximise profits. Slow-moving items were generally not considered to be cost effective as they took up space, posed distribution limitations and there was generally a lack of information on their availability. These limitations have been overcome thanks to new digital technology which allows for e-commerce, automated processes (including search engines) and digital distribution.

Anderson lists two 'imperatives' which he considers as 'the secret to creating a thriving Long Tail business'. These are summarised as '1. Make everything available; 2. Help me find it' (Anderson, 2006). Anderson's long tail appears to be more of a description of current web-based possibilities, which contrasts with traditional economic theory (based on supply and demand), rather than a prediction. It demonstrates the manner in which products (particularly those which take on a digital form, such as music, movies or e-books) may be distributed to an infinite number of consumers. The concept of the long tail is particularly valuable for organisations that are capable of recognising the opportunities that the new digital economy affords as it allows for the availability of a larger selection of goods at a low cost.

The long tail drives business from 'hits' to 'niches' through search engines and online recommendations which connect demand and supply. This allows for consumers to obtain increased accessibility to 'niches', which increases the economic potential of the long tail. Quite a few people have niche interests and new technology allows greater access to products or services related to these interests, regardless of geographical location as distance constraints may easily be overcome through new communications technologies. Niche markets are becoming increasingly available and profitable, as current technology shifts away from the influence which the mass media had in the past, when it involved communication only in one direction. Through the opportunities which technology provides, today's situation allows for increased individualised choices and increased consumer satisfaction due to the availability of such a broad range of both popular and niche products and services.

Technology has drastically shifted the locus of possibilities and niche products or services are afforded more possibilities for economic growth than ever before thanks to efficient and effective digital search facilities, e-commerce and the power and influence which individuals have acquired through online blogs, discussions and social networking sites.

Action

Knowledge and technology transfer

Research, knowlege and technology transfer play a key role in economic and social development. This involves the translation of research activities into tangible results and benefits either for an organisation, for society or for both, through the implementation of the results of research into innovative products or services. It generally involves collaboration among strategic partnerships and networks which could include universities, research laboratories, governments, communities, NGOs or organisations.

Universities, for example, possess an extensive knowledge base which may be effectively tranferred either through patents and licencing, through open source collaboration, through the creation of start-ups or through collaboration with networks, other research-based institutions, public–private consortia or private organisations. The aim of collaboration or transfer may involve the commercialisation of innovative products or processes.

External sources may provide both opportunities and challenges for knowledge and technology transfer as foreign direct investment and trade, for example, particularly when directed towards developing countries, and may serve as a channel for organisations to adopt innovative practices and implement innovative processes.

Knowledge and technology transfer may occur within an organisation across sections or divisions. This may also occur between organisations or between countries. The technological knowledge may be tangible (i.e. physical goods) or intangible (software, technical documents or training related to technical expertise).

Knowledge and technology transfer may alternatively be communicated through flows of tacit knowledge – that is, knowledge that has not been fully codified, and remains embodied in the skills of people. The knowledge may relate to the use and operation of technology or it may involve the knowledge required for a shift from one form of technology to another. It may, moreover, relate to the knowledge required to modify or replicate technologies. Technologies may be transferred from one organisation to another or from one activity to another unrelated activity.

Knowledge and technology transfer constitute an important means through which access to new knowledge is gained and technologies lead to the development of innovation capacities in an organisation or a country. Radical advances in the area of ICT allow for declining production costs and the potential extensive diffusion of knowledge and technology is one means through which social and economic activities may be transformed. Wealth creation may now be based on intangible assets based on technology.

It is through knowledge and technology transfer that the innovative results of research activities may flow from the laboratory to production and to the consumer. Technology markets may provide organisations with opportunities to sell or license technologies which they are not in a position to use, or which they do not intend to commercialise, encouraging additional investments in innovation.

Knowledge is today a commodity which acquires value when it has the potential to be commercialised or patented. Markets for knowledge and technology provide a means for the diffusion of technologies among a larger number of innovating organisations, subsequently improving their economic performance.

Summary

Most organisations accept the argument that innovation in today's economy is of vital importance to their survival and prosperity. Many have grasped the challenge with enthusiasm and actively pursue it. Others accept the logic (the why) of involvement but are less sure about *how* to proceed. This chapter presents a set of principles, models and topics that require the attention of organisations if they are to successfully innovate. Innovation is the specific tool of entrepreneurs, the means by which they exploit change as an opportunity for a different business or a different service. It is capable of being presented as a discipline, capable of being learned, capable of being practised. Entrepreneurs need to search purposefully for the sources of innovation, the changes and their symptoms that indicate opportunities for successful innovation. And they need to know and to apply the principles of successful innovation.

Discussion questions

1. What is meant by *innovation* and how does it differ from *creativity*?
2. Briefly describe the innovation process phases. In which phase/s is creativity important?
3. Compare and contrast The Idea Funnel and Stage-Gate models and indicate how their main potential weaknesses can be overcome.
4. Why do an increasing number of organisations find that hierarchical organisational structures restrict their ability to meet the challenges presented by the business environment in the current decade?
5. What are the potential advantages that result from the adoption of an organic structure? Briefly discuss and form an opinion on the statement 'mechanistic and organic structures are mutually exclusive'.
6. What are the factors that should be considered when examining whether the structure of an organisation is conducive to innovation?
7. Explain the terms *Open Innovation* and *Open Source*. What is knowledge and technology transfer and why is it important?
8. What is meant by the term *Intellectual Property*? Briefly discuss the driving role of patents in the management of innovation.
9. What is meant by 'the soft side' of innovation and why is it important?
10. Briefly explain why the term *long tail* attracts so much business interest.

Case exercise

Manley's are a light engineering company located in the UK Midlands and are seeking new products to ease the current pressure on their die-cast aluminium business. The company has held some impromptu brainstorming sessions and has generated ten possible new product ideas. Until recently the company has been a regular supplier of aluminium castings, steering components and engine parts to motor manufacturers in the UK. Manley's have an excellent reputation for quality and delivery. New product work has in the past come to the company automatically from the motor manufacturers but now with demand for their 'usual' business in decline they have decided to manage innovation for themselves.

Imagine that Manley's CEO has contacted you thinking that you are 'someone who knows about applied innovation', and has asked ou to prepare some briefing notes to assist top management (four engineers and a finance specialist) to gain 'an instant understanding' of how to introduce an innovation process to the company. The CEO is particularly interested in learning how to make Manley's organisation conducive to innovation and the finance director has specifically asked for information on 'soft' innovation.

Task

Prepare a short report (maximum of two pages of A4) and/or a short PowerPoint presentation to present to Manley's taking care to avoid and/or explain business and strategic innovation jargon.

References

Anderson, C. (2004) 'The long tail', *Wired*, October, http://www.wired.com/wired/archive/12.10/tail.html, accessed 13/04/12.

Anderson, C. (2006) *The Long Tail: Why the Future of Business is Selling Less of More*, New York, Hyperion.

Boldrin, M., Levine, D.K. and Nuvolari, A. (2008) 'Do patents encourage or hinder innovation?', *The Freeman,* Foundation for Economic Education, December, Vol. 58, Issue 10, http://www.thefreemanonline.org/features/do-patents-encourage-or-hinder-innovation-the-case-of-the-steam-engine/, accessed 13/04/12.

Chesbrough, H.W. (2003) *Open Innovation: The New Imperative for Creating and Profiting from Technology*, Boston, Harvard Business School Press.

Chesbrough, H., Vanhaverbeke, W. and West, J. (eds.) (2006) *Open Innovation: Researching a New Paradigm*, Oxford, Oxford University Press.

Dobni, C.B. (2010) 'Achieving synergy between strategy and innovation: The key to value creation', *International Journal of Business Science & Applied Management*, January, Vol. 5, Issue 1, pp. 48–58.

Dobni, C.B. (2011) 'The relationship between innovation orientation and organisational performance', *International Journal of Innovation and Learning*, Vol. 10, No. 3, pp. 226–40.

Godin, S. (2004) *Free Prize Inside: The Next Big Marketing Idea*, New York, Portfolio.

Grönlund, J., Sjödin, D.R. and Frishammar, J. (2010) 'Open innovation and the stage-gate process: A revised model for new product development', *California Management Review,* Spring, Vol. 52, Issue 3, pp. 106–31.

McDougall, P. (2005) 'IBM grants open-source developers use of 500 patents', *Information Week*, 11 January, available at http://www.informationweek.com/news/57700456, accessed 04/01/12.

NESTA (National Endowment for Science, Technology and the Arts, UK) (2009) *Soft Innovation: Towards a More Complete Picture of Innovative Change*, Research Report, July, available at http://www.nesta.org.uk/library/documents/Report%2022%20-%20Soft%20Innovation%20v9.pdf, accessed 06/01/12.

OECD (2004) *Patents and Innovation: Trends and Policy Challenges*, Paris, OECD Publications, available on http://www.oecd.org/dataoecd/48/12/24508541.pdf, accessed 04/01/12.

OECD (2011) *OECD Science, Technology and Industry Scoreboard 2011*, Paris, OECD Publications.

Raymond, E.S. (2001) *The Cathedral & the Bazaar: Musings on Linux and Open Source by an Accidental Revolutionary*, revised edition, Sebastopol, CA, O'Reilly Media.

Sethi, R. and Iqbal, Z. (2008) 'Stage-gate controls, learning failure, and adverse effect on novel new products,' *Journal of Marketing*, January, Vol. 72, Issue 1, pp. 118–34.

Shirky, C. (2003) 'Power laws, weblog, and inequality'. First published 8 February on the 'Networks, Economics, and Culture' mailing list, available at Clay Shirky's Writings about the Internet, Economics & Culture, Media & Community, Open Source. http://www.shirky.com/writings/powerlaw_weblog.html, accessed 06/01/12.

Stoneman, P. (2010) *Soft Innovation: Economics, Design, and the Creative Industries*, Oxford, Oxford University Press.

WIPO (World Intellectual Property Organisation) (n.d.) *What is Intellectual Property*, available at http://www.wipo.int/freepublications/en/intproperty/450/wipo_pub_450.pdf, accessed 04/01/12.

Websites

Seth Goden, condensed version of *Free Prize Inside*: http://www.sethgodin.com/freeprize/FreePrizeCondensed.pdf

11 Organisational climate and culture for optimising innovation

Climate, Culture. I determine how these work for that is how things are done around here.
(Anonymous client)

We must cultivate our garden.
(Voltaire, *Candide*, 1759)

Introduction

Two key elements which are essential for the effective management of innovation are organisational climate and culture. These are two distinct concepts which are often confused in the academic literature on the subject. Climate refers to the environmental factors (physical and psychological) within an organisation and include communication, trust, feedback and reward. Culture, on the other hand, involves the norms, values, beliefs and traditions of an organisation, which are often incorporated into the mission and vision statements and which constitute the philosophy and behaviour of the people who make up the organisation. The organisational climate and culture for the optimisation of innovation should also incorporate an idea management system. This chapter discusses those elements which are related to the application of innovation and to the process of innovation, discussed in the previous chapter. The chapter concludes by linking the value of culture and climate to the leadership of an organisation.

Context

Organisational attitude

Top management both inherit and fashion the attitude that an organisation takes to innovation. Some organisations stand out as concerns that place a great deal of importance in fostering and sustaining innovation. Others demonstrate interest from time to time, usually in the good times, when they have the cash to back innovation. Others tend largely to 'stick to the knitting' and base their actions strongly on the least-cost production paradigm. In reality all organisations can be said to innovate. Incremental and radical innovation initiatives should not be seen as mutually exclusive. Continuous or incremental improvements to organisational activity are generally accepted as being an essential part of management activity. Radical innovation can occur by chance through a flash of inspiration. Organisations that have secured a successful track record are the ones that displayed a consistently positive attitude to investing time and resources in innovation management.

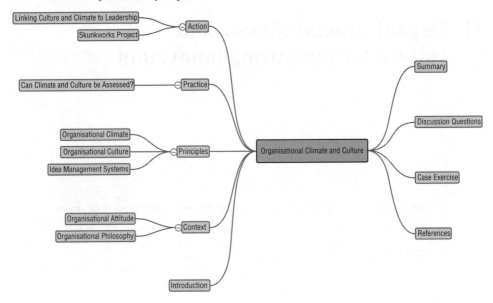

Figure 11.1 Exploring organisational climate and culture.

Developing and sustaining a strong attitude to organisational innovation is a function of a complex interaction between strategy and structure, with organisational culture and climate as important conditioning variables. Sound structure produces stability and continuity and sound strategic direction is necessary to ensure that an organisation can function successfully. While most organisations are to some extent innovative in the sense discussed above they need to place high importance on facilitating creativity and innovation in the challenging business contextual environments that face private sector, public sector, SMEs and charitable institutions.

Top management that regard innovation as important will carefully evaluate their business environments. In relatively static environments organisations are likely to be strongly focused on running their concerns efficiently in the short term. Most organisations, however, are faced with more dynamic and changing business contextual pressures and need to adopt a strong innovative orientation. This will necessitate taking care to see that their strategy and structure is carefully tuned to the development of an organisational climate and culture that facilitates business creativity and innovation. This will necessitate a careful and considered review of their *modus operandi* – the way they do things.

Organisational philosophy

Bower defines 'company philosophy' as 'the basic beliefs that people in the business are expected to hold and be guided by – informal, unwritten guidelines on how people should perform and conduct themselves. Once such a philosophy crystallizes, it becomes a powerful force indeed. When one person tells another "That's not the way we do things around here", the advice had better be heeded' (Bower, 1966). Expected patterns of behaviour are developed, either through leadership or through trial and error, until they evolve into 'a set of laws or guidelines that gradually become established'.

Key principles

Organisational climate

Interest in the literature and amongst practitioners in the link between organisational climate, culture and performance is gaining momentum. However, as yet there is no consensus even on their definitions and to compound the difficulty in examining these variables, they are dynamic, and interact with each other. Climate and culture are sometimes used synonymously. Empirical research does reveal that there is a significant positive connection between climate and organisational performance (Turnipseed, 1988; Kangis, 2000).

Generally speaking organisational climate refers to the environmental variables (physical and psychological) within an organisation and encompasses communication, trust, feedback and reward factors. Isaksen (2007) defines *climate* generally 'as the recurring patterns of behaviour, attitudes and feelings that characterize life in the organization'. Expanding this he describes a *psychological climate* that refers to 'the intrapersonal perception of the patterns of behaviour, attitudes and feelings as experienced by the individual'. Finally, he identifies an *organisational climate* that comprises the aggregation of the psychological climate and involves 'the objectively shared perceptions that characterize life within a defined work unit or in the larger organization'.

Organisational climate is determined essentially by the interaction between physical and psychological factors. People need to like going to work. Organisations that place a strong emphasis on innovation (e.g. Apple, Hewlett-Packard, KPMG, 3M, Morning Star and Semco), ensure that the physical working environment is conducive to creativity and innovation. Offices and meeting rooms are carefully designed to provide essential support services with attention also being paid to provide a stimulating environment.

Careful attention also needs to be afforded to developing a stimulating psychological climate for small as well as large businesses (Manning, 2010). People at all levels need to be seen as being important to the operation of the organisation if it is to work effectively and efficiently as a team. As we have argued in many places in this text it is vitally important for an organisation to build a climate of trust that enables staff to firmly believe that they work for a just and supportive concern. This results in an *esprit de corps* that is apparent to both internal and external customers.

Whilst attention to the physical and psychological determinants of organisational climate is necessary to stimulate creativity and innovation friction and conflict will occur. Good teams respect both their peers and leaders. A degree of conflict can be a good thing and can provide stimulation as long as it is well managed and all parties firmly believe that justice in the workplace is seen to be even-handed.

Isaksen argues that 'group problem solving, decision making, communication and coordination' are 'organizational processes', while 'psychological processes include learning, individual problem solving, creating, motivating and committing'. Collectively these influence the performance of employees, teams and the organisation as a whole.

Key Factors for developing a climate that fosters innovation

Structure. The organisational structure influences the creative climate in an organisation. As discussed in Chapter 10, Section 10.3.1, there is no magic formula for an ideal structure which may be applied. Organisations should assess their situation to ensure that the organisational structure is designed to enable the flow of communication and to be in line with its desired goals and outcomes.

Key individuals and teams. Individuals, including innovation champions, idea scouts and idea connectors, are important elements to consider where climate is concerned. Innovation champions play a key role in maintaining and sustaining the motivation of employees where idea generation and communication are concerned. Idea scouts scan the external environment for feasible innovative ideas which ensure that the organisation maintains and sustains momentum. Idea connectors create internal and external networks to be able to identify the right person who has the power to act to connect to specific ideas. Teams are constituted on the basis of their talent and skills and work on new product development and on various stages of the innovation process.

Vertical and lateral communication. An appropriate communication strategy, with a two-way flow of communication (both vertical and horizontal), is essential for the creation of the right climate for innovation. Ideas, suggestions, feedback and plans related to change should be effectively communicated to all concerned. Communication concerning planned changes should include all relevant stakeholders. The information which flows through communication may be used to create a feedback loop through which adjustments to the system may be flexibly applied whenever the need arises.

Trust. Employees trust each other in a climate which is conducive to successful innovation and where the sharing of ideas is facilitated. Trust enables social cohesion, engagement, commitment and allegiance to the values and beliefs of the organisation. It acts to increase confidence, self-esteem and honest communication and to mitigate fear of failure. The belief that what is good for the organisation is good for the individual is based on the construction of a trustful relationship.

Motivation. Motivation is linked to communication, feedback, rewards and recognition. Employees feel motivated if they know they have access to the right person with whom they may exchange their ideas and discuss issues. Challenging tasks which are assigned to the right people act as motivating forces. Feedback is important as it evokes a sense of participation and belonging. Employees are motivated if they feel that their efforts are being acknowledged, appreciated and rewarded. Emphasis on motivation as an integral element for a successful climate results in an increased commitment by employees to the organisation and reduced resistance to and fear of change.

Rewards and recognition. Leadership that is committed to nurturing a creative environment understands the motivating elements involved in rewarding employees for their efforts. Intrinsic rewards are generally considered to be more valuable than bonuses or monetary rewards. These include recognition and acknowledgement, positive reinforcement demonstrated through approval and genuine appreciation, and benefits which could include an increase in status or the assignment of a challenge or task which carries particular significance (such as representing the organisation at an important event or being assigned to a work-related trip overseas). Innovation may be self-rewarding, since the innovator may be perceived by other employees and management as an 'expert' with an enhanced reputation.

Training and staff development. This should be an on-going practice (as opposed to one-off training sessions where the skills and knowledge learnt may be forgotten in a short period of time). Employees require training in soft skills which include idea generation methods, communication skills, opportunity recognition, risk taking and leadership skills. Skills need to be practised over a period of time in order for them to be developed and applied. Follow-up training sessions to elicit feedback and to reinforce the skills learnt enables the sustaining of the benefits received during the training session.

Sustaining a creative climate is not an easy task. It requires continuous monitoring, feedback, evaluation and assessment. Successes should be celebrated and disappointments should be investigated with a positive focus on the lessons to be learnt by individuals and groups.

Organisational culture

Culture is a social concept that is transmitted from person to person. It is adaptive as opposed to static, and it may change when necessary to address the challenges or needs that it faces. Culture is social and it is visible in relationships, rather than in individuals, as it comes about as a product of people sharing agreed norms, values and beliefs. Organisations are composed of people and, just as social groups assume a social culture, so do organisations adopt a culture of their own.

Many would agree in principle that organisations would solve their problems if they were to develop working atmospheres or cultures which consistently feature trust and teamwork. This is fine as far as it goes. It represents a start; what it does not do is to address the thorny problem of *how* an organisation can change its culture.

Jaques (1952) developed a definition of organisational culture which, first, covers the dominant corporate style or operating fashion:

> The culture of the factory is its customary and traditional way of thinking and of doing things, which is shared to a greater or lesser degree by all its members, and which new members must learn, and at least partially accept, in order to be accepted into service in the firm.

Next is a description of supportive behaviours:

> Culture in this sense covers a wide range of behaviour: the methods of production; job skills and technical knowledge; attitudes towards discipline and punishment; the customs and habits of managerial behaviour; the objectives of the concern; its way of doing business; the methods of payment; the values placed on different types of work; beliefs in democratic living and joint consultation; and the less conscious conventions and taboos.

Organisations, like individuals, develop their own 'personality' (or 'character') which are fashioned by the factors described in Box 11.1.

Box 11.1 Organisational personality factors

- The organisation's unique history, including tradition, that moves from the past to the present and on to the future;
- The behaviour of the people who make up the organisation, who share the culture, and for whom it becomes a way of life;
- Norms, ideology, ideals, values and accepted ways of doing things;
- Identity which includes image, branding, symbols, rituals, traditions, dress code, myths and reputation;
- Functional and dynamic elements, including the way problems are solved and the manner in which the organisation adapts to the environment;
- Mental elements, including learned habits and social controls.

Shared values are at the centre of organisational culture. These include perceptions, beliefs and ideology. These values persist over time, regardless of changes in the member-ship of the group. They are manifest in the behaviour of people in the organisation and through expressions which include symbols, lanuage, ideology, beliefs, rituals, traditions, myths and products. Employees who join an organisation feel they need to learn how they are meant to act, what they are supposed to do, how they are supposed to do it and how they can expect others to act. This is a response to a felt need for acceptance, security, stability, safety and to avoid embarrassement.

Learning to adapt to and to absorb the culture of an organisation may come about through:

- Formal or informal induction training,
- Shadowing another employee,
- Modelling the behaviour of others,
- Trial and error,
- Intuitively,
- Through direct instructions.

As the behavioural norms, basic assumptions and values which form part of the organisa-tional culture are absorbed by new employees, they learn what the expected ways to behave are and how they should expect others to behave.

Organisations may identify various dimensions of their culture in order to assess it and to take measures, if necessary, to ensure it is directed towards and supports the innovation process.

Some dimensions of organisation culture that may be identified are summarised in Box 11.2.

Box 11.2 Dimensions of organisational culture

Cameron and Quinn (1999) identify four major types of organisational culture:

1. *The Hierarchy* – formalised, structured and stable;
2. *The Clan* – shared values, internal cohesion, teamwork, employee empowerment, loyalty and sensitivity to customers;
3. *The Adhocracy* – innovative, open to new ideas, creativity, entrepreneurship and individuality are encouraged;
4. *The Market* – focused on competitiveness, productivity and transactions with suppliers and customers.

Various tools have been developed to assess organisational culture. Cameron and Quinn (1999) devised the Organisational Culture Assessment Instrument (OCAI) which investigates the current and the desired organisational culture. The OCAI has been used extensively and it claims to be both valid and reliable. It is in the form of a questionnaire, with six groups of questions and four alternative answers to the questions.

Culture is a complex phenomenon in organisations due to its tangible and intangible effects. It is to be distinguished from climate, which is more easily observed and influenced. Culture involves the pattern of shared values, beliefs and norms which shape behaviour, in other words 'the way we do things around here'. Although it is easier to change climate than it is to change culture, innovative organisations should attend to the various manifestations of culture within the organisation to ensure that these are in line with the image they wish to project and with the norms, values and beliefs which they wish to foster in their employees.

Organisational climates and cultures are best, perhaps, viewed as different perspectives of leadership. Climates lend themselves to change more readily than cultures, which are characterised by a mix of mindsets and paradigms – some good and some not so good. The challenge for top management desirous of carrying out any serious organisational change is to achieve the 'buy in' of all staff levels. Words from the top, unless strengthened by a resource commitment, often fall on deaf ears and the organisation to all intents and purposes continues on the basis of 'business as usual'.

Top management are paid to first tell organisations where they should be going and secondly to exercise expertise in directing them to get there. Using a naval metaphor they are on the bridge of the ship and it is their function to see that the ship is functioning efficiently and steered effectively so that it will not hit the rocks. So, clear communication of clear and consistent organisational goals provides the focus for running a good ship.

In corporate situations the task of moulding strategy/structure/climate and culture to realise key goals are open to potential distraction and sometimes disaster by political power-plays. Returning to the naval analogy – at sea this would be a disaster. During times of severe organisational pressure caused by fierce environmental storms, in a slackly run business conflict and disagreement will emerge. It is top management's responsibility to see that all who may be expected to have to deal with this problem are adequately trained.

Wise corporate team leaders (those on the corporate bridge) make sure that everyone on board knows what is expected of them in their daily work and can on merit rise to positions of greater responsibility. They ensure that all on board possess a copy of the organisation's working definition of management (see Chapter 3).

Idea management systems

There are several ways in which the ideas that are generated within an organisation may be harvested. A common way of doing this is by means of an organisation suggestion scheme. In the past this generally involved the use of paper and pencil, where suggestions were written down and submitted through a suggestion box. Nowadays technology has taken over and most successful idea management schemes tend to use information technology systems such as the organisation's intranet. In this manner, ideas are communicated through specific channels, either to a team or to a department which is set up for this purpose. The team or department evaluates all the ideas which are proposed, and selects the best ones which are in line with the organisation's goals and objectives. The selected ideas are progressed toward implementation by specially tasked teams. Individuals should be kept informed of the progress of their submitted ideas and appropriately rewarded on their final adoption.

An idea management system which deals with ideas submitted by sources external to the organisation could also be adopted. This may take the form of a proprietary or open source online platform or it may adopt the process of crowdsourcing (see Chapter 9, Section 9.3.3). As discussed in Chapter 9, Section 9.3.1, idea scouts are useful for scanning the external environment for new ideas. This is, however, not sufficient, as the ideas need to be communicated to the right people who have the power to take action within the organisation.

Practice

Can climate and culture be assessed?

It is not easy to assess the climate and culture in an organisation. Although quite a few tools are available which claim to measure creativity and innovation within an organisation, to date there is no one tool which is considered reliable and valid for assessing either organisational climate or culture. Culture is more difficult to assess than climate. Ekvall (1996) and Isaksen (2007) both agree that it is very difficult to change the norms, attitudes and beliefs which constitute organisational culture. They both recommend focus on the organisational climate as this would allow for the required changes to behaviour and attitude which could, in turn, have some effect on the organisational culture. Assessing the climate for culture in an organisation is a useful exercise as it brings out strengths and weaknesses and draws attention to areas where improvement is required through intervention.

Ekvall's Creative Climate Questionnaire

Ekvall developed the Creative Climate Questionnaire (CCQ) in 1990. This is a 50-item questionnaire which covers ten dimensions of five items each. The ten factors which Ekvall identifies, which are based on theoretical and applied research and experience, are shown in Box 11.3. Ekvall maintains that this instrument is an organisational and not an individual measure as respondents are asked to contribute by taking on the position of an observer of life in the organisation.

Box 11.3 Key factors in Ekvall's Creative Climate Questionnaire

1. *Challenge*. This involves meaningfulness and job satisfaction which motivate people to invest additional energy in the tasks they assume;
2. *Freedom*. This relates to independent behaviour where information is shared, and issues discussed in a free and open manner;
3. *Idea support*. New ideas are communicated and discussed in a constructive and positive atmosphere where possibilities for testing new ideas are created;
4. *Trust/openness*. Initiatives are taken and ideas and opinions communicated without fear of failure and communication is open and honest;
5. *Dynamism/liveliness*. Life in the organisation is dynamic and lively with new things happening in a lively way;
6. *Playfulness/humour*. A comfortable and relaxed environment where jokes are shared and where laughter is often experienced;
7. *Debates*. People are keen to discuss and debate their ideas, viewpoints may clash, diversity of thought and multivocality are prevalent;

---

8. *Conflicts*. Personal and emotional tension is present, gossip, slander, plots and traps are prevalent;
9. *Risk taking*. Uncertainty is tolerated, opportunities are taken up and experimentation is encouraged;
10. *Idea time*. Slack time for discussing, testing and developing new ideas.

Isaksen's Situational Outlook Questionnaire

Isaksen's (2007) paper reports on research conducted with organisational leaders which is based on case studies and which describes the use of the SOQ (Situational Outlook Questionnaire). This tool, which is also used for assessing organisational climate, is based on Ekvall's early work and it is quite similar to his tool. Nine climate dimensions are addressed through the delivery of a questionnaire which consists of 53 questions.

Action

Onsite and offsite creativity centres

A powerful symbol of top management's commitment to innovation is their willingness to invest in onsite creativity centres, which provide an oasis for people to get away from the hum of daily life and spend time seeking inspiration. A creativity centre may contain periodicals, executive toys, pictures, art equipment, coffee machines, Post-It notes, comfy seating and so on to stimulate visitors' creativity. Some organisations (e.g. 3M) require staff to spend a mandatory percentage of their time in such centres and target them to come up with both incremental and radical innovations that reach the commercialisation phase.

In a similar vein, some organisations invest in offsite specialist locations such as skunkworks. A skunkworks project is one typically developed by a small and loosely structured group of people who research and develop a project primarily for the sake of radical innovation. The term typically refers to technology projects, and originated with Skunk Works, an official alias for the Lockheed Martin Advanced Development Programs (formerly Lockheed Advanced Development Projects). A skunkworks project often operates with a high degree of autonomy and unhampered by bureaucracy, tasked with working on advanced or secret projects. IBM set up a skunkworks to develop its original PC in 1981. Apple and GM have also used skunkworks.

Linking innovation to leadership

Whilst most top management acknowledge the importance of innovation many do not sufficiently invest in it. In a survey carried out by a consultancy in the North East of England using a sample of 150 managers drawn from the private sector, public sector, SMEs and charity organisations none of the respondents could confidently claim that their organisation was offering its employees specific creativity or innovation education or training programmes. The main factors that were identified as supporting innovation were:

- Leadership and support from top management,
- Climate and culture,

- Rewards and recognition,
- Competition, need for diversity.

Organisational culture, resistance to change, corporate structure, workloads, difficulty in accessing capital to invest in R&D activities and lack of skills were identified as the main barriers to innovation. Other telling findings revealed that there was a general lack of awareness related to:

- Creativity or innovation training programmes offered to staff,
- Idea management systems,
- Innovation metrics.

Leadership (See Chapter 13) plays a key role in creating and developing climates and cultures which are open to innovation. It is leadership that takes crucial decisions, particularly where the allocation of resources is concerned. This text seeks to encourage organisations and the students who later join them to rethink their approach to management.

Changing times demand changing responses and more leadership skills are needed. Top management attitudes to business creativity and innovation need to change as organisations strive to meet the challenges of the modern business world. Effective leadership and support from top management is crucial if organisations are to change their climates and cultures to support business creativity and strategic innovation.

There is no one single model of climate or culture that is ideal to adopt for effecting change in an organisation. Leaders should carefully assess their particular situation in order to identify a suitable model. Choice of climate and culture often depends upon the industry sector, markets and the type of work which the employees conduct. Leaders should, if feasible, attempt to conduct research to assess the manner in which climate and culture are perceived by employees and to consult with and harness their ideas concerning any planned changes.

Summary

'Climate, Culture. I determine how these work for that is how things are done around here'. This chapter has sought to encourage readers to think positively about this statement drawn recently from a client in answer to a question probing his leadership style. Our task is to contemplate the factors that will introduce and support an innovative environment.

Discussion questions

1. 'Developing and sustaining a strong attitude to organisational innovation is a function of a complex interaction between strategy and structure'. Discuss.
2. What is the difference between organisational climate and culture?
3. What are the key determinants of organisational climate?
4. How might a new recruit to an organisation learn about its culture?
5. Name an example of each of Cameron and Quinn's four major types of organisational culture.
6. How do you think climate and culture could be assessed?
7. What are skunkworks and why are they useful for managing innovation? Explain with examples.

Case exercise

Moreton Park is a country hotel in the English Midlands. It is located within easy travelling distance by both road and rail from London and the major business centres of the Midlands. The hotel occupies a late Jacobean building which has been extensively and expensively restored by the current owners. There are 15 bedrooms, all with en suite facilities. Recently the hotel's restaurant received lavish praise from two well-known chefs. The public recreation rooms are tastefully furnished and have an ambience which is both restful and in harmony with the building. In addition there is a conference suite in an adjacent stable complex that contains modern IT equipment.

Despite considerable expense being lavished on the building Moreton Park is failing to make any profitable headway in the functions, leisure and conference markets. The proprietor Sam King is a colourful gregarious man and engages well with visitors. However, his management style is hierarchical and autocratic and his staff of 25 find him distant and unapproachable. Sam believes that the building and the surrounding parkland do the work and that the role of the staff is secondary; he also believes that the staff are far too costly for what he perceives as their contribution to the business. As a result of his management style his staff suffer low morale and just do their job almost robotically. The one exception is the restaurant where the enthusiastic head chef runs an innovative and highly motivated team.

Worried by the faltering business position of the hotel Sam has recruited you to provide advice as to how the situation can be rescued. A close friend and confidant has kindly and effectively critiqued his management style and Sam has accepted that he needs to become more of a leader and to seek to develop a new relationship with his staff to earn their respect. He is also keen to harness the talents of his staff and wants them to actively support his wish to encourage innovation to provide Moreton Park with a 'market edge'. He wants to change the climate and culture of the business but does not know how to go about it.

Task

Sam King has asked you to prepare a short PowerPoint presentation and report (circa three or four pages of A4) outlining how the workplace climate and culture of Moreton Park can be changed to encourage business creativity and innovation involving all staff.

References

Bower, M. (1966) 'Company philosophy: The way we do things around here', excerpt from Chapter 2 of *The Will to Manage*, available at *Inc.* http://www.inc.com/articles/2003/04/25365.html (accessed 06/01/12).

Cameron, K. and Quinn, R. (1999) *Cameron, Diagnosing and Changing Organizational Culture*, Reading, Addison-Wesley.

Ekvall, G. (1996) 'Organizational climate for creatvity and innovation', *European Journal of Work and Organizational Psychology*, Vol. 5, Issue 1, pp. 105–23. Also available at http://stshawaii.com/research/Ekvall%201996.pdf (accessed 06/01/12).

Isaksen, S.G. (2007) 'The Climate for transformation: Lessons for leaders', *Creativity and Innovation Management*, Vol. 16, No. 1, available at http://www.cpsb.com/research/articles/climate-for-innovation/Climate-for-Transformation-Lessons-for-Leaders.pdf (accessed 06/01/12).

Jaques, E. (1952) *The Changing Culture of a Factory*, New York, Dryden press.

Kangis, P. (2000) 'Organisational climate and corporate performance: An empirical investigation', *Management Decision*, Vol. 38, Issue 8, pp. 531–40.

Manning, R.L. (2010) 'Development of the psychological climate for small businesses', *Journal of New Business Ideas and Trends*, Vol. 8, Issue 1, pp. 50–65.

Turnipseed, D.L. (1988) 'An integrated, interactive model of organisational climate, culture and effectiveness', *Leadership & Organization Development Journal*, Vol. 9, Issue 5, pp. 17–21.

12 New digital technology and organisational innovation

Progress through technology.
(Anon)

Introduction

The digital revolution has had a tremendous effect on the way most people in the Western world live their lives. Changes are evident in consumption patterns, choice and communication practices amongst others. This chapter discusses some of the effects that new digital technology is having on the management and practice of innovation and the opportunities which arise as a result of innovative technological products and services. The chapter explores topics related to innovation and digital technology including social media, the diffusion of innovation through digital technology, the effects of digital technology on organisational communication and marketing strategy, the 'creative industries' and the trend in Western countries towards what is considered to be a 'knowledge society'.

The contrasting views of Friedman (*The World is Flat*) and Florida (*Cities and the Creative Class*) are explored in an attempt to discover whether digital technology is making the 'world' more of a 'global village' with the blurring of geographical boundaries or whether population density and geographical propensity are still relevant for creativity and innovation to flourish (as claimed by Florida). The chapter concludes with a tentative glance towards the future of innovation and technology in the light of the current scenario where change has become a constant factor in most people's lives.

Context

Open innovation

The importance of harnessing ideas gleaned from sources both internal and external to the organisation was discussed in detail in Chapter 8. In order for this to be optimised, communication and other interfaces must become as permeable as possible in order for ideas to flow easily and to be directed towards those who have the authority to take action and for knowledge transfer to be effective. Although organisations have utilised external sources in their quest for new ideas for many years, the term 'open innovation' came to the fore following Chesbrough's publication on the topic in 2003. The advent of new digital technology has had a tremendous impact on the practice of open innovation, which has evolved into a strategic, systematic and effective tool for communicating with people external to

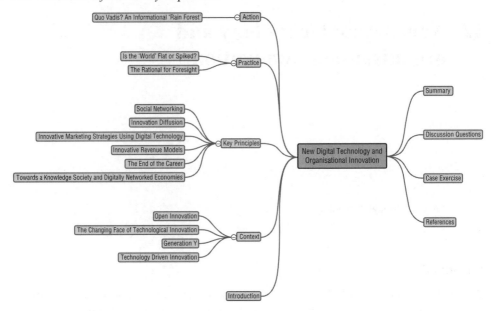

Figure 12.1 Exploring the impact of new digital technology on organisational innovation.

the organisation. The process may involve participation in communities and networks and sourcing of ideas without complete dependence on internal R&I departments.

Tracking customers' opinions, suggestions and ideas plays an important role in this process which has the potential to reduce costs, increase competitiveness and produce an endless stream of incremental and radical ideas. Organisations that specialise in cutting edge technology products or services are likely to be amongst those who benefit most from this interactive process, mainly due to the fast rate of change in this particular sector.

New technology and the possibilities it offers provides access to countless 'experts' all around the world, spanning across geographical boundaries. When invited and motivated to do so, quite a few people are happy to communicate their ideas and suggestions. This potential provides both opportunities and challenges, as although the potential pool of 'experts' is extensive, the information and ideas collected require effective management and a stringent evaluation process to separate the wheat from the chaff.

There are several degrees of open innovation which organisations may consider. The involvement of a few partners in a network where specific topics are discussed is one possible option. This could later be broadened to include a larger number of participants or a larger number of topics. It is possible for organisations to combine this with increased 'openness' where topics may not need to be specified by the organisation but are proposed by anyone who chooses to participate in the community or network which may be as open or limited as the organisation wishes it to be. Strategically managing open innovation communities or networks is not an easy task as it generally involves a process to first identify, attract (or motivate), and retain potential participants or experts.

The possibility for harnessing ideas through digital technology is so great that 'innovation brokers' or 'idea brokers' have emerged. These provide online platforms through which problems or issues requiring solutions are communicated to millions of people, with rewards for those whose ideas are selected. One such 'broker' is InnoCentive, an online platform which claims to be 'the global innovation marketplace where creative minds solve some of the world's most important problems'. It rewards ideas with cash up to £1 million and claims engagement with commercial, governmental and humanitarian organisations.

The introduction of a culture that embraces the practice of open innovation may encounter resistance due to various factors including mistrust, closed mindsets and the rejection of ideas which do not originate within the organisation itself. This resistance may be countered through placing the right people in the right positions, appointing 'idea champions', creating open communication channels, effectively disseminating information, appointing idea connectors and implementing staff training and development. Successful outcomes related to open innovation are not easy to assess. Initial 'raw' ideas are often modified, combined or adapted by various people involved in the process of transforming them into tangible and feasible innovations. As yet, however, there exists no broadly accepted tool for measuring performance where open innovation is concerned, possibly due to the difficulties encountered in identifying the variables that play a role in this complex process.

This should not deter organisations from embracing the open innovation process in a strategic manner, which involves a thorough assessment of the climate and culture of the organisation and its internal and external networks. It would be a pity for organisations that wish to take innovation seriously to forgo the benefits which open innovation offers.

Open innovation does not occur in a vacuum: strategic efforts are imperative to enable organisations to reach out to external sources and to ensure the communication of relevant and feasible ideas to key people within the organisation. Open innovation should not be viewed as a substitute for innovation within the organisation itself. Both should be fostered and sustained to ensure that the organisation makes the most of the potential which is available in order to optimise its competitiveness.

The changing face of technological innovation

Imagine a world with no laptops, no smartphones, no Skype, no internet, no chat, no social networks, no technological means of communicating. Imagine a world with no aeroplanes, no trains, no cars, no travel, no interaction amongst people in different countries. Imagine a world with no anaesthetic, no pain killers, no clean water, no sanitary facilities.

Most people today are dependent to a great extent on technology, even though some communities exist (the Amish, for example) that opt to do without it. Technology connects people globally. It provides services related to healthcare, communication, education and standards of living that most people cannot imagine living without. Technology results in the creation of new networks, new economies, new work patterns, smart cities, ambient intelligence, new means of communication (viral diffusion), new pedagogies. Although there are always two sides to a coin, if we consider the manner in which new technology has been diffused, particularly over the past decade, it is doubtful whether anyone would be keen to go back to living a life with inferior technology.

Technology fuels economic growth and it is one of the key innovation drivers. It facilitates the creation of organic network structures which enable successful organisations to move away from traditional hierarchial decision making and towards flexibility and agility. These allow organisations to locate key functions, including production, anywhere in the world; to take advantage of low cost labour, skills, expertise and natural resources. Technology allows organisations to monitor and assess trends, market developments and their own and competitors' performance.

Organisations need to challenge their current mode of thinking and to gain a better understanding of the myriad implications which change related to digital technology brings in its wake. This includes awareness of the possibility of competitors from emerging markets (such as those in India and China) which may have fewer regulatory or legislative issues to deal with and may move to market faster with more affordable products or services.

The use of cloud computing is one of the more recent technological trends that is increasingly being adopted by organisations. It involves the delivery of computing as a virtual (remote) service, where a proprietary network supplies web-based hosting services. This is generally a high speed internet-based process that enables computing resources such as data processing, data management, social networking and other IT facilities to be securely accessed and shared in a secure and scalable manner. Benefits of cloud computing include increased accessibility to data without the requirement of huge investments or particular geographical location.

Generation Y

It is not only technology but also the manner in which technology is used that plays a role when considering the changing face of innovation. Young people today, often referred to as Generation Y (or Gen Y), were born into the 'internet age' and have grown up using the internet, mobile phones and social networking sites such as Facebook for communication purposes. Born in the 1990s, their emergence onto the job market means their attitudes and the effect they will have when employed in organisations needs to be better understood.

This generation may be described as ambitious and self-confident. Some older people, particularly those known as 'baby-boomers' (born in the 1950s) may consider Gen Ys to be arrogant because they are not afraid to raise questions if something is unclear. They also have high expectations and seek new challenges. Gen Ys' entrance into the workplace could present increased opportunities to competitive organisations; having high-performing staff is an asset when demographic trends forecast potential future labour shortages. Different generations possess different values, attitudes, skills and ways of operating, but Gen Ys' are definitely one important factor to be taken into consideration in today's technologically saturated organisational environment.

Technology driven innovation

Technology is one of the main drivers of innovation and, due to its ubiquotous nature in today's world, it plays a key role in the manner in which innovative organisations function. New technology is fundamentally transforming. It will continue to transform the operating methods of most organisations as new technologies have become institutionalised globally and are having a revolutionary effect on corporate strategy. Technology allows for increased access to networks and to the creation of new networks which have the potential to span geographical boundaries, operate in real time, increase access to and disseminate relevant information, besides providing new opportunities for collaboration.

A network involves the existence of multiple nodes, the interconnections between them and the cooperative (as opposed to competitive) behaviour of these nodes. The effect of networks has been visible for many years, for example road networks, railway networks, telephone networks, electricity networks, political networks, trade guild networks, and 'old school friends' networks. New technology has, however, created unlimited possibilities for new networks, the dynamics of which play an important role where technological innovation is concerned.

Size is one relevant factor to consider in any discussion of network effects. Effective and successful networks require the establishment of a large base of participants or consumers. This makes production, collaboration and communication viable and creates increased usage. This effect is evident in the use of mobile phone communication, virtual communication or networks such as Skype or Facebook, or virtual worlds such as OpenSim and Second Life and MMORPGs (Massively Multiplayer OnLine Role Playing Games such as World of Warcraft). The concept of a large user base implies that the value of a product or service increases as the number of users, together with complementary goods or services, increases.

A consequence of the widespread use of new technology is the emergence of a new network economy. This may lead to commercial gain for organisations through the exploitation of the opportunities which new technology offers. Network externalities may be defined as the increasing utility that a user or consumer derives from the consumption of a product or service as the number of other users or consumers of the same product or service increases. Telephone networks are one example of this. When more people subscibe to a telephone network, more users can be reached, thereby increasing its usability. This also applies to credit card networks, ATM networks and social networking sites.

The actual demand for a product or service and expectations of total demand play a key role here. Customer expectations should be strategically managed as a small base of users deters motivation to subscribe to a network. The management of user expectations may give rise to confidence that the customer base may grow substantially. The more something is in demand and the more expectations for demand there are, the more valuable it becomes. This leads to increased participation, with the potential for a snowball effect if the right people are targeted during strategic expectations management. Expectations management not only applies to technological products or services but also to the purchase of items such as cars or washing machines, where there is the expectation to find spare parts and technical support over a period of time.

Successful expectations management may lead to a 'tipping point' when user or customer expectations may veer towards one network (or one service or product on the market) and away from the competition – as is the case with Windows as an operating system, Google as an online search engine and Facebook as a social networking site.

Strategy aimed towards increasing expectations may have very powerful effects. Strategic action aimed at increasing consumers' expectations of the success of a new product could result in motivating increased new users who, in turn, could influence even more users. In the mobile telecommunications industry, when mobile phones became affordable for young people (the early adopters), sales increased and more users from other segments were attracted to the market. In today's changing world, customers are uncertain about which technological standards and products will survive the test of time (remember video players and video recorders?). This will increase the need to manage customer expectations in an attempt to speed adoption rates towards 'tipping points' in the market.

Two contrasting types of network market which emerge are monopolies and regulated networks. In the latter case, efforts are made to create strong interconnections and harmonised standards, allowing users to effortlessly move from one network to another, as is the case with mobile phone network providers, ATM machines and internationally recognised credit cards. Although it is not yet the case with e-reading devices, this may be possible in the future through the launch of a new platform which may allow for interoperability.

User decisions may be interdependent as the reputation of a network and its user base increases as a result of network dynamics, with the value of the product or service increasing as its user or consumer base increases. This often follows the S-curve model (see Chapter 2, Section 2.3.6) where a point in time is eventually reached where the 'laggards' tend to join an established network. Laggards are considered as less valuable customers and the cost of acquiring new users may exceed the cost they may be willing to pay.

With the potential for globalisation which the new networked economy offers, local, national and regional boundaries blur and the need for international standards becomes more acute. The rapid growth of innovative technological products depends on operating technology standards and on production costs, for example, ATM machines and credit cards across the world must work to an agreed standard to ensure that one card may be used in different countries. Organisations that determine standards are established to reduce the cost and the uncertainty associated with adopting new standards. Negotiated standard setting guarantees the smooth exchange of information, technical components and services along different technological networks such as the telecommunications industry. The internet has a different history of standardisation to telecommunications. Standards were completely open and established within the research communities of universities.

As the internet has become a commodity for both individuals and organisations, other players are increasingly influencing its evolution, including smart phone and tablet operators, as an increasing number of people access the web through their smart phones, PDAs or tablets. With the standardisation of technology, products are becoming similar in design and quality. The implication is that suppliers may easily be replaced by organisations that offer similar products or services. The information economy is creating a network of organisations that have lower barriers of entry, but with fewer safety nets for retaining market share.

The self-organising aspect of the information economy gives rise to the concept of co-evolution. Adapting to meet the needs of other organisations may lead to more business. Through co-creation and co-evolution, organisations may avoid competition and adopt a strategy to join forces to gain more customers. Co-evolution and collaboration may be more relevant in innovative technological industries where network externalities affect organisational success.

Lock-in is the effect that occurs when users invest in the assets of a particular network platform and find the costs of switching to an alternative to be prohibitive. Lock-in may occur on an individual, social or organisational level. On a societal level, millions of users are locked into using the Microsoft Windows desktop operating system as it is, at least at present, considered to be the standard software around the world.

Telecommunications systems providers have chosen to offer new, superior technologies despite high switching costs. Switching costs and lock-in at the consumer level may be deliberately used to inhibit or prevent consumers from adopting newer technologies or from moving to alternative networks. When mobile phones were first introduced, users were bound to a particular network by contract. In the late 1990s, switching networks became easier with the introduction of 'pay as you go' cards for mobile phones. However the hidden intangible cost of switching remains, irrespective of payment structures.

The economic characteristics of network industries are dependent to a great extent on the interconnectivity and interoperability that is characteristic of new technology. Interconnectivity allows customers to view, use and link products, giving rise to virtual networks of users. It is evident that there are considerable forces promoting more cooperation and interoperability where new technology is concerned, most of which comes about as a result of new network dynamics which are self-organising and which result from innovation, flexibility and adaptation. The current growth of the smart-phone market, for example, could provide market opportunities, particularly in emerging markets where smart-phone uptake could provide users with their only access to the internet, allowing for increased mobile marketing and location-based services directed towards those who may not have the possibility of accessing the web by other means.

We are living in a world of immense uncertainty where there is a significant probability that future technological change may undermine what at present may appear as a successfully positioned product or service. Organisations need to be prepared to take risks and to adopt innovative solutions in order to survive in this technology saturated context.

Key principles

Social networking

Online social networking is creating a transformation in the manner in which organisations communicate with customers and other stakeholders. It provides the opportunity for organisations to harness ideas to communicate with users and consumers and to improve products or services or create new ones. Of course social networking existed well before the advent of new digital technology but, whether it was between members of a group with a common interest or between colleagues in the work place, communication generally took place face to face. Some examples of this include religious communities, alumni groups, trade guilds, hobby groups, associations such as Junior Chamber, Lions Club and Rotary Club, NGOs, activity groups such as ramblers or sports groups such as joggers.

Modern social networking also makes use of technology in a number of guises, such as blogs, online communities or general social networking sites (such as Facebook, LinkedIn, MySpace and Twitter) which combine a number of features. Social networking sites are popular for the following reasons:

- To make new friends and to find and reconnect with old friends;
- To communicate ideas and opinions;
- To share information, photos, videos, ideas and so on;
- To learn;
- To play games, either individual, competitive or collaborative;
- To meet others with shared interests (niche networking).

Just as some people build trust, expectations and influence in their communities, a similar process occurs in social networking where people may increase their 'status' and become influential in shaping the ideas of others.

Facebook is said to be the most popular social networking site at the moment (1 January 2012) with over 800 million active users. The manner in which Facebook has evolved follows the process of Rogers' distribution curve for the adoption of innovation (Rogers, 1962), with the exception that the 'decline' (or 'slump') does not yet appear to loom on the horizon. Facebook is so well known that a movie (*The Social Network*, 2010) has been released on its origins and evolution.

Twitter involves the communication of messages or 'tweets' with a maximum of 140 characters. Tweeters (as those who use Twitter are called) acquire followers who may choose to re-tweet a tweet – this could result in viral communication if the information and circumstances are right.

There are numerous other social networking sites, including:

- MySpace, which has similar features to Facebook, although it appears to have evolved mainly for those with an interest in sharing music (audio and video);
- HiFive, which is similar but appeals to a younger crowd, as does Bebo;
- Linkedin, which is mainly used by professionals for communicating and exchanging information through 'profiles' and groups which avail themselves of discussion boards (e.g. easyJet asked members of its Linkedin group for ideas on how to attract more business travellers).

eBizMBA, a social networking ranking site, lists Facebook, Twitter and LinkedIn as the top three most popular sites (1 January 2012). Alexa, another web ranking site, lists Google, Facebook and YouTube as the top three global sites (1 January 2012).

Facebook's popularity may be due to the services it offers which include status updates, photo and video sharing, chat and a private message service. It also offers games, quizzes and a number of applications, many of which are user-generated. Facebook's success exhibits the power of network dynamics: more users created high expectations for additional users, making it the success it is today – whether this success will be sustained remains to be seen.

Social networking sites are accessible on 'smart devices' including 'smart phones'. A survey conducted in 2010 with 50,000 people across 46 countries revealed that mobile users spend more time on social networking sites than they do on email (ITProPortal, 2010). Thanks to the increased use of smart phones, social networking is becoming one of the fastest growing internet activites.

Social networking is also possible through the creation of avatars in 3-D virtual worlds. These include Second Life (SL) and Open Sim although there are many more available. Virtual social networking sites are being increasingly used by both educators and organisations. They offer the possibility to build and nurture communities. Some religious groups and some universities or well known personalities have done this, for example, a Portugese MEP from the Azores and an American professor both use Second Life (see www.metanomics.net). IBM hold virtual meetings on their private islands on SL for people from all over the world and thus avoid travel costs and reduce their carbon footprint.

It must be noted that social networking sites may be either misused or used in what may be perceived as a 'deceptive' manner. Nerenberg (2010) draws attention to various issues, including privacy, discretion and ethical issues, where social networking sites may create problems or be misused. The media and potential or current employers are known to use social networking sites to obtain information on people; some may post information about themselves without reflecting on possible repercussions; others pretend to be someone other than themselves (a different gender or a celebrity perhaps) and still others may become addicted to such sites with serious repercussions in their real lives.

Organisations may benefit by setting up their own internal information sharing social network for use by their employees. Yammer is one provider of such a service and their website reports that:

> Deloitte Digital CEO Peter Williams posted a message on the Deloitte Australia Yammer network for a new ad campaign. Over the next 24 hours, hundreds of Deloitte Australia employees submitted thousands of taglines. As a result, Deloitte Australia utilized an

employee-submitted tagline advertising instead of hiring an advertising agency to develop the campaign. Since then, Deloitte Australia has used Yammer to start internal discussions about external information, such as reviews.

(Yammer, Success Stories, Deloitte)

This process is similar to crowdsourcing which increasingly allows organisations to collect ideas from potentially millions of people in a particular network. Yammer offers a number of services to its customers including the possibility to create private or public groups, microblogging, links to external networks and private messaging – the latter is increasingly being adopted by organisations for internal communication purposes as some organisations consider it to be an improved alternative to email.

The use of social networking by organisations allows for the gathering of information, ideas and trends as it allows organisations to tap into the market and listen to their customers through pre-existing or specifically set up online communities. Organisations that adopt social networking sites for communication purposes should recognise that the relationship between audience reach and persuasive impact is generally counter-proportional to the expense and effort expended. Although advertising and promotional media reach the largest audiences through mass media, they have the least persuasive impact. Interpersonal communication, which is possible either face to face or through online social networking sites, may reach a very limited audience, but it has the highest amount of persuasive impact.

Organisations that wish to communicate effectively through social networking sites should identify 'opinion leaders' – individuals who have the power to influence others through their opinion or advice – who then influence others. Lazarsfeld *et al.*'s 'Two-Step Flow Theory' (1944) is as valid for digital communication as it is for other media or face to face communication. The research expected to find empirical support for the direct influence of media messages on voting intentions. The results surprisingly demonstrated that informal, personal contacts were mentioned far more frequently than exposure to radio or newspapers as sources of influence on voting behaviour.

The Two-Step Flow Theory therefore claims that information from the media moves first towards opinion leaders who are capable of effectively influencing others as they communicate their own interpretations in addition to the actual media content. In today's networked and technologically saturated environment, customers follow the advice of influential opinion leaders more readily than other media messages.

A successful example of user participation by the media is CNN's iReport which allows stories, videos and photos to be uploaded on to the CNN iReport website. These are then vetted and the selected stories are endorsed by CNN. This is an efficient and cost-effective means to gather news with CNN claiming that nearly 185,000 iReports were submitted during 2011.

Organisations now have the opportunity to harness the influence of opinion leaders and the brainpower of volunteers to communicate, disseminate information, collaborate or share ideas. Social media has extended the range of potential communication to span geographical boundaries. If one influential person communicates information to friends using social media, that message could potentially reach millions of people in a very short period of time. Social media (which includes social networking) is a tool that can improve organisational performance through various means, including intelligence gathering, new product development, improved collaboration and increased customer retention and sales.

Innovation diffusion

Technological diffusion is a process through which an innovation is communicated through various channels among the members of a community. Diffusion occurs through five stages: knowledge, persuasion, decision, implementation and confirmation. If the innovation is adopted, it has the potential to spread like a virus or to be diffused through a variety of communication channels.

Prospective customers go through a series of stages of acceptance (the adoption process) when endorsing a new product or service, these are:

- Awareness: the individual becomes cognizant of the innovation but lacks information.
- Interest: the individual is stimulated to seek information about the innovation.
- Evaluation: the individual considers whether it would make sense to try the innovation.
- Trial: the individual tries the innovation on a small scale.
- Adoption: the individual decides to make full and regular use of the innovation.

These stages are adopted from Rogers' Diffusion of Innovation Theory (1962). Although diffusion is not to be equated with dissemination, some relevant information may be gleaned from this source. Rogers distinguished between 'early adopters', who explore and seek new experiences, and middle and late adopters. His Diffusion of Innovation Theory includes the identification of stages through which innovations proceed:

- Knowledge (exposure to its existence and understanding of its functions);
- Persuasion (the forming of a favourable attitude to it);
- Decision (commitment to its adoption);
- Implementation (putting it to use);
- Confirmation (reinforcement based on positive outcomes).

Rogers' views throw light on the manner in which individuals or groups may be successfully persuaded of the utility or otherwise of a policy, outcome, product or service, improving the likelihood for success.

Innovative marketing strategies using digital technology

Marketing strategies may capitalise on the use of technology to promote the launch of new products or services. This is how crowds can be attracted to stores to purchase new products or services, as was the case with the introduction of Apple's iPhone which used opinion leaders to influence potential customers with messages communicated through digital technology such as blogs, social networks and discussion forums. New technology provides the opportunity for people in marketing to tailor their messages directed towards specific interests or communities.

One tool that marketers and innovators use is BlogPulse, a website that tracks blogs through the application of automated machine-learning and natural processing techniques. It can reveal trends, tracks and captures conversations as they flow through blog posts, and provides statistics which allow for the generation of trend graphs.

Organisational success and increased competitiveness today depend a great deal on the successful communication of product or service ideas into consumer markets to attract attention and to generate interest, often before the product or service is actually launched. Increased understanding of the manner in which messages are communicated and diffused by means of new technology and how they may influence potential customers is crucial for the adoption of new products or services and for successful marketing.

Virtual worlds have been used by organisations for marketing purposes for some time. This medium offers a number of innovative possibilities including the setting up of dedicated virtual space, branding virtual goods, disseminating convincing marketing messages to opinion leaders in virtual worlds for dissemination, participating in established communities to create 'buzz' and the creation of communities for those who are interested in the particular product or service.

Innovative revenue models

Innovation is visible in the emergence of new (sustainable) revenue models which organisations are adopting and which often arise as a result of innovative technological possibilities. One example is the printer which is initially sold to customers at a relatively cheap price, but which requires a substantial input of ink cartridges which must be replaced on a regular basis. The regular need created for ink cartridges and their sale provides a steady stream of revenue as opposed to a one-off point of sale income.

On web-generated content, revenue models may be dependent on the number of visitors who click on the site since a high number of visitors attracts advertising. Web adverts generally operate as either 'pay per click' which means the advertiser pays depending on the number of times users click on the advert, or on the number of times particular information is visible on a third-party web site (pay per impression).

The end of the career?

Due to the accelerating rate of change caused mainly by the increased uptake of new technology, policy makers and organisations need to reconsider the concept of careers. Traditionally a career (perhaps in only one organisation) would comprise most of a person's working life. However, a trend towards internships for young people to gain work experience, increased job mobility and fixed-term contracts is evident. Flores and Gray (2000) claim that the career is in decline even though policy makers still consider careers to be the desirable model for employment policies and economic stability. Their claim is that 'The very idea of a career now makes less and less sense of most people's working lives'. New and less secure working patterns are emerging and the subsequent effects and implications of this shift need to be carefully assessed by both individuals and organisations.

Baby boomers born in the 1950s tended to take up opportunities for job mobility to further their career or to improve their employment position. Previous generations considered employment for life as part of their commitment to society, a practice which helped to sustain family life and communities. Generation Y have a different approach to careers, and the current economic situation no longer provides the clear career paths it may have done in the past.

A great deal of displacement is occuring through technological innovation, particularly in the service industries. Examples include travel agents, sales people in retail stores and the banking sector and the internet's effect on the publishing industry: new technologies (e-books for example) may displace the concept of the published book and newspapers.

Economies and work contexts are being transformed more rapidly than ever before and the skills required by innovative organisations today are no longer those that most people were taught in school or at university. Education should be regarded as a lifelong undertaking and employees provided with opportunities for continuous professional development and frequent retraining in order to provide individuals with the skills that organisations require, and an entrepreneurial mindset where opportunities are recognised and individuals are prepared to take risks.

Control and authority, which were traditional managerial mindsets in the past, need to give way to a new form of trust. This cannot always be constructed on a face to face basis as it was in the past. Possibilities for remote working and the blurring of geographical boundaries give rise to a new form of trust building which involves integrity, responsibility and respect. Virtual and remote communication through social networking, virtual worlds or instant messaging allow for the creation of new forms of trust building and work assessment practices. Emerging issues which need to be addressed in innovative ways include values and ethical issues. Creative thinking may play a key role in this process.

Technology unites people from all four corners of the globe. It totally erases all geographical boundaries, often eliminating political, social and cultural boundaries. The effects of innovation related to technology are impacting employment and the manner in which the digital economy operates with subsequent implications for managerial practice. Understanding these emerging trends enables organisations and policy makers to design strategies and policies that successfully address the changing context which is brought about due to innovation and technological change.

Towards a knowledge society and digitally networked economies

Many things have changed in today's organisational context including cost structures, revenue models and demand dynamics. Concepts such as added value and competitive advantage are being applied in innovative ways. Digital technology and networks play a key role in this process. It is therefore important to understand the dynamics of digitally networked economies and the consequent effects. A new network economy has emerged as a consequence of the widespread use and globalisation of innovative digital technology.

The new network economy consists of multiple nodes, interconnections and cooperative behaviour, just as traditional networks functioned in the past. The possibilities which technology offers to the network economy is similar to the manner in which neurons function in a human brain, constantly connecting and providing feedback and adjustment processes which are complex but which act on self-organising principles. Networks were traditionally one-way, creating links in one direction (television and radio are examples of this) or two-way, where links could be operated in both directions (telephones and railroads are examples of this). Technology has created a shift from physical networks to virtual networks, examples of which are online communities such as gamers, Facebook and Twitter, or open source computer software platforms where the interconnection between users is intangible, and where users remain interdependent.

Developing an understanding of how 'network economies' function is key to developing a new set of organisational strategies in today's information-based (and technological) corporate landscape. This will allow for increased possibilities for success for organisations that take innovation seriously. The internet, one example of a massive virtual network, has provided a free infrastructure for communicating information and it is creating new opportunities, the potential of which needs to be recognised and exploited. The development of the new networked economy industries may lead to increased innovation and commercial success through the exploitation of the opportunities that the world wide web offers.

What does the future hold? Some predictions claim that mature economies such as the USA will become less dominant in the future, as Brazil, Russia, India, China and South Africa (also known as BRICS) and other countries play an increasing role in the global economic scenario. At a micro level, intelligent cities and organisations based on technology are giving rise to geographical hot spots of commercial activity, created from economic networks, corporate clusters and commercial ecosystems.

Practice

Is the 'world' flat or spiked?

Knowledge is generally considered to be an intangible asset or resource and some authors claim that geographical location is one central factor to be considered when considering the possibility of innovation clusters or what are today often known as 'knowledge nodes' or 'creative cities' (Niosi, 2002).

One of the main proponents of the importance of geographical location is Richard Florida (2004) who maintains that a city must possess the three Ts if it is to attract 'the Creative Class'. These are:

- Talent (a highly talented, educated and skilled population);
- Tolerance (a diverse community consisting of, amongst others, artists, bohemians, gays, etc.);
- Technology (the technological infrastructure necessary to 'wire-up' and to fuel an entrepreneurial culture).

Florida provides an image of creative cities as 'spikes' or centres of creative activity which act as a magnet for both other creative people and for investors in the knowledge economy. Thomas L. Friedman (2005) proposes a diametrically opposed view to that of Florida. He claims that the world is 'flat' due to the possibilities which new digital technology offers. Friedman describes a global economic scenario where historical and geographical divisions are increasingly irrelevant due to the possibilities which technology networks and their related interconnections offer. Friedman's view suggests that the connectivity offered by digital technology may enable increased globalisation regardless of geographical location. One example he provides is that of call centres which are often located in countries such as India, where human resources are easily available and where costs incurred are much less than they may be in the Western hemisphere.

Nations, regions, cities or organisations may decide to select either Florida's or Friedman's views depending on their particular attributes, culture and context. Digital technology and networking across borders offers increased possibilities, particularly for small nations, cities and organisations which do not have the 'critical mass' to develop in the manner which Florida suggests they should.

Is it possible for knowledge to be as mobile as Friedman claims it is? Although knowledge may be produced anywhere in the world, it is important to recognise that some forms of scientific research require facilities which are tailor made for particular research purposes. In these cases, geographical location tends to be important, often in cities similar to the ones which Florida describes as 'hot-spots' for research activity, knowledge generation and innovation.

Although cities which appear in Florida's research as creative spikes may attract new capital investments and entice organisations and people to move to them, there are particular criteria which Florida outlines (such as that a city should have at least one million inhabitants and a number of research laboratories and universities) that may not be feasible for smaller nations. The latter could capitalise on Friedman's ideas and create networks, clusters and linkages across geographical borders – a reality which is possible thanks to new technology.

Action

Quo vadis? An informational 'rain forest'?

A number of future opportunities are emerging for organisations that take innovation in technology seriously. The global proliferation of innovative technology has created a number of dramatic changes in the manner in which organisations operate. There has been a shift from production to communication and to the use of new media to disseminate information, harness ideas and keep in touch with customers, suppliers, employees and other stakeholders. Information is more freely available and organisations may capitalise on the intelligence and data provided to support and satisfy customers' needs and to supply them with more innovative and individualised products or services.

Sifting through the plethora of information which digital technology provides is not an easy task. Neither is it easy to deal successfully with new communications technologies. New positions have been created for specific teams or consultants to deal with tasks such as business analytics and data evaluation. The use of social networking sites by innovative organisations has created a new role for teams and consultants who specialise in creating and fostering virtual relationships and with keeping users motivated to contribute their ideas on pages or sites that do not stagnate, but which are regularly updated and sustained. The role which customers and users play and their interaction with organisations needs to be rethought. Trends, competitive forces and user contributions need to be monitored and taken into consideration in planning, decision making and in the creation of new products or services. Cloud computing allows for cheaper and more efficient storage of data which allows for early identification of market trends and opportunities and the anticipation of global market shifts. Data can be mined and predictive tools (such as those used for foresight activities) utilised to test markets and create future visions and scenarios.

There are also some downsides to this picture. The new digital economy may expose governments, organisations and individuals to the escalating threat of cyberterrorism and hacking, the misuse of proprietary knowledge and intellectual property and reputational damage from influential third-party users of new media technology. Wikileaks has, for example, released and communicated a database of hundreds of documents which were held by governments and surveillance agencies on what were considered to be 'secure' sites. Anonymous, an unidentified group of hackers who apply the Anonymous label as a collective symbol, have actively collaborated since 2008 to conduct what is now called hacktivism – revealing data, undertaking protests and other actions which are often intended to sustain internet freedom and freedom of speech. The 2011 civil society protests in North Africa and the Middle East utilised technology to muster large numbers of protesters. The Occupy movement uses new media to gather together individuals who take over public or private areas, generally in central areas in large cities (such as St Paul's Square outside St Paul's Cathedral in London and New York City's Zuccotti Park where the first protest was held on 17 September 2011) for protests directed against economic and social inequality. Occupy groups make use of Meetup, a site dedicated to the creation of groups that organise meetings or protests. Organisations that adopt new media and technology need to be aware of these and other related issues and to identify means to protect their confidential data from hackers and activists.

Some weak signals and trends which emerge from the new information society include:

- The possibility of human enhancement through the implanting of 'chips' in humans for either medical reasons or to enhance human cognition and other human capabilities.
- The possibility of extending human lives for an indefinite period with the elimination of medical problems or old age. The advances in robotic technology which allow humans to do away with menial or time-consuming tasks and which allow for the automated processing of the masses of data which may be required for a project – advances in robotics are expected to be exponential in the future and it is likely that intelligent machines (or advanced-level robots) will take over a number of roles related to the caring profession just as automated processes have taken over the tasks previously conducted by support staff and tellers at commercial banks.

It is not only organisations but also nations, regions and cities that need to reflect on current trends and on the masses of information available and to consider the possibility of capitalising on them and re-designing current ways of doing things to achieve increased effectiveness, efficiency and sustainability.

Summary

The new digital economy requires new paradigms, new mindsets, new attitudes. . .What can we do to facilitate this? What understanding do we need? What type of knowledge do we need to communicate. . .to students, to educators, to organisations, to policy makers? What recommendations could be proposed?

This chapter has attempted to address these and other relevant questions. There is no doubt, however, that additional and possibly unexpected questions will arise which necessitate agility, flexibility and a holistic strategy which is capable of adapting to the changes that will come about. We need to keep in mind the fact that change, particularly concerning technology, is incremental over time and it is likely to continue in this manner. . .We cannot stop global trends. . .We need to examine threats and turn them into opportunities for the benefit of all people!

Discussion questions

1. What is meant by the term Open Innovation and how can it benefit companies and organisations?
2. How has the advent of digital technology changed our lives?
3. Who are Generation Y and what impact are they likely to have on the world of work?
4. Critically assess how technology drives innovation.
5. How is online social networking creating a transformation in the manner in which organisations communicate with customers and other stakeholders?

6.   Name the five diffusion stages and Rogers' adoption stages.
7.   How in the light of an accelerated rate of change, caused mainly by the increased uptake of new technology, might policy makers and organisations need to reconsider the concept of careers?
8.   Is the 'world' flat or spiked?

Case exercise

Task

Imagine that you have been asked to draft a brief report for a local newspaper or magazine that summarises the main impact of digital technology on organisational innovation initiatives. Prepare a one-page list of the points that you consider are important to cover.

References

Chesbrough, H. (2003) *Open Innovation: The New Imperative for Creating and Profiting from Technology*, Boston, MA, Harvard Business Publishing.

Flores, F. and Gray, J. (2000) *Entrepreneurship and the Wired Life: Work in the Wake of Careers*, London, Demos. See also http://www.demos.co.uk/files/entrepreneurshipandthewiredlife.pdf?1240939425, accessed 02/01/12.

Florida, R. (2004) *Cities and the Creative Class*, London, Routledge. See also resources on *The Creative Class*: http://www.creativeclass.com, accessed 17/04/12.

Friedman, T.L. (2005) *The World Is Flat: A Brief History of the Twenty-first Century*, New York, Farrar, Straus and Giroux. See also Thomas L. Friedman resources, articles and information: http://www.thomaslfriedman.com, accessed 17/04/12.

ITProPortal (2010) 'Social media more popular than e-mail for mobile users'. http://www.itproportal.com/2010/10/12/social-media-more-popular-e-mail-mobile-users/, accessed 24/04/12.

Jörgensen, J.H., Bergenholtz, C., Goduscheit, R.C. and Rasmussen, E.S. (2011) 'Managing inter-firm collaboration in the fuzzy front-end: Structure as a two-edged sword', *International Journal of Innovation Management*, February, Vol. 15, Issue 1, pp. 145–63.

Lazarsfeld, P., Berelson, B. and Gaudet, H. (1944) *The People's Choice*, New York, Columbia University Press.

Nerenberg, J. (2010) 'Is your doctor drunk on Facebook?', *Fastcompany*, 9 August.

Niosi, J. (2002) 'National systems of innovation are "x-efficient" (and x-effective): Why some are slow learners', *Research Policy*, February, Vol. 31, Issue 2, pp. 291–302.

Rogers, E. (1962) *Diffusion of Innovations*, Glencoe, IL, Free Press.

Websites

Alexa – global web ranking: http://www.alexa.com/topsites/global

Anonymous – AnonOps Communications: A site dedicated to reporting news about Anonymous: http://anonops.blogspot.com/

Cloud Computing: http://www.techterms.com/definition/cloudcomputing

CNN iReport: http://ireport.cnn.com/

ebizmba – Top 15 most popular social networking sites: http://www.ebizmba.com/articles/social-networking-websites

Kurzweil Accelerating Intelligence: http://www.kurzweilai.net/

Meetup: http://www.meetup.com/

Occupy Movement – Occupy Together: http://www.occupytogether.org/

The Singularity is Near: http://www.singularity.com
Tipping Point: http://www.gladwell.com/tippingpoint/
Warwick, Kevin – cyborgs and human enhancement: http://www.kevinwarwick.com/
Yammer: The Enterprise Social Network: https://www.yammer.com/
Yammer – Success Stories – Deloitte: https://www.yammer.com/about/case_studies#deloitte-story
Wikileaks: http://wikileaks.org/

Part IV

Managing change

13 The importance of leadership

A leader is a dealer in hope.
              (Napoleon Bonaparte)

I prefer the talents of action. . .to all the speculations of those mere dreamers of another
existence.
                                    (Lord Byron, Letter to Annabella Milbanke, 1813)

Introduction

Most organisations are challenged by the necessity of dealing with the impact and consequences of the paradigm change in the business environment discussed in Part I. This generally amounts to recognising and facing up to the need for change and having the resolution
to take decisions which break with the *modus operandi* of the past. Management have a
tendency to regard preserving the *status quo* as an important part of their mission and in so
doing may wittingly or unwittingly develop an unrealistic view of real-world conditions.
This attitude will result in failure to take the right mix of business decisions and can produce
a state of management confusion and myopia.

It has long been recognised that the act of management tends to be associated in many
organisations with the concept of efficiency. Managers are people who do things right
according to the established organisational culture. However, leading has more to do with
the concept of effectiveness; doing the right thing in the light of real-world conditions. This
requires an adventurous approach that identifies the need to discover a new vision for
the organisation, the determination to communicate this to staff and the collective energy
and commitment to design and energise action that will result in success. The foresight and
action necessary is, therefore, better encapsulated by the concept of leadership (Bennis and
Nanus, 1985). This chapter discusses the important characteristics of leadership and the key
tasks it is called to perform. Practical material (including an audit and a checklist) is included
to encourage readers to think through the practical implications of leadership. It should be
noted that an organisation's determination and commitment to leadership activity does not
render traditional controlling management activities redundant. Both leadership and conventional management activity are needed. It is the balance of these responses that underpins a
positive approach to operating an organisation in modern times.

One curious student posed the question in a seminar class 'What exactly is a leader?'
Reduced to basics a leader is someone others choose to follow whether or not they have a
choice in the matter. A leader is characterised by both action and trust. Such leaders provide
action and direction at a time of crisis and are immediately trusted. Leaders are also people
who others with time to think and judge also choose to follow. In the UK navy ratings have

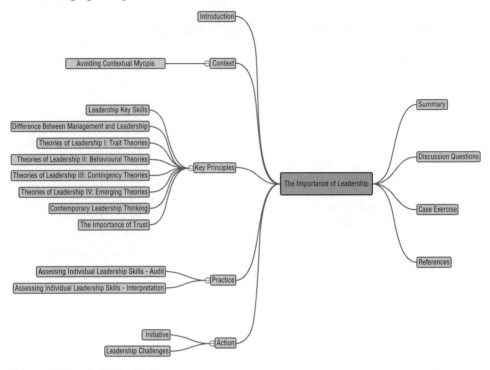

Figure 13.1 Exploring leadership.

been heard to quip 'I'll follow the man who is a leader but I won't follow the man who thinks that he is a leader'. So if there is time for people to form opinions about a leader attractive personality traits are important but not necessarily the basis of success.

Returning to the student's question, a leader appears to be someone who is recognised either immediately or over time as a person who enables individuals, groups and organisations to respond in a beneficial way within the constraints of a given environment. Within the context of an organisation this implies a sensible alignment between the needs of individuals and groups and the expressed purpose (vision) of the organisation. Traditionally leaders have often been regarded as the boss at the top. Today a fundamental shift is underway in the work of corporate leaders as they seek to create and sustain employee achievement and high levels of staff morale. It is a shift from a command and control style to one where the leader creates the conditions under which an ambition can be achieved. Thus the answer to the student's question posed earlier is: leaders are people who are able to influence others and in organisations possess managerial authority.

Context

Avoiding contextual myopia

Leaders need to assume responsibility for both successes and failures. According to Beer *et al.* (1990) they share three characteristics:

1. They harbour a strong and persistent belief that facing up to the challenges of the business environment is essential.

2. They communicate their conviction in the form of a creditable and compelling vision.
3. They have the people-skills and organisational know-how to implement their vision.

Key principles

Essential leadership skills

Much over the years has been written in the literature, both in academic articles and books, about the topic of leadership. For today's student of leadership much of this material can appear repetitive. What should an aspiring business leader read? A useful response to this question might perhaps be what is most meaningful to you in your operating environment. This reduces the library of material to that which is grounded in practice. The authors of this text have focused on the work of Bennis and Nanus (1985) who examined the behaviour and characteristics of 90 leaders. They concluded that they possess four vital competencies:

1. Management of attention – the vision of the leaders commanded the attention and commitment of those who worked for and with them in attempting to achieve it.
2. Management of meaning – the leaders were skilled communicators, able to cut through complexity in order to frame issues in simple images and language. They were excellent distillers of information.
3. Management of trust – 'Trust is essential to all organizations'. For the leaders trust was expressed through consistency of purpose and in their dealings with colleagues and others. Even though people sometimes disagreed with what they said or did, the leaders were admired for their consistency of purpose.
4. Management of self – the leaders were adept at identifying and fully using their strengths; and accepting and seeking to develop areas of weakness.

Leadership skills do develop naturally in some but can also be learnt by a manager willing to make the effort. Leadership is, however, fundamentally different from management. To survive in the twenty-first century we need a new generation of leaders not managers. Good leaders in current times require attitudes and behaviours which both attract and relate to humanity.

Differences between management and leadership

The distinction is an important one. According to Drucker (2001) 'Management is doing things right: leadership is doing the right thing'. Leaders conquer the context (Kotter, 1990) – the volatile, turbulent, ambiguous surroundings that sometimes seem to conspire against us and will surely suffocate us if we let them – while managers surrender to it. The fundamental differences between the two are illustrated in Table 13.1.

Leaders, whether good or bad, inspire trust in the people they engage and with whom they interact. Leadership is about behaviour first and skills second. With this in mind both Jesus and Colonel Gadaffi were leaders. Good business leaders do not threaten or kill their employees but rather create operating conditions in which others are encouraged to give of their best. In this sense leadership is primarily about behaviour that exhibits a positive regard and is not coercive. It involves management functions but their use is conditioned by humanitarian concern for their staff. Good business leaders earn the trust of their people by

Table 13.1 Differences between managers and leaders

Managers	Leaders
Administer	Innovate
Copy	Original
Maintain	Develop
Focus on systems and structure	Focus on people
Rely on control	Inspire trust
Inclined to take short-term view	Inclined to take long-term view
Ask how and when	Ask what and why
Eye on the bottom-line	Eye on the horizon
Accept the status quo	Challenge the *status quo*
Classic good soldier	Are their own person
Do things right	Do the right things

consistently ensuring that their behavioural attitudes are apparent and do not become submerged by management processes.

The importance of leadership in business life has been recognised for years but it assumes an especial relevance in modern buyers' market environments where the world view held by leaders needs to be realistic (Jones, 2010). This poses a number of questions such as:

- What are the necessary behavioural leadership attitudes/qualities?
- Are real leaders born and not made?
- Can leadership be learnt?
- Is it primarily a matter of behaviour?
- Is it largely a matter of contingency?
- Is it purely charisma?
- Is it visionary?
- What are the contemporary leadership issues?
- What is the essence of leadership?

The following sections address these questions.

Theories of leadership I: trait theories

Table 13.2 presents a set of personal qualities commonly believed to be exhibited by good leaders.

Table 13.2 Personal qualities of leaders

Integrity	Confidence
Honesty	Positivity
Humility	Wisdom
Courage	Determination
Commitment	Compassion
Sincerity	Sensitivity
Passion	Creativity

In the early 1940s, often as part of the Second World War effort, theorists tried to isolate the key characteristics or traits of good leaders. However, isolating important traits is one thing, observing their success in different situations (contexts) is another. Since the late 1940s through to the mid-1960s theorists turned their attention to studying behavioural styles.

Presenting a rather different view Board and Fritzon (2005) carried out some psychological research and tested 39 senior managers and CEOs from leading British companies, then compared the findings with a sample drawn from a prison. Business leaders returned results that were more alarming than the prisoners, many of whom were diagnosed with psychopathic disorders! The dominant traits they exhibited were:

- Skill in flattering and manipulating powerful people
- Egocentricity
- Strong sense of entitlement
- Readiness to exploit others
- Lack of empathy
- Lack of social conscience.

Theories of leadership II: behavioural theories

In a new attempt to isolate the fairy dust of leadership, theorists identified common leadership styles. Autocratic leaders tended to centralise all authority, dictate work procedures, make unilateral decisions, manage by email and limit and/or severely govern employee participation. On the other hand, democratic leaders involved employees in decision making, delegated authority, encouraged participation in the choice of work methods and goals and relied on feedback to coach employees. It is, perhaps, best to view these extremes as opposite ends of a continuum as many organisations will exhibit a mix of these styles.

In 1964 Blake and Mouton advocated a two-dimensional view of leadership that explored the inter-relationship between a leadership style that exhibited 'concern for people' and 'concern for production'. Their ultimate conclusion was that in most cases a team-based management approach was most effective in all situations.

The quest to fully explain leadership in terms of behaviour has generally significantly failed to explain on a consistent basis the relationship between patterns of leadership behaviour and successful situational performance.

Theories of leadership III: contingency theories

If leadership is seen as a 'doing' or responding activity it was of little surprise that theorists next began to focus on situational factors. Pinning these down reliably has also proved to be problematic but four approaches have emerged that can claim to be more reliable than most.

The Fiedler (1967) contingency model focuses on the belief that an individual's basic leadership style is a key factor in leadership success. To isolate the key determinant leadership characteristics Fiedler designed a questionnaire (least-preferred co-worker questionnaire) that was really an extension of the approach taken by trait theorists.

An approach to understanding leadership that has enjoyed a better reputation for consistency is the path-goal theory developed by House (1971). This contingency model asserts that the leaders' job is to assist individuals to attain their goals by providing the necessary direction and support. This involves matching the experienced environmental variables with the leader's evaluation of the personal characteristics of the individuals under his/her charge.

Hersey and Blanchard (1974) developed a Situational Leadership model that proposed four leadership styles – telling, selling, participating and delegating. Which style is selected by the Leader depends on the observed capabilities of individuals. As response styles improve so the Leader reduces the degree of control over and involvement with employees.

Evidence to date does not endorse any of these contingency theories as reliable explanations of leadership success. The Hersey and Blanchard model does possess an intuitive appeal but as with the other theories covered it should be exercised with caution. Larson and Vinberg (2010) researched the dimension of leadership behaviour theory and its relationship to effectiveness, productivity, health satisfaction and job satisfaction and concluded that successful leadership behaviour includes both universal and contingency elements.

Theories of leadership IV: emerging theories

Theorising is one thing but successful application is another. To answer the question 'What works in the real world', three emerging approaches – charismatic leadership, visionary leadership and transactional versus transformational leadership – have assumed increasing interest.

Charismatic leaders are self-assured; possess a clear vision of the future; are articulate; are skilled communicators (Michaelis *et al.*, 2009; De Vries *et al.*, 2010); and have a strong belief in their vision. They are prepared, if necessary, to adopt unconventional actions. They challenge the *status quo*. They are sensitive to the environment. They are prepared to think outside the box and to pursue business creativity and strategic innovation approaches. The leader's job is not to be the source of ideas but to encourage and champion ideas. Leaders must tap the imagination of employees at all ranks and ask inspiring questions. They also need to help their organisations incorporate diverse perspectives, which spur creative insights, and facilitate creative collaboration by, for instance, harnessing new technologies (Amabile and Khaire, 2008). Advocates of charismatic leadership have argued that the leader–follower value congruence plays a central role in the development of charismatic relationships; however, few studies have tested this proposition. Hayibor *et al.* (2011) found strong support for the hypothesis that perceived value congruence between leaders (CEOs) and their followers (members of their top management teams) is positively related to follower perceptions of the degree of charisma possessed by the leader.

Visionary leaders possess exceptionally clear communication skills and can explain in clear terms both the rationale for a vision and what the required actions are to manifest it both to their own staff and to all relevant third-party interests.

Transactional leaders communicate their vision clearly and develop a working environment that assists employees to motivate themselves in order to realise the vision. They also clarify the roles and tasks that are required to do so. Transformational leaders convince followers that it makes sense and is in their own best interests to work in support of the organisational change plan (Hoffman *et al.*, 2011). This generally secures a firmer 'buy-in' and thus higher-quality team performance.

Contemporary leadership thinking

As most team-sports players will confirm, good leaders gain in recognition and popularity if they are sensitive to team development issues. They tune in to the aspirations and tensions evident in teams and fine-tune their leadership skills accordingly. They represent their team to other interested third parties; act as trouble-shooters; resolve conflicts; and act as coaches.

Captaining or leading a team is a demanding occupation and calls for a high level of emotional intelligence. This involves mastering the key components of emotional intelligence – self-awareness, self-management, self-motivation, empathy and well-honed social skills.

The importance of trust

Trust is of paramount importance to individuals and groups (Castaldo *et al.*, 2010). It implies a high level of positive regard of leaders for their people. It can take a long time to build up and can be lost in a second if a leader is clumsy or inconsiderate in dealing with followers. It demands close attention to the key factors of integrity, competence, consistency, loyalty and openness. Integrity concerns leaders' honesty and truthfulness. Competence refers to their theoretical and practical ability (or know-how). Consistency relates to a leader's reliability – his/her track record in dealing with challenging situations. Loyalty relates to the leader's determination to support his/her charges through thick and thin. Openness relates to transparent communication behaviour and a determination to tell employees how it is.

Information communication technology (ICT) has in many organisations introduced remote leadership practice. Robert *et al.* (2009) and Zeffane *et al.* (2011) found that the use of ICT increased the perceived risk of team failure and therefore reduced the likelihood that team members would engage in future trusting behaviours. Regular and reliable face to face communication is a vital determinant of lasting levels of trust (Thomas *et al.*, 2009).

Practice

Assessing individual leadership skills – audit

The key to effective leadership lies in the mastery of myriad skills including those necessary to get the job done and those that are needed to ensure that subordinates are both effective and efficient. All in a leadership position should strive to build and maintain high levels of trust. This is vital for successful leadership and requires considerable technique. The word TRUST itself carries a permanent reminder to all leaders. If a leader's technique fails then the letter T disappears from the rest of Trust and all that is left is RUST – that signals decay and failure.

Readers are invited to respond to the statements in Table 13.3 to gauge their current leadership technique. Take care to ensure that you score each statement appropriately. Any temptation to 'play the game' will damage both you and your staff.

Assessing individual leadership skills – audit interpretation

When you have completed the audit add up your scores and refer to Table 13.4.

Action

Seizing the initiative

Good leaders seize the initiative and by their example create the conditions in which individuals and groups motivate themselves. They possess *know-when* and *know-how*.

Table 13.3 Leadership skills status audit

Statement	Never (score 1)	Occasionally (score 2)	Frequently (score 3)	Always (score 4)
1. I ignore employees' small mistakes and focus on more important matters				
2. I can take criticism without losing my temper				
3. I am relaxed and calm at work and in the company of others				
4. I am a confident person				
5. I am careful not to let personal relationships prejudice professional ones				
6. I am forward in praising my team when they do well				
7. I am seen to be fair in my evaluation of matters and situations				
8. I convey confidence to my team				
9. I am approachable and a good listener				
10. I am concerned to hear about and help with individual problems				
11. I am respectful of the views and opinions of people both below and above my level in the organisation				
12. I am regarded by my team as someone who can create the conditions for high levels of personal and group motivation				
13. I take care to delegate authority professionally and avoid any temptation to abdicate responsibility				
14. I demonstrate impartiality in respect of colour, religion, nationality or gender				
15. I 'roll-up' my sleeves and help out my team when necessary				
16. I choose between speed and perfection when necessary				
17. I distinguish between what is urgent and what is important				
18. I demonstrate that I am a creative person who is willing and able to think 'outside the box'				
19. I encourage all staff to be creative and innovative and welcome their ideas				
20. I take care to see that my staff receive appropriate training				
21. I am a confident and effective representative of my organisation to insiders and outsiders				
22. I generate high levels of trust in my team and organisation				
23. I keep an 'open door' and listen to my staff and others whilst being careful to distinguish between what is urgent and what can be dealt with later				
24. I keep my promises with my team and others, e.g. to give my time to helping with non-urgent matters				
Total				

Table 13.4 Interpretation of overall audit score

Score	Interpretation
32–50	Your leadership skills are weak and you have probably lost the respect and trust of your team and other work colleagues. Review the individual statement scores and study this chapter to stimulate your thinking as to how you could improve.
51–75	You are performing reasonably well but there is scope for improvement. Study the statement scores where you recorded 1 or 2 and think about how you can improve your performance.
76–100	You are a first-class leader; now to seek to improve on this!

They make decisions with due regard to context, time, task and their followers. They are action-oriented individuals.

Leadership challenges

The development and maintenance of leadership skills should assume great importance if organisational CEOs and managers are to meet the contextual changes and disturbances evident in the business environment successfully. Essentially, existing and potential leaders need to be able to meet the following challenges:

- Individual challenges:

    o   Balancing the concepts of effectiveness and efficiency
    o   Learning from others
    o   Gaining experience
    o   Preparing to lead

- Group challenges:

    o   Forming a team
    o   Delegating tasks
    o   Communicating clearly

- Organisational challenges:

    o   The importance of establishing a realistic vision
    o   The changing role of organisational leadership
    o   Corporate leaders deliver more than just financial returns; they also build enduring institutions (Kanter, 2011). Thrust of institutional logic is to build up societal value. Balance public interest with financial returns.
    o   CEOs must expand their investments to include:
    o   Employee empowerment
    o   Values-based leadership
    o   Related societal actions

The leader's role has changed and become more complex and, arguably, even more critical to an organisation's success. Leaders must:

1. Ensure that high performance-levels are achieved and sustained;
2. Handle complexity and ambiguity; enjoy leading the change process;

3.   Ensure that the organisation and its processes are constantly developed to deliver the strategy and required performance;
4.   Constantly act in the belief that, in leadership, trust between superiors and subordinates plays a quintessential role. See Kovač and Jesenko's (2010) article on the results of their empirical research completed in Slovenia.
5.   Ensure that the people within the company are motivated, developed and rewarded to produce outstanding results.

These are highly demanding tasks and skills. Developing leaders with the capacity to learn, adapt, coach, support and inspire others is a critical challenge for major companies. Meeting the challenge requires commitment, investment and creativity.

Summary

In the light of the challenges facing many organisations' operating environments it is essential for those in positions of authority to practice *real* leadership skills. This chapter has presented much for leaders to think about as, hopefully, they seek to hone their skills. Figure 13.2 presents the view from the follower's experience. A Poor Leader fails to engage convincingly with people and performs ineffectively. A Command Leader achieves an effective performance but largely on the basis of vested authority. A person to be obeyed but not one who engages with people. The best 'leaders' (Inspirational Leader) are those who are readily acknowledged and trusted by their followers. Lastly, leaders who are seen to be high on engagement but low on effectiveness (Social Animals) are often characterised by being essentially 'all talk and little do'.

Ideal leaders consistently communicate well with their staff (*engagement*); display sound contextual vision; harness professional skills to get the job done (*effectiveness*) and are generally highly rated by their *staff*.

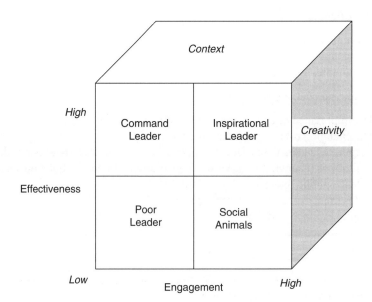

Figure 13.2 Leadership perceptions.

Changing times call for changing responses. Whilst sound management practices (see Chapter 3) are clearly required so too are strong leadership practices. Too much management (especially when it becomes micromanagement) and the desire for control that this often implies can be fatal in times of discontinuous change, when organisations are confronted and challenged by a new, and sometimes hostile environment. In such conditions creative responses, rather than academic or rule-based approaches, are required.

Sound leaders can deal with the unexpected, hold people together, stand firm in times of trial and display an acute awareness of contextual reality.

Discussion questions

1. What key competencies define a leader?
2. How do leaders differ from managers?
3. Some believe that certain individuals are born leaders and that others can never be seen as leaders. How would you argue against this assertion?
4. Leadership is about action in response to contextual challenges and involves others. How do you rate as a leader in the light of the audit in this chapter? How might you increase your leadership skills?
5. How would you define trust and why is it so important for leaders to command?
6. Name an example of a Poor Leader, a Command Leader, an Inspirational Leader and a Social Animal that you remember meeting.

Case exercise

AJM Management Development have been retained by the main board of the computer games firm Gamesoft to help them recruit a new CEO. AJM were asked to use their expertise to select suitable candidates and to draw up a shortlist of four to present to the Gamesoft board for final interview.

Gamesoft were founded in 2005 to exploit the growing market in electronic games. The company had enjoyed early success with two of its games but had failed to keep up its efforts in developing new ones. As a result the company had lost ground in the market to its main competitors. Additionally it had not fully kept up with the new game platforms that had emerged. Consequently, its market share dropped from 23 per cent to 13 per cent. For some time the board had become increasingly worried by the lack of leadership provided by their CEO and breathed a sigh of relief when he tendered his resignation citing health reasons.

In the last three years the incumbent CEO had become more and more of a recluse and had attempted to run the company by email from his home with the occasional trip to the USA to prospect for ideas. His people skills, which were once highly motivating, deteriorated and morale throughout Gamesoft fell away. Talented people left and the heart-beat of the company slowed.

The CEO had begun his time with the company on a high. He possessed sound personal skills as well as a deep understanding of the market. He inspired all who worked with him. The board of Gamesoft asked AJM to find them someone who possessed a sound blend of personal, market and technical skills.

AJM responded by advertising for the post and by analysing each application using the matrix displayed in Figure 13.2. The Poor Leader quadrant were rejected immediately and those in the Command Leader, Charismatic Leader and Social Animal quadrants sifted carefully and the top four in each quadrant called for an exploratory interview.

The four candidates regarded as possible appointees were:

1.   Bill Snaith
2.   Rob West
3.   David Bright
4.   Jeremy Stoker

During the second round of interviews AJM consultants scored each candidate on the following traits:

- Skill in flattering and manipulating powerful people
- Egocentricity
- Strong sense of entitlement
- Readiness to exploit others
- Lack of empathy
- Lack of social conscience.

Initially the Gamesoft board wondered why AJM was doing this but were convinced by their logic: exposing and rejecting all the 'actors' – the candidates whose performances just failed to convince or did not ring true.

Bill Snaith came across as resourceful, claimed to have been very successful in his previous position and presented an impressive set of references. However, two AJM consultants were unhappy with the trait scores recorded by one of their colleagues.

Rob West came across well, provided evidence of successful business practice and was currently employed by one of Gamesoft's competitors. He was persuasive, confident and fully engaged with all AJM personnel who met him with the exception of one who thought that he might need time to adjust to Gamesoft's culture. However, this was countermanded by the belief of other AJM consultants that the company's culture was in need of serious change.

David Bright was a bit of an enigma. He demonstrated excellent social skills and loved to talk about himself and his successes in life so far. Some of AJM's consultants who reviewed his presentation were concerned that he might have been hiding something.

Jeremy Stoker had risen to the rank of major in the army and provided convincing proof of his achievements as well as exhibiting an approachable manner. He was well liked by all AJM staff who met him with the notable exception of one of the consultants who was concerned that he may not separate the world of the army from that of the UK computer game industry.

Questions

1.   Using the four quadrants presented in Figure 13.2 where would you place each of the four candidates?
2.   Who would you advise the board of Gamesoft to select as a their new CEO? Explain the reasons for your choice.

References

Amabile, T. M. and Khaire, M. (2008) 'Creativity and the role of the leader', *Harvard Business Review*, October, Vol. 86, Issue 10, pp. 100–9.

Beer, M., Eisenstat, R.A. and Spector, B. (1990) *The Critical Path to Corporate Renewal*, Boston, MA, Harvard Business Publishing.

Bennis, W. and Nanus, B. (1985) *Leaders: The Strategies for Taking Charge*, New York, Harper Row.

Blake, R.R. and Mouton, J.S. (1984) *The Managerial Grid*, Houston, TX, Gulf Publishing.

Board, B. and Fritzon, K. (2005) 'Disordered personalities at work', *Psychology, Crime and Law*, Vol. 11, pp. 17–32.

Castaldo, S., Premazzi, K. and Zerbini, F. (2010) 'The meaning(s) of trust, a content analysis of the diverse conceptualizations of trust in scholarly research in business relationships', *Journal of Business Ethics*, November, Vol 96, Issue 4, pp. 657–68.

De Vries, R.F., Bakker-Pieper, A. and Oostenveld, W. (2010), 'Leadership = communication? The relations of leaders' communication styles with leadership styles, knowledge sharing and leadership outcomes', *Journal of Business & Psychology*, September, Vol. 25, Issue 3, pp. 367–80.

Drucker, P.F. (2001) *The Essential Drucker*, Oxford, Butterworth Heinemann.

Fiedler, F.E. (1967) *A Theory of Leadership Effectiveness*, New York, McGraw-Hill.

Hayibor, S., Agle, B., Sears, G., Sonnenfeld, J. and Ward, A. (2011) 'Congruence and charismatic leadership in CEO-top manager relationships: An empirical investigation', *Journal of Business Ethics*, August, Vol. 102, Issue 2, pp. 237–54.

Hersey, P. and Blanchard, K.H. (1974) 'So you want to know your leadership style', *Training and Development Journal*, February, pp. 1–15.

Hoffman, B.J., Bynum, B.H., Piccolo, R.F. and Sutton, A.W. (2011) 'Person-organisational value congruence: How transformational leaders influence work group effectiveness', *Academy of Management Journal*, August, Vol. 54, Issue 4, pp. 779–96.

House, R.H. (1971) 'A path goal theory of leader effectiveness', *Administrative Science Quarterly*, September, pp. 321–38.

Jones, M. (2010) 'The marriage of logos and mythos: Transforming leadership', *Journal of Leadership Studies*, Fall, Vol. 4, Issue 3, pp. 73–6.

Kanter, M. (2011) 'What counts as good?' *Harvard Business Review*, Kindle edition, November.

Kotter, J.P. (1990) *A Force for Change – How Leadership Differs from Management*, Glencoe, IL, Free Press.

Kovač, J. and Jesenko, M. (2010) 'The connection between trust and leadership styles in Slovene organizations', *Journal for East European Management Studies*, Vol. 15, Issue 1, pp. 9–33.

Larson, J. and Vinberg, S. (2010) 'Leadership behaviour in successful organisations: Universal or situation dependent?', *Total Quality & Business Excellence*, March, Vol. 21, Issue 3, pp. 317–34.

Michaelis, B., Stigmaier, R. and Sonntag, K. (2009) 'Affective commitment to change and innovation implementation behavior: The role of charismatic leadership and employees' trust in top management', *Journal of Change Management*, December, Vol. 9, Issue 4, pp. 399–417.

Robert, Jr., L.P., Dennis, A.R. and Hung, Yu-Ting, C. (2009) 'Individual swift trust and knowledge-based trust in face-to-face and virtual team members', *Journal of Management Information Systems*, Fall, Vol. 26, Issue 2, pp. 241–79.

Thomas, G.F., Zolin, R. and Hartman, J.L. (2009) 'The central role of communication in developing trust and its effects on employee involvement', *Journal of Business Communication*, July, Vol. 46, Issue 3, pp. 287–310.

Zeffane, R., Tipu, S.A. and Ryan, J.C. (2011) 'Communication, commitment & trust: Exploring the triad', *International Journal of Business & Management*, June, Vol. 6, Issue 6, pp. 77–87.

14 Pre-planning for change

Chance favours only the prepared mind.
(Louis Pasteur, 1854)

Introduction

The short-term performance requirements that greatly influence organisations in the West may encourage business decisions that can run counter to their longer-term performance. Activity designed to enable impressive financial results to be declared from quarter to quarter can lead to over-regulated management styles; a sort of management autopilot. A significant change in the business environment may therefore result in an organisation losing its way, failing to impress with its quarterly financial results and sliding into trouble. This chapter argues that wise organisations carefully tune their activities to prepare for success over the medium to long term. In times of global oversupply and intense competition this is of paramount importance. The alternative – not planning to achieve the right balance between effectiveness and efficiency is, sadly, to plan for failure.

Before considering, deliberating, selecting and declaring an organisational strategy, prudent top management adopt the following stages:

- Pre-planning – to decide on what shape and style of organisation is required to deliver a major change initiative successfully;
- Discussion, exploration and selection of corporate objectives;
- Cultural and functional implementation plan.

This chapter focuses on the first stage of pre-planning.

Context

The challenge of change

Managing change is of paramount importance to top management who are more aware than ever of the need to cope with and manage the process of change. However, there is much confusion about what this entails and how to proceed. Such is the pace of change that it can easily produce a tendency for organisations to carry on as usual and indulge in unclear thinking. There are no quick fixes. Instead there are many theories and models which, if introduced literally, often result in disappointment. Organisations need to blend sound theory and practical operations by developing appropriate processes.

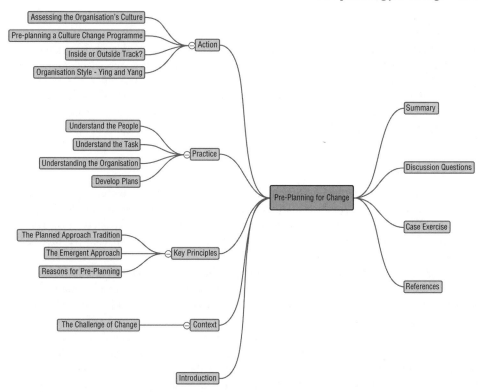

Figure 14.1 Overview of pre-planning.

The opening paragraph to this section speaks of the importance of *managing change*. This choice of words was deliberate as managing in English ends in '*ing*'. This implies that it is a skill that requires action as in driving, painting, swimming, typing, driving and so on. Better still is to blend *managing* with *leading* (or control with action) to think about *changing* an organisation to better suit modern business conditions.

Key principles

The planned approach tradition

Managers, whether individual, group or top management, are charged with the fundamental tasks of deciding *where they should be going* and *how they should get there*. This has parallels with the everyday decisions that a car driver needs to make. The planned approach tradition for a metaphorical car journey would assume that the destination was known and that to all intents and purposes there would be few questions to answer concerning choice of route and likely causes of delay. To many managers the sellers' market environment (see Chapter 1) posed few dangerous contextual challenges. Markets were there for the taking. Making money called for sound financial and supply skills in the main.

In such a climate many were keen on planning. Governments, corporations and public sector organisations were relatively flush with funds and the act of planning functional activity in a virtually given scenario was seen as sound practice. Planning took off in a big way in many organisations and assumed massive complexity. Hard systems approaches delivered the goods and all was well until performances fell short of expected levels. Potentially threatening contextual disturbances were increasingly affecting levels of achievement. Suddenly rigid planning fell short. Management could no longer expect an easy drive and had to review their assumptions.

To a degree organisational plans can be fine-tuned to take into account intermittent and relatively minor contextual changes in the business environment. However, if the disturbances to the expected conditions escalate and become more serious then organisations have to change their plans radically.

The emergent approach

Organisations can be imagined to react to external circumstances in the same way that communities react to water. This is fine in the case of a gentle shower or a usual and expected yearly rainfall pattern but a very dangerous practice if it fails to take account of even the occasional impact of floods. Sudden, massive disturbances to the expected weather conditions will result in regular emergencies.

Emergent or continuous change is a fact of life. What is important for management is the degree of severity of the change and how long it lasts. Times of discontinuous change demand a more sophisticated planning approach than relatively unchallenging times of continuous change. Some have seen organisations as systems that strive towards a state of equilibrium in which the forces of change are balanced by the forces of stability (Wilson, 1992). In real life the inherent conservatism of many organisations acts to negate stimuli for adapting to changing contexts as people opt to preserve the *status quo* (Johnson *et al.*, 2005). Consequently performance starts to drift from declared strategic goals. This can act as a stimulus for management to adopt a more realistic approach to planning by facing up to their challenges. However, too rigid an adherence to theory in the search for a potentially successful blueprint often results in too little attention being given to contextual factors. Too many business schools and top management seem to prefer to assume that environmental disturbances are temporary in nature. Responsible car drivers never do this as the risk of a negative outcome is too risky and unsafe. Crashing a car and then claiming to the police it only happened because you took your eyes off the road is no defence. Strange as it may seem if a bank is driven over the cliff the top CEO is rewarded with a generous settlement. In responsibly run organisations senior management respond strategically to the external environment (Tan and Tan, 2005). It is wise to envisage the planned and emergent approaches as not being mutually exclusive but rather opposite ends of a spectrum. Sensible top management, as Quinn (1980) argues, tune their organisations to the most appropriate position on the continuum using a combination of planned and emergent approaches.

Reasons for pre-planning

All businesses (whether private, public, small or large) should spend time thinking about their organisations before determining their overall objectives. This *pre-planning stage* is essential for later effective and efficient decision making. Key matters for the CEO to consider include:

- Does the organisation have effective and respected leaders?
- Can these leaders create the right operational conditions for their people to motivate themselves?
- Is the organisational culture suitable for a change initiative?

Ignoring or paying scant regard to the pre-planning phase is a major cause of the failure of change initiatives.

Practice

Understand the people

Unlike managing one's self, managing others demands interacting with others. A paradox that is evident in many organisations is that the top management distance themselves from middle managers and the rank and file. Some still maintain their own separate dining and relaxation rooms. People know about the top managers and read about their successes in house publications but rarely meet them. Over the last ten years there has been a declining use of the telephone and more communication by email, which tends to be impersonal. People can feel that the organisation merely gives them a payroll number, and regards them as a cost, or a digit. The trend toward the depersonalisation of staff is like a cancer that threatens business creativity.

People need to be treated as individuals who deserve, and will thrive in, a culture that values their contributions in the workplace. Organisational mindsets can turn the daily experiences of staff into a mechanical and boring experience. Many organisations become steeped in mindsets that have developed over the years during better times. Three common ones are corporate ethos, bureaucracy and process. Or put another way, 'the way we do things here'. People look to the top of an organisation to undertake a positive and interactive lead in any change programme that can be accepted as having a good chance of success.

Many organisations discover that their *modus operandi* can frustrate change and render it difficult if not in reality impossible for staff to actively contribute to a change programme and realise their potential. A change in culture is required that must begin with the demonstrable enthusiasm and involvement of top management. Once achieved it is quite common for them to realise that a great proportion of their management had been promoted because of their technical expertise rather than the ability to manage people.

So the first step for top management is to develop managers' understanding of:

- How people work,
- What motivates them,
- What demotivates them,
- How teams are run,
- How teams are led,
- Dynamics of team leadership.

It helps if top management can come up with a working definition of management (see Chapter 3) for communication to all employees. Sadly, few companies can do this effectively and as a result team briefings and actions can lose their impact. Teams represent a dominant approach to getting work done in a business environment. Creativity enables teams to solve problems and leverage opportunities through the integration of divergent thoughts and perspectives. Prior research indicates that a collaborative culture, which affects how team members interact and work together, is a critical antecedent of team creativity (Barczak *et al.*, 2010). Understanding people is of crucial importance in most business contexts and ultimately is the key to success. Few people go to work wanting to do a bad job. It is what they experience at work that prevents them giving their best. A realistic culture change programme must address those barriers that get in the way of people performing well as individuals and in teams.

Understand the task

Responsible top management need to perform up-front actions that clearly demonstrate that they understand the real position of their organisation. This means for many facing the major challenge of embarking on a change programme that it is not merely an attempt at a quick fix but rather a determined attempt to steer their organisation into clear blue water. This raises an important selection point for CEOs. Top management personnel should be supportive and active in a change initiative and not try to derail it. This challenges some age-old practices of appointing people to top positions because they are family or went to the same public school. Policies of entitlement have in the past been and still are a leading cause of contemporary business failures. Boards of directors need to be involved in effectively guiding organisational change while protecting the interests of an organisation's stakeholders (Fields, 2007).

Successful change programmes need to be planned across a declared time-frame that, depending on the organisation and business activity area, may take several years. Typically change programmes can pass through three distinct stages:

1.   *Developmental change* – typified by an audit of company skills and interests with a view to dropping those with a limited future; developing promising existing ones and preparing for the acquisition of new ones necessary for the success of the business.
2.   *Transitional change* – the programmed dropping of any 'dogs' and introduction of potential 'stars'.
3.   *Transformational change* – the completion of the original change initiative.

It is not a question of just flicking a switch. CEOs if at all possible should stick with their organisations as they pass through the change programme. Too many leave too soon for another post and by so doing can seriously undermine the programme. Depending on the size and complexity of an organisation a change programme can take five years or more to complete. An example that comes to mind is provided by the Norwegian aluminium smelter Karmoy where a CEO worked hard to engage all the staff and associated interests including union personnel in a change initiative that strongly featured business creativity activities. His premature departure removed the main driver and source of inspiration. Attention also needs to be paid to training staff in relevant existing skills and in the acquisition of new ones.

Understand the organisation

The existing hierarchy and culture may not present too many impediments to the usual business operations but may restrict and frustrate an attempt to introduce a new, radical, *modus operandi*. Top management will probably have to give serious consideration to introducing a flatter, downsized, strictly non-hierarchical structure to encourage a TEAM culture (Together Everyone Achieves More). The Morning Star (see Chapter 6, Section 6.8) and Semco cases (see below) provide top management with challenging food for thought.

Develop plans

Whilst the strategic implications of managing change are the responsibility of senior management it is important that the functional implications are delegated throughout the management structure to enable all employees to have a part to play. The TEAM approach to change initiative functional planning is a significant motivator.

Considerable pre-planning needs to precede the detailed development of organisational change initiatives. Beer and Nohria's (2000) findings that organisational change was rarely successful were corroborated by examining the experience of organisations in the UK. Argyris and Schon (1996) held the opinion that organisations found it hard to change because they built in special systems and defences that prevented them from learning and questioning their basic beliefs and assumptions. McGreevy (2009) found that empirical evidence seems to indicate that where the circumstances are right change can work provided the necessary conditions are met:

- Sound pre-planning;
- Objectives of the change process aligned with organisational objectives;
- Commitment from the top of the organisation to ensure that resources are available to manage the change effectively;
- Communications – explaining why the change is necessary;
- Participation;
- Applied project management;
- Taking a measured approach to the roll out of the change programme;
- Progress monitoring of results using metrics such as the balanced scorecard.

Action

Assessing the organisation's culture

A critical part of any pre-planning for change is to obtain a picture of an organisation's disposition toward any desired adoption of a new culture that is as accurate as possible. To adopt business creativity as a major driver within their organisations CEOs need to sound out their senior management on the six key themes that have emerged from the argument in this text, namely:

1. Context
2. Management/leadership
3. Creative response
4. Individual empowerment
5. Group empowerment
6. Organisational empowerment.

We invite you to take our Organisational Creativity Audit presented in Table 14.1. You will probably find it useful to photocopy the Audit. Tick the boxes that best describe your views and refrain from consulting with others as you complete the Audit.

Now turn to Appendix 14.1 for the interpretation of your responses.

Pre-planning a culture change programme

CEOs need to ensure that the values and energy of the organisation can cope with a major change initiative. It requires a committed attitude to stand a realistic chance of changing an organisation's culture. Mintzberg (1994) stresses the importance of managers engaging with people and leading them on a journey, seeing to it that everyone has a part to play.

Table 14.1 Organisational Creativity Audit

	Questions	Agree strongly	Agree	Disagree	Disagree strongly
1	We are a supply oriented organisation				
2	We have a working definition of management that is communicated to all our people				
3	We are aware of business creativity				
4	We encourage individual creativity				
5	We support group working				
6	We value our people				
7	We are service oriented				
8	We organise tailor-made training programmes for our people				
9	We understand what business creativity is all about				
10	We practise open communication				
11	We provide suitable training for groups				
12	We try to make the organisational culture serve the people rather than make the people serve the organisation				
13	We are a domestic organisation and do not look for business abroad				
14	We believe it best to run our organisation on hard systems thinking				
15	We are prepared to evaluate new ways of management thinking				
16	We try to provide secure employment for our people				
17	We encourage and provide time for business creativity group work				
18	We are seriously influenced by contextual factors				
19	We believe that customers are more important than our organisational culture				
20	We encourage and provide space for CPS activity				
21	We cultivate a trust culture				
22	We train people to facilitate groups				
23	We are a Learning Organisation				
24	We don't know what the market (or our internal colleagues) think of us				
25	We operate an open management style				
26	We are running or have recently run a major organisational change programme				
27	We spend as little as we can on the work environment				
28	We reward individual and group achievements				
29	We tolerate mistakes				
30	We expect loyalty upwards and downwards				

This results in a build up of enthusiasm which results in effective team-working. He paraphrases the sociologist Philip Selznick (Jaeger and Selznick, 1964) when he states that 'strategies only take on value as committed people infuse them with energy'.

Preparing for change will lead to a greater probability of success. There is resistance to change in organisations, brought about largely by the fear of the unknown. Handled correctly, using known and tested change-management techniques, change can be brought about successfully, achieving set goals and objectives and to budget. A compelling case needs to be established as a key part of the project definition, as the more people agree at the outset that the objectives of a change initiative are necessary, the more they are likely to support any change. The outcome, impact and benefits should also be defined, taking care not to over-emphasise the *process* of change over the *impact* on those involved. Any organisation operating in today's uncertain economic climate needs to know how to manage change in order to survive. It needs to react quickly to the global revolution, while at a local and national level keeping up with new technology and competition if it wants to stay ahead of the game. This viewpoint provides these organisations with a conscious approach to getting ready for change, which is likely to lead to a greater probability of success (Edmonds, 2011).

Inside or outside track?

Opinion is divided as to the best way of approaching a change programme. Some, such as Lord Sharman, a former Chairman of KPMG International, believe that 'companies can change only from the inside' (BBC, 2005). Others hold the view that to avoid the danger of top management myopia it is best to retain outside consultants to help them think, help them do and to do it for them. Whilst the first two interventions are fine the third would surrender ownership of the change initiative. Change programmes must be visibly owned by top and senior management. It is generally best not to regard the inside/outside issue as being a mutually exclusive decision. If it is viewed in the light of a continuum then top management can select an appropriate blend – drive the exercise internally but harness external expertise when and where necessary.

Organisational style – Yin and Yang

Traditional style (Yin)

Most organisations are bureaucratic and have developed a web of management practices to ensure conformity and control (Weber, 1947). They tend, especially in larger concerns, to consist of a multilayered hierarchy that can assume a life of its own. When threatened by competition, serious contextual paradigm changes or both they can find that they become resistant to change. Top management can become too dependent on hard systems with the accompanying metrics that increasingly signal declining performance. A common response of top management is to defend the *status quo* and hold fast to the claim that unforeseen turbulence in the business context is to blame. However, when aircraft pilots meet severe turbulence they find another course to avoid crashing.

Goodman (1995) has described the emergence of a scenario that he termed the *three-way stretch* in which top management, middle management and the rank and file operate in ways that cause internal strains that can destroy the organisation. People rapidly lose confidence and morale deteriorates rapidly.

The three-way stretch

The scenario develops as follows. *Top management* (directors and senior managers) sense, in the face of falling sales and mounting costs, that business is difficult. If they judge this to be a temporary blip in the expected (i.e. familiar) course of events they may decide to keep a stiff upper lip and retreat to the boardroom and executive offices. For fear of panicking the organisation, they may resort to a policy of restricting communication and/or over-using familiar hard systems tools so as to be seen to be doing something. Meanwhile, *middle management* try to hold back the tide and make repeated entreaties for help to both senior and junior colleagues. In the worse cases, top management retreat completely and middle managers find that they are placed under pressure by the *rank and file* to act decisively in the threatening conditions. This they may feel unable to do before receiving the active or tacit approval of the top management. If this response to contextual change pressures continues for long, huge fissures will start to open up in the organisational hierarchy that will threaten its very existence.

The top management will be locked in the board room, the middle management in their offices, and the rank and file (junior managers, supervisors, workers) will be calling mass meetings. This may seem a little farfetched to many readers, but let's look a little more closely at what is happening. Figure 14.2 illustrates the fundamental point. The onset of chaos has distorted the organisation so that it is in the process of breaking into three sub-organisations, each concerned about the dangers to the original organisation. The original organisation, represented by the shaded rectangle in the figure, has been pulled into the hatched polygon. Top management are conspicuous by their absence and communication with the middle management and rank and file is poor, if it exists at all. Middle management are concerned for their jobs and are trying to extract some direction from the top. The rank

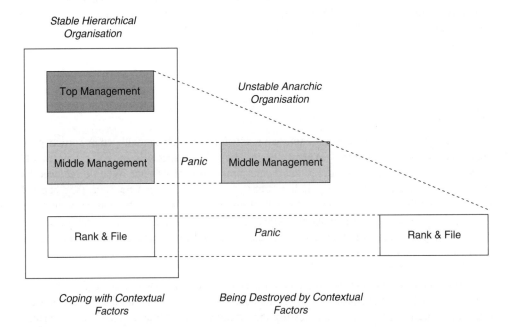

Figure 14.2 The three-way stretch.
        Source: M. R. V. Goodman, Durham University.

and file are very worried about their positions and are getting increasingly frustrated as they see the organisation disintegrating.

Since the dawn of history it has been known that a house that is divided will fall. If the organisation above is to survive, then top management have to regain control, unite the house and change their *modus operandi*. In unstable conditions, with contextual stimuli changing rapidly, a predominantly hard systems approach will probably be difficult to justify. What is needed is a new way of doing things. The old corporate mindsets must give way to a new set that will emphasise softer systems and acknowledge the value of human capital. To effect real change, top management will have to consult openly with individuals and begin to build a new climate of trust.

An alternative style (Yang)

The complete opposite to the power–command hierarchical approach is provided by self-management. Many in top management dismiss this alternative prematurely because they believe that it will lead to anarchy. This is misguided as bureaucratic and self-management styles should not be seen as mutually exclusive. They represent opposite ends of a continuum and the task of top management is to find the right blend for their organisation.

The self-management style (*Harvard Business Review*, 2011) encourages the development of trust, team-working and high morale. It resembles in many ways the operating style of a professional orchestra where performance standards are gained by a strong vision, mission and commitment of all the players. The advantages of its adoption include:

- Lower costs – absence of traditional and hierarchical managers reduces wage costs. Savings can be used to reward staff and to invest in growth.
- Encourages collegiality and internal loyalty – as people discover the benefits of working in teams where all have equal status.
- Encourages initiative – people become proactive and open to new ways of thinking and strive to increase their personal worth and reputational capital.
- Long-stay loyalty – few leave to join other organisations.
- Increased expertise – as with the individual players in an orchestra people are highly motivated to maintain high-quality work standards and to continually develop their skill sets.
- Sharper decisions – to avoid the three-way stretch phenomenon.
- Increased flexibility – orchestras can play more than one piece and perform in more than one location. The team can meet and deal more effectively with sudden surprises and challenges.

Seasoned management executives might point out that self-management has a number of drawbacks:

- Expectations – people have to perform to high standards and accept group judgement on their achievements. If both of these become lax then the self-management model can foster mediocrity.
- Pool progress issues – the absence of a hierarchy can make it difficult for people to progress to positions of greater responsibility. However, a swimming pool presents a flat surface but contains a depth continuum from shallow to deep.
- Joining experience – team-based collegiate system can be daunting to new people but also more accommodating as it is in everyone's interest that new people contribute as quickly as possible.

The self-management style can be more difficult for top management to introduce in an existing organisation than a newly formed one. However, Ricardo Semler at Semco achieved a total turnaround in the organisation he inherited from his father (see case study in Section 14.8). The CEO at Morning Star (See Chapter 6, Section 6.8) developed a strong self-management style from the start.

Summary

This chapter argues that top management should devote time to pre-planning an intended major change initiative that is under consideration as a result of significant changes in the business environment. Business leaders need to be alert to the changing landscape for, as observed by Pasteur, chance favours only the prepared mind. Readers are encouraged to complete our Organisational Creativity Audit.

There is no quick fix and to accomplish a response transformation usually requires top management to agree on the need for and to be active in introducing and driving a new organisational culture. An organisation that is open to change and the exercise of business creativity needs to pre-plan innovative activity to ensure that it has both the skills and resources to manage successful innovations. A blend of planned and emergent approaches is recommended together with a blend of bureaucratic and self-management styles.

Discussion questions

1. How does the emergent approach to change differ from the planned approach?
2. What are the key matters for a CEO to consider when contemplating a major change initiative?
3. Many people have been promoted with little management training. What are the main management skills that top management need to see that these people understand and practise?
4. What are the main advantages that external consultants can bring? What is the main danger of delegating the whole change initiative to consultants?
5. Briefly discuss the implications of the three-way stretch model.
6. What are the main advantages of the self-management organisational model?

Case exercise

In Brazil, where paternalism and the family business fiefdom still flourish, Ricardo Semler heads Semco, a manufacturing company that lets workers make corporate decisions, come to work whenever they please, and browse through the company books at will. Semco's management philosophy is anti-hierarchical and highly unorthodox. It is also a profitable concern. Democracy lets employees set their own working conditions and control production. Profit sharing rewards them for doing well. Information tells them how well they're doing. As part of its effort to eliminate hierarchy, the company has cut management layers to three. It limits the size of operational units to fewer than 200 people. Workers share the after-tax profits of their own divisions according to formulas they vote in. Every employee gets a balance sheet, a profit-and-loss analysis and a cash-flow statement every month, along with a course in how to read them. Managers set their own salaries. This kind of unconventional management has produced a growth rate of 40 per cent.

Once you say what business you're in, you put your employees into a mental straitjacket and hand them a ready-made excuse for ignoring new opportunities. So rather than dictate his company's identity, Semler lets his employees shape it through their individual efforts and interests. 'I don't know what Semco is', he writes in his account of his company's expansion from manufacturing to internet services. 'Nor do I want to know'. Ten years ago, Semco employees who were selling cooling towers to owners of large commercial buildings heard customers complain about the high cost of maintaining the towers. The sales people proposed a new business in cooling tower maintenance, and the venture is now a $30 million property-management business. That initiative led to the creation of an online exchange to facilitate the management of commercial construction projects. The exchange is revolutionising the construction process in Brazil and has become a springboard for further web initiatives such as virtual trade shows. Some of the lessons that can be learnt from this approach are:

- Forget about the top line.
- Never stop being a start-up.
- Don't be a nanny (treat your employees like adults).
- Let talent find its place.
- Make decisions quickly and openly when it comes to reviewing proposals for new businesses.
- Partner promiscuously: 'Our partners', Semler says, 'are as much a part of our company as our employees'.

Task

Write a brief report summarising the similarities of approach between Semco and Morning Star (See Chapter 6, Section 6.8). Include a discussion of the advantages and disadvantages of the self-management organisation styles.

References

Argyris, C. and Schon, D.A. (1996) *Organisational Learning II*, Reading, MA, Addison-Wesley.

Barczak, G., Lassk, F. and Mulki, J. (2010) 'Antecedents of team creativity: an examination of team emotional intelligence, team trust and collaborative culture creativity and innovation management antecedents of team creativity', *Creativity & Innovation Management*, December, Vol. 19, Issue 4, pp. 332–45.

BBC (2005) *Mastering Change*, London, BBC Books.

Beer, M. and Nohria, N. (2000) 'Cracking the code of change', *Harvard Business Review*, May–June, pp. 133–41.

Edmonds, J. (2011) 'Managing successful change', *Industrial & Commercial Training*, Vol. 43, Issue 6, pp. 349–53.

Fields, D. (2007) 'Governance in permanent whitewater: The board's role in planning and implementing organisational change', *Corporate Governance: An International Review*, March, Vol. 15, Issue 2, pp. 334–44.

Goodman, M.R.V. (1995) *Creative Management*, Upper Saddle River, NJ, Prentice Hall.

Hamel, G. (2011) 'First, let's fire all the managers', *Harvard Business Review*, December, Vol. 89, Issue 12, pp. 48–60.

Harvard Business Review (2011) 'The road to self management', December, Kindle edition.

Jaeger, G. and Selznick, P. (1964) 'A normative theory of culture', *American Sociological Review*, October, Vol. 29, Issue 5, pp. 653–69.

Johnson, G., Scholes, K. and Whittington, R. (2005) *Exploring Corporate Strategy: Text and Cases*, 7th edn, Hemel Hempstead, FT Prentice Hall.

Maresco, P.A. and York, C.C. (2005) 'Ricardo Semler: Creating organizational change through employee empowered leadership', *Academic Leadership – The Online Journal*. http://www.newunionism.net/library/case%20studies/SEMCO%20-%20Employee-Powered%20Leadership%20-%20Brazil%20-%202005.pdf, accessed 24/04/12.

McGreevy, M. (2009) 'Why change works sometimes', *Industrial & Commercial Training*, Vol. 41, Issue 6, pp. 305–13.

Mintzberg, H. (1994) 'The fall and rise of strategic planning', *Harvard Business Review*, January–February, pp. 107–14.

Quinn, J.B. (1980) 'Managing strategic change', *Sloan Management Review*, Summer, pp. 3–20.

Semler, R. (1989) 'Managing without managers', *Harvard Business Review*, September/October, Vol. 67, Issue 5, pp. 76–84.

Semler, R. (1993) *Maverick: The Success Story Behind the World's Most Unusual Workplace*, New York, Warner Books.

Semler, R. (1994) 'Why my former employees still work for me', *Harvard Business Review*, January/February, Vol. 72, Issue 1, pp. 64–71.

Semler, R. (2000) 'How we went digital without a strategy', *Harvard Business Review*, September/October, Vol. 78, Issue 5, pp. 51–8.

Semler, R. (2004) *The Seven-Day Weekend: Changing the Way Work Works*, New York, Warner Books.

Semler, R. (2007) 'Out of this world doing things the Semco way', *Global Business & Organizational Excellence*, July/August, Vol. 26, Issue 5, pp. 13–21.

Tan, V. and Tan, N.T. (2005) 'Change management in times of economic uncertainty', *Singapore Management Review*, Vol. 27, Issue 1, pp. 49–68.

Weber, M. (1947) *The Theory of Social and Economic Organisation*, Glencoe, IL, Free Press.

Wilson, D.C. (1992) *A Strategy of Change*, New York, Routledge.

Appendix: Organisational creativity audit interpretation

1. Transfer your ticks from Table 14.1 to the six factor boxes below.
2. The factor boxes present a picture of your views of case material or your organisation.

Table 14.2 Organisational Creativity Factor Analysis

Context-related factors					
	Statement	*Agree strongly*	*Agree*	*Disagree*	*Disagree strongly*
1	We are supply oriented				
7	We are service oriented				
13	We are a domestic organisation and do not look for business abroad				
18	We are seriously influenced by contextual factors				
24	We don't know what the market (or our internal colleagues) think of us				

Table 14.2 cont'd

Management-related factors

	Statement	Agree strongly	Agree	Disagree	Disagree strongly
2	We have a working definition of management that is communicated to all our people				
8	We organise tailor-made training programmes for our people				
14	We believe it best to run our organisation on hard systems thinking				
19	We believe that customers are more important than our organisational culture				
25	We operate an open management style				

Creativity related factors

	Statement	Agree strongly	Agree	Disagree	Disagree strongly
3	We are aware of business creativity				
9	We understand what business creativity is all about				
15	We are prepared to evaluate new ways of management thinking				
20	We encourage and provide space for CPS activity				
26	We are running or have recently run a major organisational change programme				

Individual empowerment factors

	Statement	Agree strongly	Agree	Disagree	Disagree strongly
4	We encourage individual creativity				
10	We practise open communication				
16	We try to provide secure employment for our people				
21	We cultivate a trust culture				
27	We spend as little as we can on the work environment				

Table 14.2 cont'd

Group empowerment factors

	Statement	Agree strongly	Agree	Disagree	Disagree strongly
5	We support group working				
11	We provide suitable training for groups				
17	We encourage and provide time for business creativity group work				
22	We train people to facilitate groups				
28	We reward individual and group achievements				

Organisational empowerment factors

	Statement	Agree strongly	Agree	Disagree	Disagree strongly
6	We value our people				
12	We try to make the organisational culture serve the people rather than make the people serve the organisation				
23	We are a Learning Organisation				
29	We tolerate mistakes				
30	We expect loyalty upwards and downwards				

15 Strategy for change

Not so much a programme, more a way of life.

(Anon)

If one does not know to which port one is sailing, no wind is favourable.

(Seneca, *Epistulae Morales*, no. 71)

Introduction

Organisations that suddenly find themselves severely affected by unexpected changes in their business environment are often tempted to look for a 'quick fix'. Johnson *et al.* (2005) define strategy as follows: 'Strategy is the *direction* and *scope* of an organisation over the *long-term:* which achieves *advantage* for the organisation through its configuration of *resources* within a challenging environment, to meet the needs of *markets* and to fulfil stakeholder expectations'.

This chapter draws on much of the argument covered in previous chapters to provide guidelines for top management intent on designing a change management initiative. Every organisation is different and there is no easy quick fix. Chapter 14 argued for the importance of thoroughly thinking through the approach to change. This chapter expands the discussion and provides general advice on how to go about setting strategic objectives and developing a sustainable organisational culture to deliver change successfully.

Context

View from the boardroom

The business world is unpredictable and characterised by instability and chaos. In many organisations top management stare out of the boardroom windows at a turbulent business environment and at each other for inspiration. A crucial personal skill needed for this decade is to manage radical change. The changes now facing managers are more significant and broad-ranging than ever before. The many manifestations of change affect:

- Technology – the information technology (IT) revolution continues apace.
- Organisations – new organisational structures are emerging, emphasising and enabling speed of response.
- Individuals – people are having to learn new skills and adapt to an uncertain business environment.

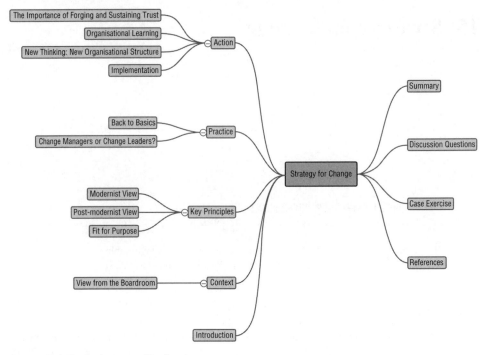

Figure 15.1 Exploring strategies for change.

- Society – the role of employment and organisations in society is questioned and debated.
- Markets – are becoming increasingly demanding and changing at an ever increasing pace.

Boards that clearly recognise the need for a major change initiative are faced by the following key and challenging questions:

1. Why have business contexts changed so much?
2. What should the organisation be doing?
3. Who should be actively involved in managing change?
4. When should top management launch a change initiative?
5. How can they proceed?

The complexity facing top management calls for a new and innovative response. As there is no quick fix solution CEOs have to encourage and facilitate their senior managers to explore multiple ways of approaching change.

Key principles

Modernist view

This sees change as being a natural phenomenon that is evolutionary, incremental and exploits humans and nature (Ketola, 2009). Business life is governed by the principle of cause and effect. To achieve a required outcome all that is needed is an appropriate functional response. This suits some organisations in particularly favourable business environments and links to the familiar hard systems approach to change that focuses on planned as opposed to emergent change. However, in times of rapid and discontinuous change, another paradigm is needed to achieve genuine corporate sustainability.

Postmodernist view

This is the opposite view and sees the business world as being complex, non-linear and characterised by chaos. What postmodernism has to offer business is not rules, but questions that raise issues of responsibility (Gustafason, 2000). It observes humans and nature. It requires a mix of hard and soft systems and does not relate easily to recognised academic change models. According to Weiss (2000) it calls for a flatter, organic (self-management) and flexible organisation. Those who sympathise with postmodernism are addressing the question of what is good. Postmodernists, it is argued, wish to engage in advocacy for values and preferences that they view as putting them in radical opposition to the *status quo*. To facilitate such advocacy they call for the repudiation of 'modernism', in particular the key modernist notion that there is an objective truth that can be sought out rationally and systematically. Postmodernists adopt, instead, a relativist philosophy, which contends that 'truth' must be considered merely subjective, such that one's view of truth is only relative to one's circumstances. Although taking the position that no-one can say what is or is not 'true' puts them in opposition to mainstream science, it supports their ability to discredit views they oppose, and simultaneously provides a defence against those who would claim that the postmodernist's view is not 'true'.

A new ensemble of organisation development (OD) practices have emerged that are based more on constructionist, postmodern and new sciences premises than the assumptions of the early founders. These include practices associated with appreciative inquiry, large group interventions, changing mindsets and consciousness, addressing diversity and multicultural realities, and advancing new and different models of change. Marshak and Grant (2008) propose that the emerging field of organisational discourse offers sympathetic concepts and research that could add additional insights and theoretical rigour to the new OD. In particular, studies of organisational discourse based upon social constructionist and critical perspectives offer compelling ideas and practices associated with the establishment of change concepts, the role of power and context in relation to organisational change, and specific discursive interventions designed to foster organisational change.

Ketola (2009) describes a Pre-Morphean paradigm which presents an alternative to modern and postmodern paradigms of corporate sustainability that stresses the importance of understanding and caring for humans and nature.

Fit for purpose

The strategist's first task is to challenge the prevailing assumptions with the questions:

- Why do we do what we do?
- Are we fit for purpose?

This might, perhaps, be followed by a third question: What is strategy? Strange as it may seem, many organisations have a problem communicating a common internal and external description of their strategy. Does it describe what the organisation is actually doing? What it says it is doing? Or what it ought to be doing? Then how should top management develop a strategy? Should it start with an internal audit of key competencies or with an assessment of what the market or administrative recipient needs? Or a combination of both approaches?

In the current business environment the traditional methods of formulating and implementing strategy are increasingly questioned. The conventional approach can be summarised in the acronym MOST:

M mission
O objectives
S strategy
T tactics

This offers an orderly progression from creating a mission to making a strategy happen. Life is no longer so straightforward. Top management need to be wary of relying too heavily on the rational analytical approaches to strategy formulation. Intuition is needed to capture top management's reading of the business environment. Executive skill comes into play when top management combines both analysis and intuition to formulate a suitable strategy. Organisations should be able to describe the main tenets of this on a single sheet of paper rather than in a hundred page report. A clear executive summary provides a clear focus for internal and external publication. This is why some of the case exercises in this text call for short responses.

The globalised economy has resulted in new business concerns, where future success depends on how well change is managed (Kalyani and Sahoo, 2011). Competitiveness is the best parameter to determine the survival of enterprises and organisational excellence in this scenario. Marković (2008) developed a profile for an organisation that would be best suited to the business environment in the new economy and concluded that the successful companies in the future will be the ones which are wise enough to harness the full potential of the entire organisation in the rapidly changing business environment. Winning organisations will be the ones that are responsive to challenges and adroit in both creating opportunities and capturing them. In other words, to match the business environment that is more networked within and among companies, the ability to deliver value will have to be distributed across the company to a much greater extent than in the past.

Under these circumstances, managers also need to transform themselves. They need to have a better framework for thinking about and understanding organisational change. Continuous learning is the key competency required by any organisation that wants to survive and thrive in the new knowledge economy.

Practice

Back to basics

Strategy is essentially about seeking answers to the following questions:

- Where is the business trying to get to in the long term? (Direction).
- Which markets should a business compete in and what kind of activities are involved in such markets? (Markets; scope).
- How can the business perform better than the competition in those markets? (Advantage).
- What resources (skills, assets, finance, relationships, technical competence, facilities) are required in order to be able to compete? (Resources).

- What external, environmental factors affect the businesses' ability to compete? (Environment).
- What are the values and expectations of those who have power in and around the business? (Stakeholders).

The approach adopted by top management to deliver change is of paramount importance and needs to be determined before embarking on detailed functional planning. Failure to commit enough time and thinking to the pre-planning stage is a frequent and fundamental cause of frustration and disappointment. The recently concluded American intervention in Iraq (December 2010) and the current allied operations in Afghanistan provide stark warnings. This text argues that the basic strategy questions set out above should be considered in the light of the Pre-Morphean paradigm within organisation style that is a finely tuned balance of the traditional and self-management approaches.

Change managers or change leaders?

Our text argues that organisations must take up the challenge of 'doing things differently' if they are to survive and prosper in times of discontinuous change exacerbated by intermittent minor and major financial crises. This implies synthesising theories of leadership, empowerment and business creativity (Zhang and Bartol, 2010). Empirical research finds that empowering leadership positively affects psychological empowerment, which in turn influences both intrinsic motivation and creative process engagement. The latter two variables have a positive influence on business creativity. Empowerment role identity moderates the link between empowering leadership and psychological empowerment and the encouragement of creativity by management moderates the connection between psychological empowerment and creative process engagement.

Figure 15.2 illustrates the route that our text has followed to assist both scholars and practitioners to appreciate the potential role that business creativity can play in organisational renewal. Once the case for business creativity has been made and some suggestions advanced

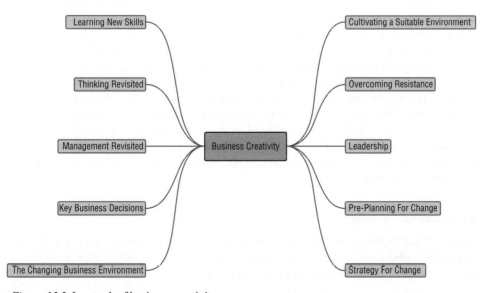

Figure 15.2 In search of business creativity.

as to how it might be introduced top management needs to turn their attention to developing strategic innovation (see Chapters 8–12, 16). This will require firm leadership by all managers and in particular from the CEO. Every organisation needs to forge its own response style. Most success is likely to come from a well considered blend of traditional and self-management approaches of leading and managing skills.

Action

The importance of forging and sustaining trust

Trust and commitment do not just happen; they are forged and maintained through effective communication, leadership and management (Zeffane *et al.*, 2011). In leadership and management, trust between superiors and subordinates plays an important role. Ingenhoff and Sommer (2010) in a survey of over 200 firms in Switzerland found that companies are more trusted than CEOs. This emphasises the need for CEOs to lead effectively and stay the course of a change initiative. Regretfully many choose to move on before the task is successfully completed.

In leadership, trust between superiors and subordinates plays a very important role. Empirical research by Kovač and Jesenko (2010), covering the connection between the level of trust within an organisation and leadership styles, selected delegation, communication and control as important elements in the leadership process. The results obtained indicated a clear connection between the level of democracy in leadership styles and the level of formalisation in delegation, communication and the control of the tasks of one's subordinates. Di Virgilio and Ludema (2009) confirm that communication clearly plays an important role in the development of trust within an organisation. They propose that effective leaders generate energy for action by engaging people in conversations that provide them (and themselves) with a sense of autonomy, competence and relatedness. Energy is expressed in the form of support, time, money and resources, which contribute to the success of the work. Continuous attention to conversations that invite the co-creation of desired futures creates upward spirals of energy and increases the probability of successful change over time.

While a number of researchers have studied the relationship of trust and communication, little is known about the specific linkages between quality of information, quantity of information, openness, trust and outcomes such as employee involvement. Thomas *et al.* (2009) tested these relationships using communication audit data from 218 employees in the oil industry. Using mediation analysis and structural equation modelling, they found that quality of information predicted trust of one's co-workers and supervisors while adequacy of information predicted one's trust of top management. Trust of co-workers, supervisors and top management influenced perceptions of organisational openness, which in turn influenced employees' ratings of their own level of involvement in the organisation's goals. Their study suggested that the relationship between communication and trust is complex, and that simple strategies focusing on either quality or quantity of information may be ineffective for dealing with all members in an organisation.

Organisational learning

Organisational learning is vitally important if top management want to secure a sustainable competitive advantage (Stata, 1989) and is crucial for any major change initiative. Organisational learning was and still is of major interest for academicians, organisational development experts and researchers because of its inherent ability to generate competitive advantage. Senge (1990) and his colleagues at the Massachusetts Institute of Technology did much to establish the importance of the learning organisation. Their philosophy was based on the humanist view of organisational change that emphasises that businesses actively improve the conditions that motivate their people. Organisations need to build core competencies to innovate and outperform their rivals. Businesses need organisations that are proactive, futuristic, strategic in thinking, are capable of adaptability and are flexible in acquiring new learning. This requires a strong and sustained commitment from top management. It requires a major emphasis on the sharing of information and its interpretation. The concept of a learning organisation has widespread acceptance, and is equally important and applicable in educational, business, private or public organisations. Scholars present different views about organisational learning.

New thinking: new organisational structure

Developments in organisational thinking (Akhtar and Khan, 2011) often lead to new forms of organisational structure. Increases in organisational complexity and operational connectivity have intensified the need for coordinated decision taking at and among all levels of an organisation. This means that the ability to work in teams has become a core competence in work environments where collaboration is at a premium. Empowered teams consist of people with complementary skills who are committed to a common purpose or a set of performance goals for which they hold themselves mutually accountable. The power and authority traditionally held exclusively by the manager is passed to the team. Contemporary organisations often demonstrate examples of such work teams, showing exceptional job performance and production of innovative solutions. Consequently, there has been great interest in understanding what makes these teams what they are, and how they function.

Laszlo *et al.* (2009) researched the characteristics of high-performance teams and explored the possibilities and implications for developing such teams into evolutionary learning communities. The significance of their work resides in the focus it lends to advancing beyond the traditional operational benchmark of the high-performance team to a new benchmark identified as the evolutionary learning community. Organisations that embrace this new construct not only raise the bar in terms of team standards for efficient and effective operations but also create organisational dynamics that foster quality of work life and business cultures that are vibrant, alive and thriving.

Implementation

Organisational excellence is at a crossroads today. The drastic change in the business scenario calls for a speedy transformation of mission, vision, core values, core competence, management style, policy framework, management system, structures, process, renewal mechanism and so on of an organisation. Any change programme revolves around people – changing their mindset, behaviour and motivational level (Kalyani and Sahoo, 2011; Westover, 2010). The question is, how do organisations manage this change and how might people be affected by it? Handy (1994) laments that many managers have been brought up in the era of sellers' markets on a diet of power, divide and rule and have been preoccupied with authority rather than making things happen. The successful implementation of a major change programme demands a new management approach. Change literature emphasises the significance of aligning change at a systemic level for sustained effectiveness of strategic change initiatives. While this body of literature stresses the significance of psychological and process dimensions of managing change, research on an integrated and strategic approach to deploy, track, measure and sustain large-scale changes has been limited and inconclusive.

Jayashree and Hussain (2011) address this gap in the literature and propose a holistic conceptual framework for identifying, formulating, deploying, measuring, aligning and tracking strategic changes in organisations. The suggested approach draws significantly from the Balanced Scorecard (Kaplan and Norton, 1996) framework and focuses on the use of formal steps such as developing change themes and results, setting change objectives, and developing lead and lag performance measures for measuring strategic change objectives. Furthermore, their proposed framework also provides directions on how to track the progress of change initiatives with respect to the desired objectives. They conclude that 70 per cent of all change efforts fail. While some fail due to incomplete diagnoses, others fail due to gaps in deployment or measurement. However, there is uncertainty about how to prevent change failure. A rigorous and practical approach to deploy change systematically with a continuous focus on strategic alignment has specifically been found missing in the literature. Jayashree and Hussain's framework fills this gap and offers managers and organisational decision makers a holistic and practical tool to successfully navigate the complexities of their strategic change efforts by measuring strategic alignment in a step-wise manner throughout the change process.

During periods of strategic change, maintaining the congruence between new configurations of resources and activities (strategic investments) and how these new configurations are communicated to external organisational constituents (strategic projections) is an important task facing organisational leaders. One part of this activity is to manage organisational identity, to ensure that the various strategic projections produced by organisational members are coherent and support the new strategic investments. Little is known, however, about how organisational leaders accomplish this crucial task. Ravasi and Philips's (2011) study of strategic change at Bang & Olufsen highlights the internal identity work – or identity management – that organisational leaders engage in to preserve this congruence. The findings also complement the current emphasis in the literature on the social validation of organisational identities. Their research found an important link between identity claims and beliefs, strategic projections and the material reality of their organisational structures and outputs. Gans (2011) discusses change management and recommends that before implementing new practices firms should assess their impact on their employees and formulate a support strategy. Ideally a team should be formed to handle change management, as well as a team leader to oversee it. Prior to embarking upon change, it is crucial to identify key executives who can become visible advocates for change.

Top management must understand the importance of managing organisational change in today's uncertain economic climate (Edmunds, 2011). Training in change management delivered by a business school or consultancy agent can help to provide a deeper knowledge of its principles and an understanding of how to implement and manage change in an organisation. Edmunds found that there is resistance to change in organisations, brought about largely by peoples' fear of the unknown. Handled correctly, using known and tested change management techniques, change can be brought about successfully, achieving set goals and objectives and to budget. As every organisation is different, there is no template for successful organisational change management. In reality, change cannot be wholly prescribed by management; it will emerge naturally once a strategy for change is in place.

A compelling case needs to be established as a key part of the pre-planning stage of a change initiative, as the more people agree at the outset that the objectives of a change initiative are necessary, the more they are likely to support it. The outcome, impact and benefits should also be defined, taking care not to over-emphasise the process of change over the impact on those involved. Lastly, the implementation plan tasks should be structured in ascending order of achievement difficulty to provide staff with the opportunity to boost their confidence after every successful win (Amabile and Kramer, 2011).

Gaining a corporate 'competitive edge'

The best advice for organisations is to be positively different in the judgement of customers than the competition at an acceptable cost (Ohmae, 1982). To strive for an appropriate balance between the concepts of effectiveness and efficiency. This can be achieved by:

- Focusing on key strengths or factors of success;
- Building on relative advantages over the competition;
- Pursuing aggressive tactics to undermine the perceived strengths of the competition;
- Seeking through sustained innovation opportunities that are unseen by competitors.

Summary

It is important for any organisation to continually reappraise the business environment and think about how it might change. Without change there is no innovation, creativity or incentive for improvement. Be wary of basing future strategy decisions on past ideas. Being ready to respond to change with pre-planned and well developed plans should result in success. Strategies for change should not be occasional exercise programmes but more a way of life.

Discussion questions

1. What are the key questions that top management should address when contemplating a change initiative?
2. Explain the difference between modernist and postmodernist views.
3. What is the best parameter to ensure the survival of enterprises?
4. Managing or leading? What is best for major change initiatives?
5. Why is trust such an important factor for top management to deliberate when embarking on a strategic change exercise?
6. What is meant by the term *learning organisation*? Why is it so important for organisations progressing a strategic change project?
7. Explain why top management should arrange training in change management skills and techniques before setting strategic objectives and developing implementation plans.

Case exercise

James Roberts had been recently appointed as CEO of a light engineering firm that was performing poorly, following a change initiative planned by Grahams and Partners, a local consultant and friend of his predecessor. He commissioned the consultant to assess the level of trust of his rank and file employees. When the consultant presented his findings, two weeks late, he was both disappointed and disillusioned. The report was full of theory and contained irrelevant academic references and statistical analysis. The findings were couched in so many unrealistic assumptions that he sank back into his chair in despair. Gaining no satisfaction from his questions he thanked the consultant, paid his invoice and turned to a small consulting firm (Heathways and Partners) recommended by a friend. A week later Heathways' consultant reported in terms that were easily understood by him and his senior managers. Their report stressed that Roberts' organisation had too many indirect employees and needed to quickly 'shape up or ship out'. Heathways found that the employees in Roberts' organisation were 'blindly governed and morosely facing disaster'. Shocked at first by this disclosure but feeling it to be true he knew things had to change. Heathways' detailed findings presented a highly distressing picture of the level of motivation and trust in his organisation and it all rang true. Their advice was to scrap the poor change initiative of his predecessor, move forward and start all over again.

The Heathways consultant gave each of the senior management team a sheet of paper on which was written his opening comment that the employees were 'blindly governed and morosely facing disaster'. Then he asked them to advance the initial letters of the main words (i.e. 'b', 'g', 'm', 'f' and 'd') by one letter, keeping the 'a' in the same place. This they found spelt out the word CHANGE.

Executives don't realise it, but a hierarchy of managers exacts a hefty tax on any organisation: managers are expensive, increase the risk of bad decisions, disenfranchise employees and slow progress. In fact, management may be the least efficient activity in any company. Yet it's clear that market mechanisms alone can't provide the degree of coordination and control that many companies require. Is there any way to get the flexibility of a market system and the discipline of a tightly knit hierarchy without a management superstructure? Morning Star, the global market leader in tomato processing, proves that there is. Morning Star, which has seen double-digit growth for the past 20 years, has no managers. That's right – no bosses, no titles, no promotions. Its employees essentially manage themselves.

Workers negotiate responsibilities with their peers, anyone can issue a purchase order and each individual is responsible for acquiring the tools needed to do his or her work. Compensation decisions are handled by local committees elected by the employees, and pay reflects the contributions that people make, not their status. And if staff find themselves overloaded or spot a new role that needs filling, they simply go ahead and initiate the hiring process. Morning Star's self-management model has two cornerstones: the personal mission statement, and the Colleague Letter of Understanding, or CLOU. In a personal mission statement, each employee outlines how he or she will help the company achieve its goals. The CLOU, which must be hammered out every year with colleagues, is an operating plan for fulfilling it. A CLOU covers as many as 30 activity areas and spells out relevant performance metrics. The system isn't without its challenges, and it isn't for everyone. But it has produced a dedicated workforce with exceptional initiative and expertise. And its success shows that it is possible for organisations to transcend the seemingly intractable trade-off of freedom versus control.

Tasks

- What are the cornerstones of Morning Star's self-management model?

Draft a brief report for James Roberts indicating how this self-management model could be adapted for his light engineering firm.

References

Akhtar, N. and Khan, R.A. (2011) 'Exploring the paradox of organizational learning and learning organization', *Interdisciplinary Journal of Contemporary Research in Business*, January, Vol. 2, Issue 9, pp. 257–70.

Amabile, T.M. and Kramer, S.J. (2011) 'The power of small wins', *Harvard Business Review*, May, Vol. 89, Issue 5, pp. 70–80.

Di Virgilio, M.E. and Ludema, J.D. (2009) 'Let's talk: Creating energy for action through strategic conversations', *Journal of Change Management*, March, Vol. 9, Issue 1, pp. 67–85.

Edmunds, J. (2011) 'Managing successful change', *Industrial & Commercial Training*, Vol. 43, Issue 6, pp. 349–53.

Gans, K. (2011) 'Should you change your thinking about change management?', *Strategic Finance*, October, Vol. 93, Issue 4, pp. 48–50.

Gustafason, A. (2000) 'Making sense of postmodern business ethics', *Business Ethics Quarterly*, July, Vol. 10, Issue 3, pp. 645–58.

Handy, C. (1990) *Inside Organisations: 21 Ideas for Managers*, London, BBC Books.

Handy, C. (1994) *The Empty Raincoat*, London, Hutchinson.

Ingenhoff, D. and Sommer, K. (2010) 'Trust in companies and in CEOs: A comparative study of the main influences', *Journal of Business Ethics*, September, Vol. 95, Issue 3, pp. 339–55.

Jayashree, P. and Hussain, S.J. (2011) 'Aligning change deployment: A Balanced Scorecard approach', *Measuring Business Excellence*, August, Vol. 15, Issue 3, pp. 63–85.

Johnson, G., Scholes, K. and Whittington, R. (2005) *Exploring Corporate Strategy Texts and Cases*, Harlow, Pearson.

Kalyani, M. and Sahoo, M.P. (2011) 'Human resource strategy: A tool of managing change for organizational excellence', *International Journal of Business & Management*, August, Vol. 6, Issue 8, pp. 280–86.

Kaplan, P. and Norton, D.P. (1996) *The Balanced Scorecard*, Boston, MA, Harvard Business Publishing.

Ketola, T. (2009) 'Pre-Morphean paradigm – an alternative to modern and post-modern paradigms of corporate sustainability', *Sustainable Development*, March/April, Vol. 17, Issue 2, pp. 114–26.

Kovač, J. and Jesenko, M. (2010) 'The connection between trust and leadership styles in Slovene organizations', *Journal for East European Management Studies*, Vol. 15, Issue 1, pp. 9–33.

Laszlo, A., Laszlo, K.C. and Johnsen C.S. (2009) 'From high-performance teams to evolutionary learning communities: New pathways in organizational development', *Journal of Organisational Transformation & Social Change*, Vol. 6, Issue 1, pp. 29–48.

Marković, M.R. (2008) 'Managing the organizational change and culture in the age of globalization', *Journal of Business Economics & Management*, Vol. 9, Issue 1, pp. 3–11.

Marshak, R.J. and Grant, D. (2008) 'Organizational discourse and new organization development practices', *British Journal of Management*, March, Supplement 1, Vol. 19, pp. S7–S19.

Ohmae, K. (1982) *The Mind of the Strategist*, New York, McGraw Hill.

Ravasi, D. and Phillips, N. (2011) 'Strategies of alignment: Organizational identity management and strategic change at Bang & Olufsen', *Strategic Organization*, May, Vol. 9, Issue 2, pp. 103–35.

Senge, P. (1990) 'The leader's new work: Building learning organisations', *Sloan Management Review*, Autumn, pp. 7–22.

Stata, R. (1989) 'Organizational learning – the key to management innovation', *Sloan Management Review*, Spring, pp. 63–74.

Thomas, G.F., Zolin, R. and Hartman, J.L. (2009) 'The central role of communication in developing trust and its effect on employee involvement', *Journal of Business Communication*, July, Vol. 46, Issue 3, pp. 287–310.

Weiss, R.M. (2000) 'Taking science out of organization science: How would postmodernism reconstruct the analysis of organizations?', *Organization Science*, November/December, Vol. 11, Issue 6, pp. 709–31.

Westover, J.H. (2010) 'Managing organizational change: Change agent strategies and techniques to successfully managing the dynamics of stability and change in organizations', *International Journal of Management & Innovation*, Vol. 2, Issue 1, pp. 45–50.

Zeffane, R., Tipu, S.A. and Ryan, J.C. (2011) 'Communication, commitment & trust: Exploring the triad', *International Journal of Business & Management*, June, Vol. 6, Issue 6, pp. 77–87.

Zhang, X. and Bartol, K.M. (2010) 'Linking empowering leadership and employee creativity: The influence of psychological empowerment, intrinsic motivation, and creative process engagement', *Academy of Management Journal*, February, Vol. 53, Issue 1, pp. 107–28.

16 Foresight methodologies for coping with change

> There is always one moment…when the door opens and lets the future in.
> (Graham Greene, *The Power and the Glory*, 1940)

Introduction

Strategy design and the implementation of policies to arrive at a desirable future scenario require knowledge of strategic innovation. The creation of future visions requires skills related to all the other topics discussed in this text. Several foresight methodologies are available and these may be applied in the areas of policy (e.g. ICT, science and technology, environment and energy), society (climate change, green issues, ageing population, etc.) and in private organisations (corporate foresight).

This chapter provides a toolbox of methods which organisations may use to design a desirable future. Foresight, which involves thinking about the future and designing future scenarios, is necessary in times of discontinuous change. Foresight may be considered from two points of view: theoretical or applied. The practice of foresight is based on key theoretical underpinnings and on 'foresight cycles' which build on previous experience and on expertise within and outside the practice.

Various methods may be used during foresight activities, many of which involve the participation of stakeholders, resulting in a democratic process. The outcomes of a foresight exercise may be incorporated into an organisations' strategic plan; these may include awareness raising, networking and learning on the part of those involved in the process. The use of foresight methodologies allows for creative possibilities and innovative solutions. The various methods facilitate the process of designing a strategy, a roadmap or a journey towards a future which is desirable, feasible and viable.

Context

Foresight: the predictive power of strategic planning

Foresight incorporates a number of theories, tools and practices which deal with planning for the future. The topic has attracted interest recently with numerous publications spanning both theoretical and applied aspects. Although much emphasis has been placed on technological foresight and policy making, the tools and methods can be applied to social, economic, environmental and organisational issues.

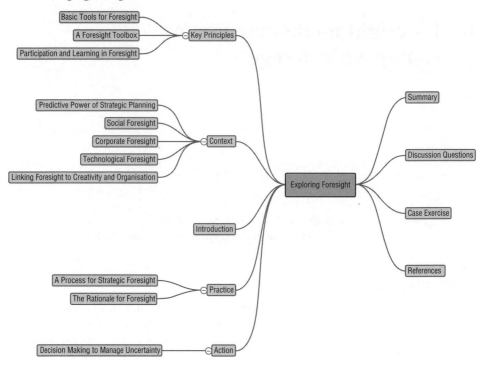

Figure 16.1 Exploring foresight.

Foresight is relevant because we are living in an era where change is exponential and where we cannot allow chance to regulate future events. Strategic intervention is, therefore, essential and may come about through the use of foresight methods and foresight activities. 'Good foresight should always include a sense of what would be involved in the implementation of specific recommendations or analysis' (Mack, 2005). Although foresight is still a fledgling discipline it involves tried and tested methods and procedures with proven benefits.

Social foresight

Social foresight is defined by Foresight International as 'the ability to create…sustain and apply a variety of high quality images and understandings about futures in a range of socially useful ways'. It involves both reflection on and an investigation of the way in which individuals and societies react to issues which affect them (security, welfare, climate change etc.). The social consequences of planning, problem solving and decision making (which form part of the outcomes of foresight activities) should be given serious consideration, particularly since the issues addressed are complex and cannot always simply be reduced to seemingly mechanical or linear sub-issues. When conducted successfully, foresight involves learning, synergy and a holistic view of a situation or issue.

One area where social foresight may be of increasing relevance is the work conducted by NGOs (non-governmental organisations), in particular when societal needs (clean water, sanitation, environmental issues, security, education and social justice) are involved (see Chapter 8, Section 8.4.2).

Corporate foresight

Some difficulties may arise when attempting to introduce foresight practice into an organisation as managers may be unfamiliar with the techniques and tools (see Chapter 7). Resistance to change involves fear, risk and a loss of security. Resistance to the adoption of foresight practices in organisations may be considered as similar to that which emerges when other novel avenues and strategies are pursued. Evident barriers could include financial issues, an emphasis on crisis management, inflexible mindsets and adversity to risk taking.

Corporate foresight activities may choose to focus on a number of factors:

- Technological
- Social
- Environmental
- Economical
- Ecological or political
- Trends (social, political, economical or technological)
- Horizon scanning
- Demographics
- Consumption patterns
- Value systems and innovative emerging market opportunities.

Corporate foresight may result from two motives:

1 Reactive: in response to companies' business operation demands a long-term orientation (such as industries with long product cycles);
2 Proactive: to better cope with uncertainties in the business environment in general.

Additional rationales for corporate foresight include the following:

- An early warning system in fast-changing sectors (such as consumer goods and ICT) to identify future threats and opportunities;
- To prepare for possible '*wildcard*' events and sudden shocks (earthquakes, tsunamis, terrorist threats, oil crises, financial crisis, political upheavels etc.) in the political, economic and social sphere;
- To better understand the social and cultural context related to the use and diffusion of technology;
- To build up knowledge and expertise about emerging technologies and their future users in technology intensive sectors (for example, Philips, Ericsson, IBM, Siemens);
- To open up the organisation to the outside world and to find starting points for innovation transfer, co-operation and best practices;
- To identify important background information about the future conditions and contexts in which the organisation will have to operate.

Foresight activities that focus on the business environment serve as the starting point for the development of corporate strategy and enable the embedding of it in the socio-economic context. This may come about through:

- Anticipatory intelligence (early warning);
- Direction-setting and strategy formulation (corporate strategy);

- Determining priorities (to guide R&I funding decisions);
- Innovation catalysing (stimulating innovation processes).

Foresight is one method with which to tackle the complexity and dynamics of the globalised economy, both in terms of long-term challenges and present-day decisions to construct a better future (Godet, 2010). However, 'foresight can be wrong and still be useful to business…it's a working metaphor, and the value for business is as a way of thinking strategically…*(being)* ready for whatever comes' (Mack, 2005).

Technological foresight

According to Irvine and Martin (1984):

> Technology Foresight is a process which seeks to look into the longer term future of science, technology and economy and society with the aim of identifying the areas of strategic research and the emerging generic technologies likely to yield the greatest economic and social benefit.

Another definition describes technology foresight as 'a systematic means of assessing those scientific and technological developments which could have a strong impact on industrial competitiveness, wealth creation and quality of life' (Georghiou, 1996). Technology foresight activities are an appropriate tool for strategic planning, decision making, connectivity, networking and awareness raising about future technologies.

Barré (2002) provides three major objectives for technology foresight which refer to 'the innovation system':

1   Supporting science and technology priority setting and resource allocation;
2   Improving the connectivity and efficiency of the innovation system;
3   Increasing awareness of future technologies, opportunities and strategies and their impacts.

Technology is not the only key factor to consider when conceptualising future visions and it should not be isolated from other relevant considerations (Godet, 2010).

Linking foresight to creativity and innovation

If foresight is to be considered as a new discipline, it must necessarily be closely linked to both creativity and innovation. How do these links emerge? Thinking about the future requires the use of the imagination and a positive attitude towards change and all that it brings in its wake. Creativity involves the generation of ideas without censure, where thinking 'out of the box' is encouraged. This is often referred to as divergent thinking, which provides a stark contrast to linear, analytical or logical thinking. Successful foresight activities are concerned with the long-term future in an effort to 'eliminate' or 'ignore' current obstacles, blockages or conservative mindsets which may act as deterrents. Foresight may feed into the innovation process at various levels, in particular, where innovation policy and research and innovation are concerned. This is mainly due to the prioritisation factors which often play a key role in the foresight process.

Successful foresight activities require both linear, logical and analytical thinking *together with* imaginative, creative (and therefore 'non-linear' and at times, apparently 'irrational') thinking (Gavigan *et al.*, 2001). As discussed above foresight is a participatory and democratic process which explores the generation of possible (generally long-term) future scenarios and which aims to be action oriented. One similarity which emerges between foresight and innovation concerns the concept of incremental and radical innovation.

Forecasting is generally considered to rely on quantitative tools, with predictions being based on existing conditions and trends. The focus is on incremental as opposed to long-term change. Futurists, on the other hand, create alternative scenarios and they may use both (or either) qualitative and quantitative tools (The University of Houston, n.d.).

The three characteristics that distinguish foresight from forecasting are, according to de Lattre-Gasquet (2009):

- It uses a pluridisciplinary approach of systemic inspiration, based on the principle that the problems we face cannot be correctly understood if reduced to one dimension and divided into several parts.
- It integrates the long-term dimension, past and future. It looks at past tendencies (retrospective) to better envisage the future. It considers that some variables have a relatively profound inertia (i.e. demography, ecosystems) whereas others have shorter timescales (i.e. technological innovation, foreign exchanges).
- It integrates breakthroughs, whether technological, social (i.e. human desire to change the rules of the game) or economic (i.e. market saturation).

An area where foresight appears to be taking over certain areas of strategic management is the corporate context. This is not an entirely new practice, as Shell, for example, was one of the first private organisations to use foresight tools in the late 1960s. It is to be admitted, however, that there is a great deal of potential for foresight in the corporate context that has not yet been realised, and some resistance has been reported (see, for example, Graves, 2007).

'Scenarios are…the most powerful vehicles I know for challenging our "mental models" about the world and lifting the "blinders" that limit our creativity and resourcefulness' (Schwartz, 1996).

Key principles

Basic tools for foresight

There is no single method, technique or set or mix of methods and techniques which predominate in a foresight exercise. The mapping of foresight exercises carried out by the European Foresight Monitoring Network (EFMN) (Popper, 2009) identified four categories of method:

- Qualitative methods
- Semi-quantitative methods
- Quantitative methods
- Other methods

Qualitative methods: a selection of these activities is shown in Table 16.1. They allow space for creative and subjective thinking, but cannot be scientifically corroborated.

Table 16.1 EFMN qualitative methods

EFMN Categories	Activities
Qualitative methods	Backcasting
	Brainstorming
	Citizen panels
	Environmental scanning
	Essays
	Expert panels
	Futures workshops
	Simulation gaming
	Interviews
	Literature review
	Morphological analysis
	Questionnaires and surveys
	Relevance trees
	Scenarios
	SWOT analysis

Semi-quantitative methods use mathematical principles together with expert opinions. Table 16.2 presents a selection of these activities.

Table 16.2 EFMN semi-quantitative methods

EFMN Categories	Activities
Semi-quantitative methods	Cross impact/structural analysis
	Delphi surveys
	Key/critical technologies
	Multicriteria analysis
	Quantitative scenarios
	Stakeholder mapping and (technology) roadmapping

Quantitative methods are where statistical techniques are applied to process and analyse data. Examples of some popular activities are shown in Table 16.3.

Table 16.3 EFMN quantitative methods

EFMN Categories	Activities
Quantitative methods	Bibliometrics
	Modelling and simulation
	Trend extrapolation

Other methods include a variety of activities as shown in Table 16.4.

Table 16.4 EFMN other methods

EFMN Categories	Activities
Other methods	Benchmarking
	Patent analysis
	Wild cards
	Science fictioning
	Genius forecast
	Acting/role play
	Voting/polling
	Indicators

Popper (2009) further classifies these methods according to their ability to gather or process information, based on the following four key considerations:

- Evidence
- Expertise
- Interaction
- Creativity.

The above concepts are not exclusive and may at times overlap, or they may be combined. This implies that the use of one method, brainstorming, for example, may involve a large percentage of creativity combined with smaller elements of evidence, expertise and interaction. Proactive efforts need to be put into place if creativity is to be awarded priority where foresight methodologies are concerned (Godet, 2010).

A foresight toolkit

Some of the more well-known methods used in foresight activities are described in Appendix 16.1. (For a more detailed description of further methods see Popper, 2008.)

An investigation of the literature on foresight exhibits a plethora of methods, some of which have been found to be more effective than others. A comprehensive understanding and skill acquired in the use of some of the more well-known foresight methods is necessary as the selection of the methods to be used in a foresight activity constitutes an integral component of the 'pre-foresight' planning exercise that is essential for a successful outcome.

Participation and learning in foresight

It is better to strive towards a desirable future rather than to be 'stuck' in the *status quo* or simply to react to events as they occur. Emphasis on foresight as a process (as opposed to focusing on the actual 'content' which emerges as an 'output') tends to lead to strategy and to action. Foresight becomes 'embedded' in practice and it subsequently tends to become a more powerful force which has increased potential for informing research, increasing organisational competitivity and adding value (Kristóf, in press).

The learning process includes awareness raising, not only on the topic of the foresight exercise but also on the importance of reflecting on future possibilities. One of the 'core' learning objectives of a foresight exercise is 'Moving individuals and groups away from pre-determined paths and patterns of behaviour to explore alternative ways forward' (FOR-LEARN).

The involvement of policy makers in the foresight process may be a debateable topic and a challenging process. Policy makers may find it more convenient to delegate foresight activities to others who they believe may be more competent. Their direct participation, however, enables increased ownership of outputs (Da Costa *et al.*, 2008).

The main lessons to be learnt include:

- An increased appreciation of future possibilities;
- Empowerment through the acquisition of foresight methods and skills;
- Knowledge acquired through debate and dialectic processes;
- Networking with other key people, stakeholders and experts on a particular topic;
- An appreciation of the democratic processes which form part of the foresight activity;
- Participatory leadership.

Practice

A process for strategic foresight

Foresight involves a dynamic process where individuals, communities, groups, stakeholders or experts interact with each other and where context, ideas, methods, information, objectives and goals play a key role. Three phases are generally identified in a successful foresight process: pre-foresight, foresight and post-foresight. The first stage involves the preliminary activities which are required before the foresight itself commences. This is sometimes known as 'scoping' and it involves setting clear objectives, decision making on the methods to be used, the identification and selection of participants and the collection of information or data.

Miles (2002) separates the recruitment phase (where the key stakeholders and experts are identified and their support and commitment is ensured) from the pre-foresight phase. A strategic plan is formulated and this should include a clear outline of the allocation of tasks, milestones to be achieved and budget distribution. Horton (1999) describes this phase as consisting of 'the collection, collation and summarization of available information…and results in the production of foresight knowledge'. Miles (2002) splits this phase into the 'Generation Phase' and the 'Action Phase'. Dissemination is an important factor to consider in the foresight process.

The generic foresight process which Voros (2003) describes is composed of four phases:

1. Inputs: a creative stage which may use methods such as Delphi (see Appendix 16.1) and environmental scanning (or 'strategic scanning'), brainstorming, etc.
2. Foresight at work. This involves three stages, each of which feeds into the next step:

    (a) Analysis: this addresses the question, what seems to be happening? Tools used include trend analysis, cross-impact matrices and other analytical techniques.
    (b) Interpretation: the question here is, what is really happening? This involves probing deep beneath the surface to reveal insights and interrelationships.

(c) Prospectation: Voros coins this word to reflect both 'prospective thinking' and the French term *prospective*. The question raised at this stage depends on the type of potential futures under consideration. Scenarios and visions are created as alternative future possibilities.

3. Outputs: the question raised at this stage relates to action. Outputs may be tangible (possible future options) and intangible (insights generated and changes in thinking processes). Foresight ends here with the outputs, which are communicated through workshops, reports and so on, being considered as inputs for strategy.
4. Strategy: this involves implementation and action through strategy development and strategic planning. A feedback loop may be created to cater for improvement, learning and continuous re-assessment.

Dingli (in press) discusses the challenges which tend to occur at the dissemination phase and provides a list of questions which could be considered in the pre-foresight phase for the subsequent maximisation of the effects of dissemination which, in turn, may lead to action.

In a discussion on the topic of evaluation and impact, Georghiou and Keenan (2008) list 'three basic tests' which they suggest could be applied as part of 'a generalised evaluation framework', these being:

1   *Accountability*: this questions the efficiency of the foresight activity and evaluates funding issues;
2   *Justification*: this questions whether it is justified to continue or to extend the process;
3   *Learning*: this examines the lessons learnt in the process and considers how things could have been done in a better way.

Georghiou and Keenan (2008) further identify three 'classic criteria of evaluation' which are:

1   *Efficiency of implementation*. This evaluates the selection of participants such as stakeholders and experts, the manner in which the activity was managed and structured and the choice of methodology.
2   *Impact and effectiveness*. This evaluates outputs and outcomes, although as Georghiou and Keenan point out, 'outputs measure only activity and not its significance'. It may therefore be appropriate to consider both qualitative and quantitative measures of effectiveness.
3   Appropriateness. This looks into the rationale of the foresight activity and raises questions concerning what the alternatives to intervention would have been and whether there are any additional effects, which could include the adoption of new ways of thinking and behaviour. As Georghiou and Keenan state, 'foresight may be best evaluated ultimately in terms of its ability to change values and behaviour in these directions'.

Caution should be exercised on issues related to a situation where the 'owners' of a foresight activity are also the persons involved with resources for implementation. A foresight process should always include clearly stated objectives. The dynamism which processes bring into foresight activities cannot be underestimated (Rescher, 1996).

The rationale for foresight

There are a number of reasons for foresight exercises to be conducted, although the prioritisation of choices for investment and policy concerning innovation, science and technology is one aim that is often accentuated. Miles *et al.* (2008) outline a number of valid reasons for foresight activities, including the generation of 'more compelling scenarios, and more accurate econometric models'. Additional reasons for foresight activities include social, technological, political and cultural issues, and the contexts in which foresight is applied are wide ranging.

The focus on social factors is a relatively recent trend in foresight. Decision making, problem solving and dealing with issues related to the future all have an impact on society at large and these must be taken into consideration. This focus on society and on social factors was not so evident in the past.

Attempts have also been made to 'cluster' foresight rationales into five main groups (Miles *et al.*, 2008):

1   Directing or prioritising investment in STI (setting general research directions by identifying previously unknown opportunities);
2   Building new networks and linkages around a common vision;
3   Extending the breadth of knowledge and visions in relation to the future;
4   Bringing new actors into the strategic debate;
5   Improving policy making and strategy formation in areas where science and innovation play a significant role.

The use of foresight for purposes of innovative public policy is beneficial to enable organisations to move away from 'lock-in' failure and to recognise and adopt opportunities related to new technology or new markets. Foresight activities, in particular those that utilise methods which involve creativity, may be viewed as one possible way to tackle market failure and 'lock-in'.

Innovative policy intervention may result in the creation of new and more dynamic networks, with increased expertise and synergy, either for establishing standards (in telecommunications, for example) or for new structures to emerge which give rise to innovative strategies, as opposed to previous ingrained (and possibly more conservative) ways of operating.

Network externalities may also be more dynamically activated through the involvement of stakeholders and experts who work together in a complementary manner, thus allowing for increased synergy and subsequent success in achieving pre-set objectives.These results may not have been possible without public intervention through the creation of foresight activities.

The rationale for foresight activities has evolved a great deal during its brief lifespan. Further changes relevant to context and circumstances are to be expected in the future, particularly since innovation practices get to play a more important role in both public-and private-funded foresight activities. The shift appears to have been mainly from an initial tendency to identify emerging technologies which were expected to yield both social and economic benefits, towards the creation of networks and a raising of awareness concerning the strategic planning of future action.

Whereas the rationale for foresight in the 1990s was generally related to setting up both national and regional systems of innovation, with an emphasis on R&I policy initiatives, there is today more awareness of the importance of embedding a culture of foresight amongst key movers and shakers. An increased emphasis on an acknowledgement of the current context as a knowledge intensive one which incorporates a globalised learning economy and which is not bereft of social implications and repurcussions is evident.

As a result, a new paradigm which is oriented towards shaping an efficient and adaptable innovation system has emerged. This new policy paradigm focuses on creating adaptable innovation systems by:

- Stimulating learning institutions and economic actors;
- Developing integrative and coordinated policy visions and instruments for enhancing innovation;
- Creating the conditions for a more agile and flexible policy making process which is learning and adapting constantly to the new demands and conditions of the economy.

The range of national foresight objectives has therefore been extended to incorporate:

- Priority setting;
- Reorienting the science and innovation system;
- Bringing new actors into the strategic debate;
- Building new networks and linkages across fields, sectors and markets or around problems.

The above objectives may be operational at an organisational, local, regional, national or supranational level. Timescale may range from the immediate future to an extended horizon within the distant future. The key actors may be drawn from a number of sectors which include 'firms, governments, business sectors, voluntary organisations, social movements and technical experts' (Miles *et al.*, 2008). Foresight is a 'disruptive' process which raises questions such as 'What if?', strategic planning is 'goal-oriented' and 'pragmatic' as it deals with the steps required at the implementation or action phase of a project (Voros, 2003).

Action

Decision making to manage uncertainty

The preceding sections have described various perspectives related to foresight, with particular emphasis on the manner in which creativity and innovation play a role in the foresight process.

'Grand challenges' and 'global problems'(Popper, 2009) have and will continue to play a key role in foresight activities. Both decision making and prioritisation (particularly when making choices related to funding) play a role in this process. Resources are never as plentiful as one may wish. De Lattre-Gasquet (2009) draws attention to some consequences of 'inadequate choices'. 'Crises have always existed, and financial and economic crises are even cyclical...It seems they are related to inadequate choices and a loss of sense of personal responsibility and responsibility towards one another and for the natural environment'. Strategy should be formulated and action taken in an attempt to address and prioritise these global problems and experience has demonstrated that foresight is a useful activity to adopt.

Foresight does not only address issues related to decision making or problem solving. In a similar way to business creativity, foresight may address issues where no apparent problem solving or decision making is required, but where innovative ideas facilitate strategy and action.

Not all foresight activities result in consensus. It may be argued that too much consensus leads to a decrease in creativity and imagination due to homogeneity of thought and action which reduces focus on multiple future possibilities. Foresight involves a dynamic process that allows for the freedom to construct a future which presents multiple choices. It emphasises the importance of being proactive and of broadening current perceptions through the use of intuition and imagination. Realism, feasibility and sustainability play a role in the process (de Lattre-Gasquet, 2009). The foresight process should be considered just as important as the content or outcomes. Creativity, innovation and foresight need to be tempered with facts, context and reality, and social elements should always be given serious consideration (Mack, 2005).

Way back in 1989 Alan Kay, at the time a fellow at Apple Computer Inc. and later Head of R&D at Disney Imagineering, said: 'the best way to predict the future is to invent it. This is the century in which you can be proactive about the future; you don't have to be reactive. The whole idea of having scientists and technology is that those things you can envision and describe can actually be built'. Well over 20 years later Kay's words still ring true. Foresight is one activity which may be successfully used to facilitate and enable mindsets which are open to future possibilities and the creation of new future scenarios and visions. The future is not pre-determined. The use of foresight enables us to design possible scenarios and future visions and to utilise the imagination in order to creatively envisage and enact strategies to realise a desirable future.

Summary

We live in tempestuous times and wise organisations seek to anticipate how likely future events will affect their business operations. Most will need to be flexible enough and prepared to deal with various possible futures. This chapter provides a toolbox of methods which organisations may use to design a desirable and relevant future.

Discussion questions

1   What is foresight and how can it be considered?
2   Why is foresight attracting attention and what can foresight methodologies bring to strategic planning?
3   Define social foresight and briefly discuss why it is important.
4   What are the key motives that lead organisations to become interested in corporate foresight?
5   Name the three major objectives for technology foresight which refer to 'the innovation system' suggested by Barré (2002).
6   Explain briefly how foresight links with creativity and innovation.
7   Name the three characteristics that distinguish foresight from forecasting.
8   What categories of method were identified by the European Foresight Monitoring Network (EFMN) foresight mapping exercises?
9   List the five main cluster groups of foresight rationales.
10 What are the main benefits to be gained from participating in the foresight process?

Case exercise

HMV is a British global entertainment retail chain and is the largest of its kind in the United Kingdom and Ireland. It is currently a leading brand in the retailing of music, film, games, consoles, books and tickets. The HMV group issued its third profits warning in April 2011 following increased trading difficulties. The group owns 285 HMV stores and 314 Waterstone's bookstores in the UK and Ireland. In May 2011 it agreed to sell its Waterstone's book chain to a fund controlled by Russian billionaire Alexander Mamut for £53m. In addition the international arm of its business comprises 125 stores in Canada, five in Hong Kong and two in Singapore.

Buffeted by fierce competition from supermarkets and online retailers such as Amazon and iTunes the group closed 60 stores in 2011 as a result of falling sales. Over Christmas, sales dropped 13.6 per cent in the UK and Republic of Ireland. Like-for-like sales for the five weeks to 31 December 2011 were down 8.1 per cent.

As pressure mounted on the HMV group any benefits from being the last major chain on the High Street had now largely disappeared. Seymour Pierce analyst Kate Calvert said that HMV's strategy was not working. 'The speed of deterioration in profitability of this business confirms that management's strategy is not arresting the very real structural pressures on the core retail business from online'. However, technology sales reported a big jump after a change in focus. Half year losses circa £46m, were up from £27m in 2010 (Wood, 2012).

Task

Draft a brief note for the HMV board outlining in clear language how foresight processes can assist them in understanding their present situation and how they can help to identify viable strategic options for the future.

References

Barré, R. (2002) 'Foresights and their themes: Analysis, typology and perspectives', paper at the conference The Role of Foresight in the Selection of Research Policy Priorities, Seville, 13–14 May.

Da Costa, O., Warnke, P., Cagnin, C. and Scapolo, F. (2008) 'The impact of foresight on policy-making: Insights from the FORLEARN mutual learning process', *Technology Analysis and Strategic Management*, May, Vol. 20, Issue 3, pp. 369–87.

de Lattre-Gasquet, M. (2009) *Foresight. CTA: Knowledge for Development*, 21 April. http://knowledge.cta.int/en/Dossiers/S-T-Issues-in-Perspective/Foresighting/Articles/Foresight, accessed 03/04/11.

Dingli, S.M. (in press) 'The dissemination and implementations of results of forecast activities', in Borch, K., Dingli, S.M. and Jørgensen, M.S. (eds.) *Participation and Interaction in Foresight: Dialogue, Dissemination and Visions*, Cheltenham, UK, Edward Elgar.

Foresight International (n.d.) 'What is social foresight?' http://www.foresightinternational.com.au/what-social-foresight, accessed 27/12/11.

FOR-LEARN (n.d.). 'Corporate foresight. Online Foresight Guide', *JRC European Commission*. http://forlearn.jrc.ec.europa.eu/guide/9_key-terms/corporate.htm, accessed 27/12/11;

FOR-LEARN (n.d.) *JRC European Commission*, The FOR-LEARN *Online Foresight Guide*. http://forlearn.jrc.ec.europa.eu/guide/0_home/index.htm, accessed 04/04/11.

FOR-LEARN (n.d.) 'Why is communication so important to the success of a foresight exercise?' *JRC European Commission*. http://forlearn.jrc.ec.europa.eu/guide/3_scoping/set_com_important.htm, accessed 28/12/11.

Gavigan, J.P. *et al.* (2001) *A Practical Guide to Regional Foresight*, FOREN Network, STRATA Programme, European Commission Research Directorate General. http://foresight.jrc.ec.europa.eu/documents/eur20128en.pdf, accessed 17/04/12.

Georghiou, L. (1996) 'The UK technology foresight programme', *Futures*, Vol. 28, No. 4, pp. 359–77.

Georghiou, L. and Keenan, M. (2008) 'Evaluation and impact of foresight', in Georghiou, L., Cassingena Harper, J., Keenan, M., Miles, I. and Popper, R. (eds) *The Handbook of Technology Foresight*, Prime Series on Research and Innovation Policy, Cheltenham, UK, Edward Elgar.

Godet, M. (2010) 'Future memories', *Technological Forecasting & Social Change*, Vol. 77, pp. 1457–63. http://en.laprospective.fr/dyn/anglais/articles/future-memories-tfsc-2010.pdf, accessed 27/12/11.

Graves, T. (2007) 'Stealth foresight for innovation: Creating support for creative change in large organisations in Australia', *Journal of Futures Studies*, November, Vol. 12, Issue 2, pp. 121–28.

Horton, A.M. (1999) 'A simple guide to successful foresight', *Foresight,* Vol. 1, Issue 1, pp. 5–9.

Irvine, J. and Martin, B. (1984). *Foresight in Science: Picking the Winners*, London: Francis Pinter.

Kristóf, T. (in press) 'Learning theory in foresight', in Borch, K., Dingli, S.M., Jørgensen and M.S. (eds) *Participation and Interaction in Foresight: Dialogue, Dissemination and Visions*, Cheltenham, UK, Edward Elgar.

Mack, T.C. (2005) 'Organizational and management dynamics in foresight', *Journal of Futures Studies*, February, Vol. 9, No. 3. http://www.jfs.tku.edu.tw/9–3/E01.pdf, accessed 27/12/11.

Miles, I. (2002) *Appraisal of Alternative Models and Procedures for Producing Regional Foresight.* Report prepared by CRIC for the European Commission's DG Research Funded STRATA-ETAN Expert Group Action, Manchester, CRIC.

Miles, I. (2003) 'Foresight tools – scenario planning', UNIDO – Technology Foresight for Practitioners, training course, 6–10 October 2003, Prague, Czech Republic, PREST, University of Manchester, United Kingdom.

Miles, I., Cassingena Harper, J., Georghiou, L., Keenan, M. and Popper, R. (2008) 'The many faces of foresight', in Georghiou, L., Cassingena Harper, J., Keenan, M., Miles, I. and Popper, R. (eds) *The Handbook of Technology Foresight: Concepts and Practice*, Prime Series on Research and Innovation Policy, Cheltenham, UK, Edward Elgar.

Popper, R. (2008) 'Foresight methodology', in Georghiou, L., Cassingena Harper, J., Keenan, M., Miles, I. and Popper, R. (eds) *The Handbook of Technology Foresight, Concepts and Practice*, Prime Series on Research and Innovation Policy, Cheltenham, UK, Edward Elgar.

Popper, R. (2009) *EU Report Mapping Foresight: Revealing how Europe and other World Regions Navigate into the Future.* http://ec.europa.eu/research/social-sciences/pdf/efmn-mapping-fore-sight_en.pdf, accessed 10/04/2011.

Rescher, N. (1996) *Process Metaphysics: An Introduction to Process Philosophy*, Albany, NY, SUNY Press.

Schwartz, P. (1996) *The Art of the Long View: Planning for the Future in an Uncertain World*, New York, Currency Doubleday.

The University of Houston (n.d.) Futures Studies program. http://tech.uh.edu/programs/graduate/futures-studies-in-commerce, accessed 08/11/2010.

Voros, J. (2003) 'A generic foresight process framework', *Foresight*, Vol. 5, Issue 3, pp. 10–21.

Wood, Z. (2012) 'HMV insists it will survive despite Christmas sales fall', *The Guardian*, 10 January, Kindle edition.

Appendix: A foresight toolbox

Some of the more well-known methods which are used in foresight activities are described in the following paragraphs. (For a more detailed description of further methods see Popper, 2008.)

Delphi is an established survey method which takes its name from the famous oracle. It involves repeatedly polling the same individuals. However, each subsequent poll includes a feedback mechanism which allows for the responses from previous polls to be incorporated into the next round. This allows for better judgement and avoids the influence which strong personalities may have on others within a group during face to face discussion sessions since Delphi surveys are mainly conducted online. A Delphi survey generally consists of two rounds of polls conducted with the same individuals.

Horizon scanning is based on an enhanced perception of current and future contexts, based on: 'Looking ahead – beyond usual timescales. Looking across – beyond usual sources. Seeing things – you don't normally see'. Horizon scanning allows for the identification of trends, drivers, weak signals and wildcards which provide key inputs for the scenario development process.

Weak signals/Wildcards. Weak signals are early signs of possible significant changes, while wildcards are low probability and high impact shocks or disruptions. Wildcard thinking provides an effective means for making policies more robust and resilient to the occurrence and effects of wildcard events. By learning from past wildcards, it may be possible to adapt and mitigate their potential impact and to counteract undesirable human-caused wildcards.

Futures workshops are structured events which include a mix of presentations, discussions, debates and workshops.

Brainstorming allows for the removal of inhibitions as it allows for freedom of thought and for the generation of creative ideas. It may be used either in face-to-face group meetings or online. Brainstorming may be incorporated with workshops, scenarios, extrapolation or scanning. This is a useful divergent thinking method for generating original ideas.

Trend extrapolation involves the assumption that the future is a sort of linear continuation of the past. This method utilises past trends to envisage the future through the extended continuation of that which has been observed or measured in the past. Care should be taken when utilising this method as although it may be useful for topics which include demographics or other statistical data, the exponential changes which are currently being experienced imply the possibility of disruptive events (which require more imaginative thinking), rather than regular trends which move smoothly from the past into the future.

Science fictioning involves the use of utopian or distopian scenarios expressed in imaginative stories as a source of inspiration for thinking about the future. It may also be used to illustrate a particular point through a story when a report which deals with future scenarios is being compiled. Some renowned science fiction authors have been successful in predicting future inventions such as the internet, air travel or high rise buildings. Science fiction may provide creative inspiration for foresight activities that deal with particular topics, such as artificial intelligence.

SWOT Analysis may be applied in a variety of situations and is mainly used for decision making, problem solving and strategy formulation. It involves addressing a topic, event or issue and listing the Strengths, Weaknesses, Opportunities and Threats. This is followed by an attempt to build on the strengths, to overcome the weaknesses and to turn the threats into opportunities. Strategy and policy formulation to capitalise on the opportunities which are identified and to act on them would follow.

Simulation gaming (which may involve role play and acting) has been used for many years, particularly in the military as war gaming. Online virtual worlds, which simulate the model battlefields of the past, may be used for this purpose. Role play, which involves acting out a script by adopting one or more particular roles, generally occurs in face to face settings. The main goals of simulation gaming are an increased understanding of tactics and motivations, the exploration of various possibilities (including 'action' or 'reaction' strategies) or the eventual implementation of action plans.

Roadmapping involves planning for the future in an attempt to design a strategy or 'roadmap' which would include time frames in order to achieve a desired result in the future. This method requires input from experts and desk research. It may be useful for communicating shared visions and future expectations to key stakeholders who are involved in the implementation of the strategy.

Scenario development and **scenario writing** are based on imagining the future effects and consequences of current trends and present-day decisions, together with surprise events and breakthroughs which may occur. As Georghiou (1996) states, they do not predict the future but 'expand the "possibility space" on how the future might unfold'.

Scenarios are constructed through a systematic approach which is often based on the identification and discussion of emerging trends and drivers. A driver is a factor that significantly influences the goals of a foresight activity. Through scanning, an initial list of drivers is generated and classified. A useful way to classify drivers, and to ensure that a full range has been considered, is to apply a framework to prompt participants' thinking. The most commonly applied is STEEP and its variant STEEPV (an acronym for Social, Technological, Economic, Environmental, Political and Values) or PEST (Political, Economic, Social and Technological). Scenarios are developed based on the opinions and judgements of participants about the nature, direction and prominence of the drivers. The key drivers need to be carefully selected and, where necessary, clustered or combined.

The **success scenario approach** is a normative and action-based approach, developed at the University of Manchester in England, which is designed to build a common vision of future success among key stakeholders in an area. Miles (2003) identifies the following key aspects of the approach:

- Desirability: capturing a vision of what could be achieved or aspired to by the sponsoring organisation or the wider community that it represents;
- Credibility: the scenario is developed with the assistance of, and validated by, a sample of experts in the area chosen to reflect a broad range of interests and usually including both practitioners and researchers.

The success scenario approach helps to create a shared vision among stakeholders of what success in the area would look like. This is specified in terms of goals and indicators which begin the process of developing a roadmap.

Epilogue

The text has explored business creativity and strategic innovation in 16 chapters.

> Now they sit and map out a wider view
> Galaxies appear and have been set free
> Explorers set out to see the new
> Steer out beyond any fixed decree.

We exhort you to 'Steer out beyond any fixed decree' and continue to explore the concepts, models and techniques that the text has featured.

The figure below summarises key points covered in the text. A realistic understanding of context should stimulate a fresh approach to response and a redefinition of management that is managing plus leading. Fresh creative thinking and the empowerment of employees to think creatively and generate ideas is the first major step. The second concerns the development of an appropriate organisational strategy, structure and a sustained intent to develop a climate and culture that is conducive to successful innovation.

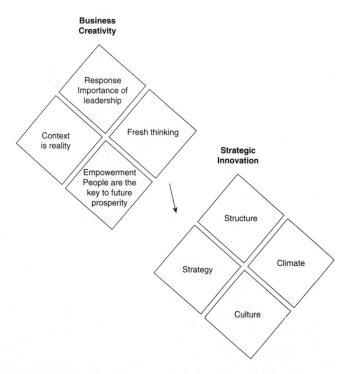

Academic Index

Subject Index